BEYOND THE ICON

STUDIES IN COMICS AND CARTOONS

Jared Gardner, Charles Hatfield, and Rebecca Wanzo, Series Editors

BEYOND THE ICON

Asian American Graphic Narratives

Edited by Eleanor Ty

THE OHIO STATE UNIVERSITY PRESS
COLUMBUS

Library of Congress Cataloging-in-Publication Data
Names: Ty, Eleanor Rose, 1958– editor.
Title: Beyond the icon : Asian American graphic narratives / edited by Eleanor Ty.
Other titles: Studies in comics and cartoons.
Description: Columbus : The Ohio State University Press, [2022] | Series: Studies in comics and cartoons | Includes bibliographical references and index. | Summary: "By looking at storytelling, form, and style in graphic novels and comics such as *Ms. Marvel*, George Takei's *They Called Us Enemy*, Thi Bui's *The Best We Could Do*, Gene Luen Yang's *The Shadow Hero*, and others, this volume demonstrates how Asian American creators in the twenty-first century employ graphic narrative to show Asian Americans as complex, nuanced individuals"— Provided by publisher.
Identifiers: LCCN 2022028020 | ISBN 9780814214947 (cloth) | ISBN 0814214940 (cloth) | ISBN 9780814282458 (ebook) | ISBN 0814282458 (ebook)
Subjects: LCSH: Graphic novels—Asian American authors—History and criticism. | Comic books, strips, etc.—Asian American authors—History and criticism. | American literature—Asian American authors—History and criticism. | Storytelling in literature. | Asian Americans in literature.
Classification: LCC PN6714 .B49 2022 | DDC 741.5/97308995073—dc23/eng/20220712
LC record available at https://lccn.loc.gov/2022028020
Other identifiers: ISBN 9780814258514 (paper) | ISBN 0814258514 (paper)

Cover design by Laurence J. Nozik
Text design by Juliet Williams
Type set in Palatino Linotype

CONTENTS

ILLUSTRATIONS

ACKNOWLEDGMENTS

We wish to express gratitude to our family, friends, and colleagues who have nurtured us and sustained our work over the years. We are grateful for the support of our Asian American and comics studies communities.

Eleanor Ty would like to thank the Research Office at Wilfrid Laurier University and the Social Sciences and Humanities Research Council of Canada for providing funding for research and dissemination. The initial idea for this volume came from a course Ty taught at the Department of Asian American Studies, University of California, Santa Barbara in 2019, where she held a Fulbright Canada Visiting Research Chair. She would like to acknowledge the help of her wonderful student assistant, Deborah Hernandez, with the preparation of the index.

Asian American Literature and Asian American Graphic Novels

ELEANOR TY

Beyond the Icon examines the crucial development of Asian American literature into the genre of graphic narratives in the second decade of the twenty-first century. Early scholars of Asian American literature, such as Elaine Kim, Shirley Geok-lin Lim, Amy Ling, and King-Kok Cheung, anticipated the flourishing of literature, mostly fiction, poetry, and drama, by Asian authors in the North American diaspora over two decades ago. Starting around the 2000s, the expansion of Asian American literature moved into the fields of graphic novels and nonfiction narratives. According to statistics from publishing, comics and graphic novel sales have been steadily expanding since 2012 in North America (see MacDonald). Rob Salkowitz reports that in 2020, the "graphic novel outperformed at all levels; even during the worst periods of uncertainty, sales were up significantly." In their informative and well-researched chapter on Asian American graphic narrative for the *Oxford Research Encyclopedia of Literature,* Monica Chiu and Jeannette Roan contend that works by Asian Americans "have become significant presences in the contemporary graphic narrative world" (1). While there are now many excellent studies of Asian American literature, this volume is notable because it examines the vibrant and growing body of graphic narratives by Asian North American creators. Twenty-first-century Asian American comics authors have made great strides in their efforts to rewrite official history; re-present the everyday, unexoticized experiences of Asian Americans; intervene in collective fantasies about American heroes and superheroes; and participate in debates about the environment, technology, and disability.

The idea for this volume began in 2019, before the pandemic that shut down almost every country in the world. The questions that engaged us as Asian American scholars—those of identity, representation, historical inequity, and racial injustice—became pressing and urgent issues in 2020 and 2021. Asian Americans came into the media and the public's attention as tensions mounted due to COVID-19 restrictions and frustrations, fueled in part by former president Donald Trump's repeated references to the virus as the "China virus" (see, for example, Reja). Violence against Asians and anyone who looked Asian in the diaspora increased in North America and Europe. These anti-Asian acts ranged from microaggressions like shunning, verbal abuse, and vandalism of Asian-owned restaurants, to spitting and coughing on Asian Americans, and finally, to physical assaults. Anti-Asian hate incidents and crimes increased in the US and Canada, as reported by Stop AAPI Hate and Fight Covid Racism (see Yam; Liu). The horrific and tragic shootings where six Asian Americans were murdered at three massage parlors in Atlanta brought the issue of anti-Asian racism, exclusion, and class inequalities precipitously into the public's purview.

The violent acts that escalated during the pandemic are evidence of a history of racism against Asian Americans dating back to the late nineteenth century, a narrative well known to scholars in ethnic and Asian American studies, but apparently, not familiar to the average member of the American or Canadian public. A number of Asian American scholars were interviewed or else published useful and informative op-eds pointing out the history to counter the prevailing myth of Asians as the model minority. Mae Ngai, Adrien De Leon, and Renee Tajima-Peña, among others, explained the history of Anti–Asian American marginalization and racism, beginning with the exclusion laws to keep out "unassimilable" Chinese in the late nineteenth century, through the incarceration of Japanese Americans and Canadians during World War II on the grounds that they were an "enemy race"; the exoticization and use of Asian women as prostitutes by American servicemen in Vietnam, Korea, the Philippines, and Okinawa; the anxiety about Japanese economic ascendancy, which led to the murder of Vincent Chin in 1982; and the continued exploitation of migrant domestic, sex, and farm workers (see Chotiner; Ngai; De Leon).

Comics and graphic novels, like novels, poems, plays, and films, though not primarily meant to be didactic, go a long way in countering misrepresentations and myths of Asian North Americans by providing full and complex depictions of Asian diasporic subjects, by telling our forgotten or silenced histories, by presenting strong and positive examples, and by explaining structures of inequality that shape our lives. Because comics tell stories by using the pictorial and visual as well as textual, educators remark that they are accessible and are a "powerful educational tool, . . . able to combine story and information simultaneously, more effectively and seamlessly, than almost every other medium" (Blake). In his seminal book, *Understanding Comics*, Scott McCloud argues that we identify with "simple and basic" faces rather than a realistic drawing (36). McCloud has famously proclaimed that the power of comics comes from the way it enables us to "reach beyond ourselves" (40). He explains, "By de-emphasizing the appearance of the physical world in favor of the idea of form, the cartoon places itself in the world of concepts" (41). Similarly, Robert Petersen writes about the immediacy of using pictures and texts, and notes that in comics and graphic narratives, the "human figure provides the reader with a vehicle for emotional empathy" (xvii). Comics and graphic novels can effectively be used to inform, transform, question assumptions about, and inspire positive perceptions of Asian Americans in the twenty-first century.

This easy identification with characters, while useful, does pose some risks. In his introduction to a special issue on graphic narrative and multiethnic literature in *MELUS* in 2007, Derek Parker Royal discusses the effectiveness and dangers of using referential icons in comics. Because comics rely heavily on stereotyping, authors, he notes, "may expose, either overtly or through tacit implication, certain recognized or even unconscious prejudices held by them and/or their readers, . . . [and] there is always the all-too-real danger of negative stereotype and caricature" (8). In literature, film, and popular culture, Asian American and Asian Canadian authors have had to engage with and resist assumptions and prejudices about their beliefs, habits, and lifestyles based on their race. While some progress has been made in terms of discriminatory practices and media representation in the last decade, popular culture still has a "problematic relationship to ethnic difference" (Royal 8). As Min Hyoung Song remarks, "It is precisely because literature can seem so personal to raced subjects like Asian Americans that the race of the author, the race of the characters it focuses on, and the racial nature of the themes it develops are such intense objects of scrutiny in both scholarly and lay discussions" (*Children* 6–7).

In light of the burgeoning work by Asian American comics creators, this volume offers critical readings of works produced by Asian North American creators in the twenty-first century that address and challenge historical and present-day race relations in the United States and Canada; that explore intersectional links between gender, class, and ethnicity; that, in a few cases, do not engage with issues of racial identity at all. As Charles Hatfield notes, "Comic art, after all, is a potentially complex narrative instrument, offering forms of visual-verbal synergy in which confused, and even conflicting points of view can be entertained all at once" (127). Recent artists represent their views of the world not only in the form of autobiographical comics but also by playing with genres, borrowing from manga, superhero comics, sci-fi, and fantasy. Making the most of words and images, they theorize and are self-reflective about the writing and drawing process; they use images to rewrite history and question cultural memory, the way our memories are shaped by symbols, media, institutions, and social practices (Erll 9). They employ innovative techniques and use different conventions, including those from nonfiction documentary, the refugee narrative, popular films, and myths. In their volume of essays focusing on multiethnic comics and history, Martha Cutter and Cathy Schlund-Vials point out the versatility of the comics form: "Using the open and flexible space of the graphic narrative page—in which readers can move not only forward but also backward, upward, downward, and in several other directions—contemporary multiethnic writers present history as a site of struggle where new configurations of the past can be manipulated and alternate conceptualizations of present and future histories might be envisioned" (2). Such flexibility of form also allows Asian American graphic artists to use their textual/visual narratives to express trauma, loss, and feelings of shame and guilt. They show crucial links between politics, power, and the well-being of marginalized people in our society, how emotions and affects "shape individual as well as collective bodies" over different historical periods (Ahmed 15).

This volume presents chapters on contemporary graphic novels authored by Asian American artists and creators rather than on comics by non–Asian Americans that feature "Oriental" and Asian American protagonists. These Asian American artists use their works to resist what have become "iconic" and exaggerated representations of Asian Americans in popular Western culture. Asian Americans have had to deal with negative media representations for more than a hundred years. Among others, Robert G. Lee has examined the tradition of "Orientalism" in newspapers and popular culture since the late nineteenth century. In *Orientals: Asian Americans in Popular Culture*, Lee looks at the tradition of "yellowface" and "racial grotesques that had illustrated broadsides, editorials, and diatribes against Asians in America since the mid-nineteenth century" (1). He reminds us that "yellowface exaggerates 'racial' features that have been designated 'Oriental,' such as 'slanted' eyes, overbite, and mustard-yellow skin color" (2). As noted by a number of scholars, in newspapers, books, and Hollywood films during the first half of the twentieth century, Asians were caricatured as sinister villains, exotic temptress figures, or else asexual servants with characters such as Fu Manchu, Lotus Blossom, and Hop Sing (Hagedorn, Preface; Gates, ch. 2; Marchetti, ch. 2). Marvel Comics adapted Sax Rohmer's supervillain Fu Manchu (later called Zheng Zu), who first appeared in 1973 and who was a genius, a master of disguise, a martial arts expert, and a skilled medical practitioner/sorcerer. Asian Americans were perceived to be aliens during the yellow peril period of the late nineteenth and early twentieth centuries and later, as foreigners who were threatening because of their otherness.[1] Jachinson Chan explains that "the unwillingness of the entertainment industry to move beyond racial stereotypes is determined by a logic of familiarity. Stereotypes effectively reduce the unfamiliar to the familiar and familiarity provides a convenient environment to minimize, or maximize, social conflicts" (8). More recently, Lori Kido Lopez observes, "Asian Americans have historically been portrayed as noncitizens—as unassimilable perpetual foreigners" (16), but they have also become the model minority, someone who is "passive and nonconfrontational, possesses an aptitude for math and science, and is the picture of discipline and obedience" (17). Lopez notes that it was not until the 1970s that Asian Americans began to organize, fight for cultural citizenship and belonging, and protest racist media imagery (17–18).

In order to create multiplicity and complexity in their narratives, Asian American graphic creators resist and attempt to go beyond one-dimensional characters, racist iconography, and stereotypical representations. In his well-cited work on representation, Stuart Hall notes that "stereotypes get hold of the few simple, vivid, memorable, easily grasped and widely recognized characteristics about a person, *reduce* everything about the person to those traits, *exaggerate* and *simplify* them, and *fix* them without change or development to eternity," rendering them "abnormal" and "unacceptable" (258). In order to challenge the negative iconography and stereotypes, Asian American graphic creators often have to invoke them and rework, rewrite, and resituate them. In art, Hans Lund argues that paintings such as Edvard Munch's *The Scream*, "the stereotypical face of anxiety," can be

---

1. Jachinson Chan notes that "Fu Manchu represents the xenophobia towards Chinese laborers while Charlie Chan conceals the underlying ethnic-specific racism in American culture by upholding a model minority group while vilifying other racial minority groups in the 1920s and 1930s" (6).

"paraphrased" and put into new context, including into comic strips. In graphic narratives by Asian Americans, iconic photographs and images are redrawn, pastiched, transposed into new temporal and cultural contexts. For example, Lynda Barry repurposes childhood objects and photographs into collages; Gene Luen Yang invokes nineteenth-century images of the China-man and puts them into contemporary America. Familiar literary techniques such as imitation, parody, adaptation, and translation are used to question and critique cultural assumptions about Asian Americans.

Asian American Literature and the Graphic Novel: Historical Context 1970s–2000

The development of the graphic novel, particularly autobiographical com-ics, and of Asian American literature, particularly autobiographical novels by Asian American women, intersected in ways that facilitated the growth of Asian American graphic narrative. Both the graphic novel and Asian American literature emerged in the 1970s. As comics scholars have noted, the term "graphic novel" was first used by Will Eisner in *A Contract with God—A Graphic Novel* (1978). Eisner was influenced by underground comix but wanted to promote "serious comics to the general book trade and a gen-eral readership" (Hatfield 29). Charles Hatfield argues that the underground comix movement transformed comic books into a commodity for adults as it "conveyed an unprecedented sense of intimacy, rivaling the scandalizing disclosures of confessional poetry but shot through with fantasy, burlesque, and self-satire" (7). By the 1980s, the publication of several novel-length vol-umes that had originally been serialized, such as Art Spiegelman's *Maus* (1986), Frank Miller's *The Dark Knight Returns* (1986), and Alan Moore and Dave Gibbon's *Watchmen* (1987), established the graphic novel in the book trade (Hatfield 30). Autobiography soon became one of the common genres within graphic novels. Robert Petersen writes of the rise of stories detail-ing "an artist's difficult childhood and budding sexuality," such as Ches-ter Brown's *The Playboy* (1992), Craig Thompson's *Blankets* (2003), David Beauchard's *Epileptic* (2005), Alison Bechdel's *Fun Home* (2006), and Marjane Satrapi's *Persepolis* (2007). This trajectory overlaps with the development of Asian American literature in significant ways.

The term "Asian American," introduced after the civil rights movements and the strikes at San Francisco State University in the 1960s, was meant to bring together Chinese, Japanese, and Filipino Americans, each with their own histories and relation to imperialism, their different means of entry into the US, into a strategic pan-ethnic political coalition.[2] Published in 1974, the volume *Aiiieeeee! An Anthology of Asian-American Writers*, edited by Frank Chin, Jeffery Chan, Lawson Inada, Shawn Wong, and others, was an effort to unite Filipino, Chinese, and Japanese American writers, but the editors' notions of who qualified as Asian American turned out to be masculinist and limited to those who were American born. The editors outlined issues facing Asian Americans then, such as racism, Orientalism, ghettoed communities, and class issues, which have remained important for Asian American resistance movements. But as David Leiwei Li observes, the editors did not figure out "how differently racism affects people of different backgrounds and how their different responses are expressed in writing" (35).

A few years later, Maxine Hong Kingston's *The Woman Warrior* (1976) and Joy Kogawa's *Obasan* (1981), both autobiographical novels, appealed more broadly to the sensibilities of Asian and non-Asian American readers and became iconic texts of Asian American and Canadian literature in the 1980s and 1990s. Weaving together history, myth, stories, and memory, both Kingston and Kogawa presented their oral or "talk story" narratives from a feminist perspective, and dealt with topics such as silence and speech, women's oppression in a patriarchal system, racial exclusion, and prejudice. In her study of Hisaye Yamamoto, Maxine Hong Kingston, and Joy Kogawa, King-Kok Cheung points out that these three writers "question the authority of language . . . and speak to the resources as well as the hazards of silence. They articulate—question, report, expose—the silences imposed on themselves and their peoples, whether in the form of feminine and cultural decorum, external or self-censorship, or historical or political invisibility; at the same time, they reveal . . . that silences—textual ellipses, nonverbal gestures, authorial hesitations . . . can also be articulated" (*Articulate Silences* 3–4).

Kingston's *Woman Warrior* was praised for its feminist elements, for its depiction of "female condition and female anger" by many reviewers and critics (Johnson 19). Sidonie Smith writes, "No single work captures so powerfully the relationship of gender to genre in twentieth-century autobiography as Maxine Hong Kingston's *Woman Warrior*. . . . Using autobiography to create identity, she breaks down the hegemony of formal 'autobiography' and breaks out of the silence that has bound her culturally to discover a

---

2. Before the term "Asian American" was first used by activists and academics in 1968 in Berkeley, there were already works published by Asian Americans, including books by biracial sisters born in Montreal, Edith Maude (1865–1914) and Winnifred (1875–1954) Eaton; Filipino-born Carlos Bulosan (1913–56); Louis Hing Chu (1915–70); Jade Snow Wong (1922–2006); and others. The works of these writers have been retrospectively claimed as "Asian American."

resonant voice of her own" (150–51). However, it also garnered strong negative criticism from some Asian American authors and critics who denounced
it for pandering to white readers and for its use of negative stereotypes of
Chinese men. For example, Frank Chin claimed that Kingston's autobiographical form was "fake," not Chinese, but based on the Western meta-
physical tradition and the Christian confession (Chin 3). David Li explains
that Kingston's work was caught between many opposing factions: "new
immigrants with their diasporic sensibility" and the "native-born generations whose sensibilities are formed by a colonial education and the structures of exclusion" (50). It was also ensnared in debates about its generic
classification and with its claims as a real account of life. Furthermore, Li
says, "First, the work of ethnic art inevitably shoulders, as historical cir-
cumstances obligate it, the burden or representing the whole humanity of
its people in culture and politics, a task no single work is capable of. Second,
ethnic writers are unwillingly caught in the struggle for the hard-to-obtain
position of the community representative" (52–53). Thus, by the 1990s, critics were advocating for more and varied forms of Asian American representation. There was a concerted effort to promote diversity of ethnicity, class,
age, culture, and religion, as suggested by the celebration of "heterogeneity,
hybridity, multiplicity" by Lisa Lowe.

Asian American Literary and Cultural Criticism: Developments Pre- and Post-2000

In the late 1990s, Lisa Lowe, King-Kok Cheung, and a number of other
Asian American literary scholars emphasized "heterogeneity and diaspora"
(Cheung, *Interethnic Companion* 1) and the ethno-cultural and sexual diversity of Asian Americans. Rachel Lee highlighted the importance of "gender
and sexuality" in the way "Asian American writers conceive of and write
about 'America'" (3), noting the "changing terrains of Asian American gender critique with its new sources in theories of subaltern womanhood and
the gendering of international labor" (11). There was a push to go beyond
the boundaries of nation and gender. Gayatri Gopinath used the term "queer
diasporas," arguing that "suturing 'queer' to 'diaspora' thus recuperates
those desires, practices, and subjectivities that are rendered impossible and
unimaginable within conventional diasporic and national imaginaries" (11).
At the beginning of the twenty-first century, otherness was often discussed
through Freudian-inspired psychoanalytic discourse, including "Asian
abjection" (Li 6), the "racial castration" of Asian American masculinity (Eng

2), and mourning and the "melancholy of race" (Cheng ch. 1). The common thread in these theories is the view that Asian Americans are "othered" by dominant culture and live as "others" in America. Consequently, in *Imagine Otherwise*, Kandice Chuh urges us to imagine Asian American identity differently: "To imagine otherwise is not about imagining as the other, but rather, is about imagining the other differently" (9). Chuh offers the notion of "subjectlessness" as a conceptual tool, arguing for "strategic *anti*-essentialism" instead of "problematic assumptions of essential identities" (10). Subjectlessness can open up "various components of differences (gender, class, sexuality, religion, and so on)," as well as "help to identify and trace the shifting positionalities and complicated terrains of US American culture and politics articulated to a globalized frame" (10–11).

Another literary scholar who proposed a compelling reassessment of Asian American critical practices in the twenty-first century is erin Khuê Ninh, whose book *Ingratitude: The Debt-Bound Daughter in Asian American Literature* cautions against putting all the blame of intergenerational conflicts on "externally imposed racialization and stereotype" or "institutional racism and media representation" (4, 5). Instead, Ninh examines the Asian American family itself, reading the "immigrant nuclear family as a special form of capitalist enterprise," where the Asian immigrant family is a "production unit . . . for a particular brand of good, capitalist subject" (2). She contends that the daughters in novels by Jade Snow Wong, Maxine Hong Kingston, Evelyn Lau, Fae Myenne Ng, and others are subjected to threats of disownment, the regulation of sexuality, and other forms of familial power by their families. Aimee Bahng's *Migrant Futures* similarly critiques the negative effects of capitalism but through a comparison of "fiction, finance, and futurity" (1). Bahng uses the trope of speculation, of speculative finance and speculative fiction "as two forms of extrapolative figuration that participate in the cultural production of futurity" (2). Wishing to imagine the future otherwise, Bahng writes, "In the face of a seemingly monolithic financialized future, as conceived by investment banks and international development funds, this book . . . sets out to think speculation from below and highlights alternative engagements with futurity emerging from the colonized, displaced, and disavowed" (7).

In the same way, the scholars in this volume are interested in how Asian American graphic artists imagine not just the past but the future differently. Given the variety of scholarly methodology critics have used to examine Asian American literature and culture over the last two decades, it is not surprising that the contributors to this volume also employ a wide range of approaches to discuss contemporary graphic novels. In spite of my cursory summary of scholarly criticism, there is not a straight chronological path of theoretical approaches from heterogeneity, gender, diaspora, melancholia, Otherness, and anti-essentialism to affect and futurism in Asian American literature. As Asian American studies scholars working in comics studies, we have benefited from these theoretical approaches as well as historical, critical insights and terminology from film studies, visual culture, critical race theories, and feminist studies. Henry John Pratt points out that "comics and film use many of the same narrative techniques. . . . The art forms arose at about the same time, both are products of a mass culture and its associated means of reproduction and dissemination, and most importantly, comics and film alike are typically a hybrid of the verbal and the visual" (113). Terms such as "composition," "framing," "distance of framing," and "shot/reverse-shot sequence" are used in comics and film studies, while some comics studies scholars use terms from visual art such as "chiaroscuro," "collage," "color hues," "cross-hatching," and "realistic" (Molotiu). Feminist and gender theories shape the essays by Oh, Ninh, Roan, and de Jesús; critical race and postcolonial theories underlie the discussions by Davé, Dong, Lee, and de Jesús; affect, trauma, and film and visual culture studies inspire the readings of Chiu, Oh, Ninh, Roan, and Ty. Finally, posthuman, environmental, ethics, and disability studies figure in the chapters of Ty and Oh. What links the chapters together is the way all the contributors read the graphic narratives through the lens of Asian American cultural criticism, politics, and history.

Asian American Graphic Novels, 2000–2010: Key Texts

The popularity of literary works by Asian North Americans showed that there was interest in stories of racialized others and that you could talk about personal experiences of marginalization, alienation, dislocation, and injustice in fiction. At the same time, a parallel development of the confessional mode was happening in comics. Tracing the roots of autobiographical comics to Robert Crumb's "The Confessions of R. Crumb" (1972) and Justin Green's *Binky Brown Meets the Holy Virgin* (1972), Elisabeth El Refaie notes that "what these underground-inspired works have in common is the apparent desire of their creators to use brutally honest—even exhibitionist— accounts of personal experiences as a way of challenging puritanical American society and its concept of the 'normal'" (38). Thus, not coincidentally, the first Asian American graphic novel to emerge in the early 2000s was Lynda Barry's *One! Hundred! Demons!*, a first-person account of a mixed-race young girl growing up in a poor neighborhood in Seattle with her Filipina mother and grandmother. In the section that follows, I discuss four key graphic narratives that have become staples in comics studies as well as in Asian American literature. They were all produced in the first decade of the twenty-first century and contain some autobiographical elements, characteristics of early comics. Though these graphic novels share themes of exclusion and alienation, their graphiation and choice of protagonists are very different, demonstrating the variety of styles and imaginative possibilities in the comics genre. These four graphic novels have been most influential in the field and are the most often taught works in courses on the Asian American graphic novel. The following section provides brief overviews of the main concerns and quintessential scholarly criticism that have been written about them.

LYNDA BARRY'S *ONE! HUNDRED! DEMONS!* AND AUTOBIOGRAPHY

Lynda Barry's *One! Hundred! Demons!*, first published semimonthly online at Salon.com from April 7, 2000, to January 15, 2001 (de Jesús 1), is probably the best-known of the four. It can be read through various subgenres of fiction: as a thinly veiled fictional autobiography, a bildungsroman, a graphic novel about abuse, an ethnic or immigrant story, and a mother-daughter narrative. It is also a work that has been read from different theoretical approaches—feminist, life writing, race, trauma, and comics studies. The book, a collection of nineteen linked stories in the form of comic strips, straddles "high" and "mass" culture, according to Hillary Chute (109). Some of the stories are drawn on yellow lined paper, suggesting a homemade quality, while other strips are set against pastel-colored backgrounds that give them a vibrant, lively tone. Most notable are the double-page collages that serve as the title pages to each story and are richly decorated and textured. Chute describes these collage pages as "dense and accumulative. . . . a piling on of sundry materials, including strips of brightly colored fabrics; cardboard; magazine pictures; tissue paper; the scalloped edge of a paper bag; photographs; the printed insides of bank envelopes; interior candy bar and gum wrapping; dried flowers; bits of doilies; glitter globs; Ric Rac; Chinese postage stamps; origami creatures; a stuffed animal; and pieces of old pajamas" (110). The inclusion of these items, used in crafts and associated with the feminine, suggest a valorization of domestic arts, and the tendency to collect, save, and reuse what might be considered scraps, memorabilia, or rubbish.

Not all critics call Barry an "Asian American" artist, but she writes about many of the themes found in Kingston's and Kogawa's works, such as imposed silences, oral stories, racial marginalization, invisibility, and shame. Barry was influenced by underground comics' sense of intimacy, self-satire, and humor and used them to question negative stereotypes of mixed-race Asian Americans in her "autobifictionalography" (Barry, table of contents). In essence, Lynda Barry was using the comics form to do the same work as Kingston and Kogawa did in their autobiographical novels—to put together from objects and documents a version of one's life story to counter official history, to remember and imagine a narrative from the bits and pieces left behind. Critic Manina Jones calls Joy Kogawa's work a "documentary collage" (122) because Kogawa's "citation of history through the quotations of historical documents" exposes "gaps in the record" kept by the Canadian government about the forced relocation and dispersal of Japanese Canadians during World War II (130). Similarly, Barry's visual and material collage becomes a kind of remembering and reimagining of what she could not say or fully understand as a child. Susan Kirtley notes, "While Barry prefers not to speak of her girlhood, images of girls came to dominate her works in all genres, and eventually her own personal story as a girl began to emerge in later works" (15). While childhood and/or girlhood are often viewed as a time of simplicity, Leigh Gilmore and Elizabeth Marshall point out that this view is a cultural myth: "Centering women of color as analysts of oppression and injustice casts a new light on the fiction of childhood innocence and the myth of protecting children. The innocence of childhood is a racialized construct. To place girls of color, and by extension, mothers of color, as the agents of an autobiographical tradition invested in testimony and justice is to recast the mutual construction of childhood and innocence as a function of whiteness" (Introduction). Though Barry's work is not strictly a graphic memoir, it attempts to delineate the artist's struggle with her difficult childhood, sexuality, and feelings of alienation in the same way as white/non-Asian American comic artists and Asian American novelists of the period.

Barry engages readers through what Gillian Whitlock calls "autographics" (966), where Whitlock repurposes Gilmore's term "autobiographics" to call attention to the "specific conjunctions of visual and verbal text in this genre of autobiography, and also to the subject positions that narrators negotiate in and through comics" (966). Through the juxtaposition of the child and the adult on the same page, for example, Barry is able to compress time and space in an economical way to show the changing subject positions of the narrator as she matures. Speaking of women graphic artists such as Marjane Satrapi, Phoebe Gloeckner, and Lynda Barry, Chute says, "They use the inbuilt duality of the form—its word and image cross-discursivity—to stage dialogues among versions of self, underscoring the importance of an ongoing, unclosed project of self-representation and self-narration" (5). In the story called "Lost Worlds," Barry inserts one panel of the narrator as an adult, drawn as a red-haired woman with glasses, sitting in an airplane amidst the recollection of herself as a freckled child energetically playing kickball on the streets. Playing kickball using manhole covers as bases reveals the working-class neighborhood of her childhood, but the memory of those days is one of nostalgia and spontaneity rather than a sense of deprivation. While the child Lynda tries to wave to people in the airplane from the ground, the adult Lynda's realization that "you can't see VERY MUCH FROM AN airplane WINDOW. BIG THINGS, YES, but the little things are lost" becomes a literal metaphorical statement about loss—of memories, of innocence, of childhood friendships and play—as she notes that people and "whole neighborhoods of children" (33) tend to disappear from a geographical and temporal distance. The juxtaposition of images highlights the importance of perspective in our efforts to recreate the past, offering a somewhat ironic and, at the same time, nostalgic view of childhood. Her work demonstrates how visual narrative in graphic novels can be used to convey "the little things" that are "lost," how silences can be effective.

While Asian American novelists employ "articulate silences" in prose (Cheung, *Articulate Silences*) as a strategy, many comics creators use comics devices, such as gutters, to narrate the unspeakable (see Postema, ch. 2). One specific rhetorical device of comics that Barry makes use of is what Thierry Groensteen has called braiding or *tressage*. Groensteen explains that one type of braiding is "repetition . . . with or without variation," which can enrich and supplement the reading experience, producing "an enhancement, a layering, a deepening of meaning" (Groensteen). Melinda Luisa de Jesús has looked at Barry as a "vanguard feminist or 'wimmin's' cartoonist" (3) who articulates the Filipina American perspective.[3] De Jesús focuses on "The Aswang" chapter (originally published in Salon.com), noting that Barry uses the myth of the vampire-like dog monster to represent her "estrangement/ alienation" from her mother, who fears the *aswang* and her bond with her grandmother, who retells the monster story to fit her purposes (8). One panel in this chapter represents Lynda's very angry mother, with one arm outstretched, swearing that "There is NO ASWANG" (92). Emanata, specifically plewds, or teardrop shapes, emanate from the mother's head to express her embarrassment and her worry, and jarns, quimps, nittles, and grawlixes (squiggles, stars, and other glyphs that substitute for curse words) come out

---

3. De Jesús situates Barry among other Asian American women writers, like Evelyn Galang and Kingston, who also use mother-daughter stories in order to show how the daughter "constructs a hybrid new identity" for herself (4, 5).

FIGURES 0.1A AND B. Panels from Lynda Barry's *One! Hundred! Demons!* (a) There is no aswang. (b) Stop that. © Lynda Barry. Used by permission from Drawn and Quarterly.

of her mouth (Friedman). This image of the mother, pictured on the bottom right corner of a panel and looking to the left, is repeated several times in *One! Hundred! Demons!* to emphasize not only the mother's irascible character but also the mother's negative behavior and its lasting influence on Lynda.

The braiding of this image occurs most obviously in the story/chapter "Dogs," where there are two panels featuring this same angry stance at the bottom right corner. Lynda as an adult is shown yelling at her dogs, and this is mirrored on the opposite page with her mother yelling at Lynda for crying about Lassie on TV as a child (172–73). Lynda has internalized the anger and self-loathing from her mother, and from her has learned to be verbally abusive toward the weak. The repetition of the figures with the same pose makes the problem apparent. Braiding occurs within a story/chapter and also between stories in *One! Hundred! Demons!*, linking them thematically, enabling readers to understand the cumulative effects of ostracization, marginalization, and racial abjection. Using visual and textual means of telling the story, Barry's graphic memoir, like Kingston's and Kogawa's books, recounts and gives voice to these intergenerational issues, as well as revealing how feelings of shame and lack of self-worth affect the subjectivities of Asian American children.

GENE LUEN YANG'S *AMERICAN BORN CHINESE*: CONTESTING STEREOTYPES

A number of Asian American graphic artists employed genres other than autobiography at this time. Using what Min Hyoung Song describes as "the twin poles of realism and genre fiction" ("How Good" 76–77), Gene Luen Yang, in *American Born Chinese* (2006), similarly explores issues of "identity and belonging," through three intertwined story lines (Dong, "Reimagining" 232). Yang's graphic narrative appeals to, and is suitable for, both mature and young adult readers as it deals with many of the issues, such as the difficulties of assimilation, desiring to be white, old versus new world cultures, and generational conflicts, raised by Asian American authors of the 1990s and 2000s. Yang deliberately draws a fine "distinction between the American-born generation and their immigrant parents" (Dong, "Reimagining" 232) with the intertextual retelling of the Monkey King legend alongside a story about an Asian American boy set in contemporary San Francisco. Yang's representation of Chin-Kee, Danny's Chinese cousin, risks what Derek Parker Royal warns as "negative stereotype and caricature" (8). However, Song situates Chin-Kee historically, noting that the character is "a grotesque stereotype of the Chinese as racially alien, a stereotype first cast in the nineteenth century as Western imperial countries chipped away at China's sovereignty and Chinese workers began to populate California and the rest of the American West in visibly large numbers" (Song, "How Good" 78, 80).

Thus, Chin-Kee seems exaggerated and repulsive to Danny and to readers, but Yang is actually drawing an image "formalized in newspapers and popular entertainment and later largely disseminated through the growth of popular media" (Song, "How Good" 80). Dong notes that "Yang's creation of Chin-Kee stands the enduring images of the 'Heathen Chinee' and the Chinaman on their heads and provides criticism in visual as well as textual representations" (Dong, "Reimagining" 242). Toward the end of the novel, Chin-Kee reveals himself to be the Monkey King, and Danny and his friend are also not who we believe them to be. Song notes that "these dizzying revelations emphasize the ways in which *American Born Chinese* is interested in what is hidden from view. Outward identities lead inexorably to secret identities, and bodies are always capable of transforming themselves— much like the transformer robots that Jin and Wei-Chen liked to play with when they first met" (Song, "How Good" 83). Just as Barry uses repetition to articulate what has been lost and forgotten, Yang uses the intertextual references of these visual images to give a sense of depth and complexity to his characters. Jin learns to stop wishing he were someone else, because appearances are not always indicative of one's character. In her chapter in this volume, scholar Jin Lee elaborates on the function of the anachronistic character Chin-Kee to illuminate the existence of century-old stereotypes in our contemporary culture.

ADRIAN TOMINE'S *SHORTCOMINGS* AND ASIAN AMERICAN MASCULINITY

Responding specifically to assumptions about Asian American sexuality and masculinity, Adrian Tomine creates an unlikeable antihero, Ben Tanaka, in *Shortcomings* (2007; originally serialized in *Optic Nerve* #9–11). Tomine uses his fictional insecure, yet slightly obnoxious Japanese American male protagonist to demonstrate the psychic damage of negative media stereotypes on Asian American males. Ben, who remarks to his girlfriend that not everything has to be a "big statement about race" (Tomine, *Shortcomings* 13), nevertheless is deeply affected by the popular films and videos that he consumes. Stella Oh observes, "In an effort to assert his own Asian American masculinity, historically feminized and emasculated, he watches porn featuring white women and sexually desires white women, thus gendering and racializing them as ideal feminine commodities" (108). Ben desires, but is unable to execute his fantasies with, white women. Oh notes, "The visual syntax and the spatio-temporal framing of the panels in *Shortcomings* signal the distance between expectations for intimate connection and the shortcomings of attaining such intimacy" (110–11). The distance between expectations and reality here reveals what is hidden from view, the unexpressed pain experienced by Asian American men. The framing of the narrative through surveillance cameras, film and TV screens, and photographic lenses reveals "interpellative viewing practices," how others see us and how we, in turn, see ourselves (Oh 114). Through a series of failed relationships experienced by Ben, Tomine raises uncomfortable questions about "ideals of white beauty," the "hypersexualized Asian women," and the "emasculation of an Asian American man" (Oh 117). These are critical and ongoing issues that have affected Asian American male and female subjectivities that have been discussed further by Asian American film scholars, such as Celine Parreñas Shimizu and Jane Chi Hyun Park.

MARIKO TAMAKI AND GILLIAN TAMAKI'S *SKIM*: QUEER AND OTHER

Published originally in a shorter form as a special edition of the magazine *Kiss Machine* in 2005 (Saltman), Mariko Tamaki and Gillian Tamaki's *Skim* has become a YA favorite, nominated for four Eisner Awards in 2009 and winning the 2008 Ignatz Award for Outstanding Graphic Novel and the Best Book at the 2009 Doug Wright Awards. *Skim* echoes some of the themes of alienation, isolation, and racial otherness found in other Asian North American literature, but also deals with depression, queer identity, and teen suicide. It is a novel about growing up Japanese Canadian and queer, yet the textual narrative does not articulate Skim's sense of outsiderness. As Monica Chiu notes of Skim's secret relationship with her English teacher, there is no "verbal corroboration" for lesbian encounters so that readers need to "ascertain for themselves the reality or fiction of these homosexual encounters" (29). Similarly, "Skim's visible physical features (almond eyes, black hair) denote her Asian heritage without a single verbal articulation of race" so that the novel "successfully pictures that which has been rendered unspeakable in her school" (Chiu 29). Skim's depression comes from her race, her lesbian desire, but also her body weight and her parents' divorce. Eleanor Ty points out that Skim is unable to participate in what Sara Ahmed calls the "happiness commandment," which entailed conforming to the aspirations of her parents and their ideas of happiness and success (Ty 41). The use of the diary format gives an "authentic adolescent voice" to the narrative, while Jillian Tamaki's monochromatic drawings, panels varying in size and placement on the page, framing, and perspective call attention to Skim's loneliness, her adolescent confusion, her yearning, and her desire for validation (Saltman). Similar to Barry, Yang, and Tomine, Mariko Tamaki and Gillian Tamaki's graphic novel expresses, through verbal and nonverbal narratives, the difficulties of articulating the self, especially as a queer Asian North American subject.

Contemporary Asian American Graphic Novels: Chapter Summaries

Asian American graphic creators after the first decade of the twenty-first century continue to use their work to scrutinize and resist Orientalist stereotypes, challenge social and cultural marginalization, and reconstruct personal and political histories. Many of them have also taken on large social issues, such as the misuse and overuse of technology, environmental problems, and media misinformation. They demonstrate the intersectional relationships between race, class, gender, and disability. The essays in this volume examine selected contemporary Asian American graphic artists and storytellers who are keenly aware of the power of representation in history, literature, popular media, and comics. Pulitzer Prize winner Viet Thanh Nguyen has repeatedly emphasized the importance of Asian American representation in the media and in culture: "It is still a struggle in the US for populations that are minorities or unrepresented or marginalized in some way to have people access to the means of production and representation to get their stories out there," he observed in an interview (Villano). "What we need is a situation in which there are thousands of stories about us so that when one story screws up, it doesn't matter," he said. "That's why white people can go to watch a movie and if they don't like it, they'll say, 'It's just a story.' Because it doesn't matter. They have a million stories about them" (J. Nguyen). For minorities and people of color, however, representation in history and the popular media is an ongoing struggle. As our title suggests, the graphic narratives examined in this volume not only reject stereotypical icons but also break other boundaries by "imagining otherwise" (Chuh), resituating media and popular culture representations of Asian Americans, using nonrealist and experimental techniques, using humor, irony, and parody to present a fuller and broader picture of Asian American experiences.

The first section, "Retelling History," consists of two chapters that discuss the ways comics artists have the power to highlight and refocus our attention to untold stories of the past. Both *They Called Us Enemy* and *The Best We Could Do* present personal accounts of historical events that have been important for Asian Americans, namely, the internment of Japanese Americans and the Vietnam War. By visualizing aspects of history that have been elided in the media and in historical accounts, they perform the work of re-presentation, reinvesting old sites with new meaning. Cutter and Schlund Vials discuss historical comics that "turn to the past not only or necessarily to create a new factual history but instead to ask readers to resist stabilizing the past's meaning as a totalizing narrative about what 'really' happened" and "to envision polyphonic, diverse, complicated narratives of history" (16). *They Called Us Enemy* recounts *Star Trek* actor and activist George Takei's childhood experience of being imprisoned in camps with other Japanese American families during WWII after the bombing of Pearl Harbor in 1941. Monica Chiu's chapter on George Takei, Steven Scott, and Justin Eisinger's graphic memoir focuses on three camp icons that appear with regularity in internment literature, film, and photography: sentry towers, barbed wire fences, and latrines. Chiu argues that the images provided by the graphic novel counter the visual censorship of these camps. Through the perspective of George, the child's-eye view, Chiu notes that these objects and images become "differently meaningful" across Japanese Americans and non-Japanese Americans, encouraging readers to identity with the plight of the "enemy aliens."

Thi Bui's highly acclaimed *The Best We Could Do* was a finalist for a number of awards, including the National Book Critics Circle (2017), the American Book Award, and the Eisner Award for Reality-Based Comics. Based on Bui's family story of migration from Vietnam, the graphic memoir depicts Bui's search for her identity and the family's experience of war, trauma, and assimilation into US society. It has been taught in a number of college and university courses and was the UCLA First Year Experience Common Book for 2017–18 (UCLA First Year Experience). The chapter by Stella Oh and erin Khuê Ninh points out how Bui rewrites media and filmic representations of the Vietnam War by delineating the effects of colonization and the war on individuals, especially on women. Oh and Ninh observe that *The Best We Could Do* engages in "a form of ethical storytelling," offering "new perspectives of the Vietnam War through the lens of motherhood and family." The chapter offers two different ways of approaching and teaching the graphic memoir, one from an upper-division course in women's and gender studies and another from a course on Vietnamese American experience in an Asian American studies program. Oh's course highlights the way Bui's novel can be used to link class discussions to current debates on refugees and migration and the way personal experience can reflect a "larger collective memory." Ninh discusses the way Bui's memoir avoids sensationalism of the past through her muted visuals. In addition, drawing on Mimi Thi Nguyen's notion of the "grateful refugee," Ninh reminds us not to succumb too easily to readings that focus on the good refugee story and refugee gratitude, which can become, for refugees and children of refugees, a "dangerous definition of freedom."

The three essays in the second section, "Subverting Stereotypes," examine comics that challenge racialized stereotypes of the meek and compliant Asian, counter the model minority myth, and combat the abjection of the Filipina girl. The comics studied in this section present Asian American women who are strong and who are survivors of racism and trauma. They show the fantasy and outdated tendencies of Orientalist icons and racial categories that are still prevalent today. Jeanette Roan looks at one issue of the feminist dystopian comics series *Bitch Planet* that features a female character of Asian descent to show how it deconstructs stereotypes using Anne Anlin

Cheng's theory of "ornamentalism." The comics series, set in an imaginary outpost, parodies women-in-prison exploitation films of the '60s and '70s. Created by Kelly Sue DeConnick and Valentine De Landro, *Bitch Planet* is an "exaggerated parody of a patriarchal society" and reveals, in a satiric tone, the oppression and objectification of women. Roan notes that in this particular issue, Meiko, the Asian female character, surprises the other prisoners with her athletic agility. She is petite but can run "like a cheetah" and impresses others when she and another player team up to win a game the prisoners play. Roan analyzes the visual and textual narratives in Meiko's backstory compared to those of an African American character, showing the dangerous and unsettling ways Asian and African American women have been categorized and exoticized. The comic ends with a strong critique and subversion of the notions of "good Asians," challenging the Asian American model minority myth.

Looking at the reappearance of stereotypes that are more than fifty years old in contemporary graphic novels, Jin Lee points out that the anachronistic presence of racist figures is revealing and is used by Gene Yang and Fred Chao to "remind us of the legacies of racialized histories in America." Taking advantage of the ability of comics to "spatialize temporality," Lee argues that *American Born Chinese* and *Johnny Hiro* counter the representation of Asian Americans as homogeneous through a "structure of splitting and displacement." Using Homi Bhabha's notions of nation, territory, and tradition, Jin Lee argues that characters who embody multiple temporalities show the "anachronistic continuation of racism" and the "history of segregation" for Asian Americans.

Melinda Luisa de Jesús's chapter examines two emerging Filipina comics artists, Trinidad Escobar and Malaka Gharib, through the lens of girls' studies, Pinay aesthetics, and decolonization. Aside from scholarly work on Lynda Barry, there have been few studies on Filipina American graphic artists. Pinay North American comics creators, such as Escobar, Gharib, Lorina Mapa, and Emmanuelle Chateauneuf, have recently published works about growing up Filipina in the US and in Canada. Their stories represent their fascinating cross-cultural, transnational experiences due to the US's neocolonial relationship with the Philippines. Using what she calls "peminist" theory, de Jesús raises issues about belonging, adoption, mixed-race families, girlhood, trauma, and memory.

The third section of the volume looks at superhero comics that feature Asian American protagonists. Superhero comics remain one of the most popular forms of comic books and are enormously influential, especially for young adult readers. Comics featuring a "heroic character with a selfless, pro-social mission; with superpowers—extraordinary abilities, advanced technology, or highly developed physical, mental, or mystical skills . . . and iconic costume" appeared after the Great Depression, featuring characters such as Superman, Batman, Captain Marvel, Wonder Woman, and Captain America (Coogan 30). Produced primarily for young male readers by DC and Marvel, superhero comics presented mainly white, male superheroes—until recently. Shilpa Davé's and Lan Dong's chapters provide discussions of how representations of superheroes who are nonwhite can empower Asian American communities. Davé's chapter studies the comics superhero *Ms. Marvel*, arguing that Ms. Marvel's Pakistani and Muslim identity makes her a significant post-racial superhero across multiple media platforms. With her shapeshifting abilities, Kamala Khan assumes the mantle of her idol Carol Danvers, the white superhero otherwise known as Captain Marvel. Davé notes that *Ms. Marvel* changes what is conventionally seen as "normal" through the depiction of Kamala's daily life representations of her family, food, clothing, and religious practices.

Lan Dong argues that Gene Yang and Sonny Liew's *The Shadow Hero* "plays with Orientalist imagery," situating the Chinese American superhero within the stereotypical "family and community life of a fictional 1940s Chinatown." The comic functions to disrupt the superhero genre through humor and exaggeration at the same time as it becomes an "expression of Asian American history and culture." Dong looks at the significance of details—of costumes, insignias, and skin color—pointing out that these visual markers bear witness to the industry's gradual progress in representations of racialized superheroes.

The fourth and last section demonstrates how Asian American comic creators engage with broader, current issues of ecology, inclusivity, and otherness. Moving away from stories about growing up, which was the subject of Mariko and Jillian Tamaki's most popular graphic novel, *Skim*, Jillian Tamaki's *Boundless* deals with a range of important topics, including the use of social media, the difficulty of forming lasting social bonds, speciesism, illness, and aging. Eleanor Ty's chapter reads four stories from *Boundless* that deal, in particular, with anthropomorphism, with what Cary Wolfe calls "posthumanist" concerns. In "World Class City," "Bedbugs," "Boundless," and "1.Jenny," Tamaki highlights the importance of nonhuman animals in our world through animal focalization. Using humor and fantasy, Tamaki also comments on the significant role social media apps like Facebook play in the construction and development of our identity. Ty points out various ways the drawing techniques used by Tamaki reflect the theme of "boundlessness." Tamaki shows the dissolution of the boundaries between animal and human, male and female, and real and virtual, and how our well-being is intimately connected to the nonhuman, to those we have deemed as Others.

In a similar way, Stella Oh examines an important issue that concerns our contemporary society's efforts to be more inclusive. She looks at the "interplay between verbal and visual modalities combining text and image" in a story about a disabled character from Adrian Tomine's *Killing and Dying*. Using Emmanuel Levinas's theory of ethics and optics, Oh studies not only what is "visible and pictorially embodied" but also the "absent and missing that challenge us toward ethical responsibility" as we "engage meaningfully with difference." Her chapter approaches graphic narratives through ethics, disability studies, and feminist gaze theories in order to problematize old ways of seeing.

Beyond the Icon: Asian American Graphic Narratives does not provide a chronological survey of Asian North American graphic novels but instead looks at ways graphic novels by Asian Americans have moved beyond iconic representations, thematically and stylistically, in the twenty-first century. Many of the creators question essentialist notions of race; their ways of telling stories, their "graphiation" (Baetens and Frey 137), or their drawing styles reflect the desire to move beyond referential icons and stereotypes. As the contributors note, these graphic novels offer exciting new ways of envisioning Asian Americans as multiply constituted subjects, as subjects involved in the movement toward social justice, self-representation, and empowerment in arts, culture, and the community. The volume opens up and provides vital conversations between Asian American studies, ethnic studies, and comics studies scholars.

Works Cited

Ahmed, Sara. *The Cultural Politics of Emotion*. Routledge, 2010.

Baetens, Jan, and Hugo Frey. *The Graphic Novel: An Introduction*. Cambridge University Press, 2015.

Bahng, Aimee. *Migrant Futures: Decolonizing Speculation in Financial Times*. Duke University Press, 2018.

Barry, Lynda. *One! Hundred! Demons!* Sasquatch Books, 2002.

Blake, Corey. "The Benefits and Risks of Comics in Education." *CBR*, 30 January 2013, https://www.cbr.com/the-benefits-and-risks-of-comics-in-education/.

Chan, Jachinson. *Chinese American Masculinities: From Fu Manchu to Bruce Lee*. Routledge, 2001.

Chateauneuf, Emmanuelle. *Queen Street*. Chapterhouse, 2017.

Cheng, Anne Anlin. *The Melancholy of Race: Psychoanalysis, Assimilation, and Hidden Grief.* Oxford University Press, 2000.

Cheung, King-Kok. *Articulate Silences: Hisaye Yamamoto, Maxine Hong Kingston, and Joy Kogawa.* Cornell University Press, 1993.

———, editor. *An Interethnic Companion to Asian American Literature.* Cambridge University Press, 1997.

Chin, Frank. "Come All Ye Asian American Writers of the Real and the Fake." *The Big Aiiieeeee!: An Anthology of Chinese American and Japanese American Literature,* edited by Jeffery Paul Chan et. al., Meridian, 1991, pp. 1–18.

Chiu, Monica, editor. *Drawing New Color Lines: Transnational Asian American Graphic Narratives.* Hong Kong University Press, 2015.

Chiu, Monica, and Jeannette Roan. "Asian American Graphic Narrative." *Oxford Research Encyclopedia of Literature,* 26 September 2018, doi:10.1093/acrefore/9780190201098.013.784.

Chotiner, Isaac. "The History of Anti-Asian American Violence." *The New Yorker,* 25 March 2021, https://www.newyorker.com/news/q-and-a/the-history-of-anti-asian-american-violence.

Chuh, Kandice. *Imagine Otherwise: On Asian Americanist Critique.* Duke University Press, 2003.

Chute, Hillary L. *Graphic Women: Life Narrative and Contemporary Comics.* Duke University Press, 2010.

Coogan, Peter. *Superhero: The Secret Origin of a Genre.* MonkeyBrain Books, 2006.

Cutter, Martha J., and Cathy J. Schlund-Vials. *Redrawing the Historical Past: History, Memory and Multiethnic Graphic Novels.* University of Georgia Press, 2018.

de Jesús, Melinda Luisa. "Of Monsters and Mothers: Filipina American Identity and Maternal Legacies in Lynda J. Barry's *One Hundred Demons." Meridians: Feminism, Race, Transnationalism,* vol. 5, no. 2, 2004, pp. 1–26.

De Leon, Adrian. "The Long History of US Racism against Asian Americans, from 'Yellow Peril' to 'Model Minority' to the 'Chinese Virus.'" *The Conversation,* 8 April 2020, https://theconversation.com/the-long-history-of-us-racism-against-asian-americans-from-yellow-peril-to-model-minority-to-the-chinese-virus-135793.

Dong, Lan. "Reimagining the Monkey King in Comics: Gene Luen Yang's *American Born Chinese." The Oxford Handbook of Children's Literature,* edited by Julia Mickenberg and Lynne Vallone, Oxford University Press, 2011, pp. 231–51.

———. *Teaching Comics and Graphic Narratives: Essays on Theory, Strategy and Practice.* McFarland, 2012.

Doughty, Jonathan. "More Than Meets the 'I': Chinese Transnationality in Gene Luen Yang's *American Born Chinese." Asian American Literature: Discourses and Pedagogies,* vol. 1, 2010, pp. 54–60.

El Refaie, Elisabeth. *Autobiographical Comics: Life Writing in Pictures.* University Press of Mississippi, 2012.

Eng, David L. *Racial Castration: Managing Masculinity in Asian America.* Duke University Press, 2001.

Erll, Astrid. *Memory in Culture.* Translated by Sara B. Young, Palgrave MacMillan, 2011.

Friedman, Nancy. "Word of the Week: Emanata." *Fritinancy,* 14 July 2008, https://nancyfriedman.typepad.com/away_with_words/2008/07/word-of-the-week-emanata.html.

Gates, Philippa. *Criminalization/Assimilation: Chinese/Americans and Chinatowns in Classical Hollywood Film*. Rutgers University Press, 2019.

Gilmore, Leigh, and Elizabeth Marshall. *Witnessing Girlhood: Toward an Intersectional Tradition of Life Writing*. Fordham University Press, 2019.

Gopinath, Gayatri. *Impossible Desires: Queer Diasporas and South Asian Public Cultures*. Duke University Press, 2005.

Groensteen, Thierry. "The Art of Braiding: A Clarification." *European Comic Art*, vol. 9, no. 1, 2016, pp. 88–98, https://doi.org/10.3167/eca.2016.090105.

Hagedorn, Jessica, editor. *Charlie Chan Is Dead 2: At Home in the World (An Anthology of Contemporary Asian American Fiction)*. Penguin, 2004.

Hall, Stuart, editor. *Representation: Cultural Representations and Signifying Practices*. Sage, 1997.

Hatfield, Charles. *Alternative Comics: An Emerging Literature*. University Press of Mississippi, 2005.

Johnson, Diane. " Ghosts." *New York Review of Books*, 3 February 1977, pp. 19–21.

Jones, Manina. *That Art of Difference: Documentary Collage and English Canadian Writing*. University of Toronto Press, 1993.

Kirtley, Susan E. *Lynda Barry: Girlhood through the Looking Glass*. University Press of Mississippi, 2012.

Lee, Rachel. *The Americas of Asian American Literature: Gendered Fictions of Nation and Transnation*. Princeton University Press, 1999.

Lee, Robert G. *Orientals: Asian Americans in Popular Culture*. Temple University Press, 1999.

Li, David Leiwei. *Imagining the Nation: Asian American Literature and Cultural Consent*. Stanford University Press, 1998.

Lim, Shirley Geok-lin, and Amy Ling, editors. *Reading the Literatures of Asian America*. Temple University Press, 1992.

Liu, Stephanie. "Reports of Anti-Asian Hate Crimes Are Surging in Canada during the Covid-19 Pandemic." *CTV News*, 17 March 2021, https://www.ctvnews.ca/canada/reports-of-anti-asian-hate-crimes-are-surging-in-canada-during-the-covid-19-pandemic-1.5351481.

Lopez, Lori Kido. *Asian American Media Activism: Fighting for Cultural Citizenship*. New York University Press, 2016.

Lowe, Lisa. "Heterogeneity, Hybridity, Multiplicity: Marking Asian American Differences." *Diaspora: A Journal of Transnational Studies*, vol. 1, no. 1, Spring 1991, pp. 24–44.

Lund, Hans. "Edvard Munch's *The Scream* as Cultural Icon." *Cultural Icons*, edited by Keyan Tomaselli and David Scott, Left Coast Press, 2009, https://doi.org/10.4324/9781315431017.

MacDonald, Heidi. "Comics and Graphic Novels Sales top $1.21B in 2019—the Biggest Year Ever." *The Beat Comics Culture*, 15 July 2020, https://www.comicsbeat.com/comics-and-graphic-novel-sales-top-1-21b-in-2019-the-biggest-year-ever/.

Mapa, Lorina T. *Duran Duran, Imelda Marcos and Me*. Conundrum Press, 2019.

Marchetti, Gina. *Romance and the "Yellow Peril": Race, Sex, and Discursive Strategies in Hollywood Fiction*. University of California Press, 1993.

McCloud, Scott. *Understanding Comics: The Invisible Art*. Harper Perennial, 1994.

Molotiu, Andrei. "List of Terms for Comics Studies." *Comics Forum*, 26 July 2013, https://comicsforum.org/2013/07/26/list-of-terms-for-comics-studies-by-andrei-molotiu/#:~:text=The%20tendency%20of%20a%20comic,reading%20can%20be%20dubbed%20iconostatization.

Ngai, Mae. "Racism Has Always Been Part of the Asian American Experience." *The Atlantic*, 21 April 2021, https://www.theatlantic.com/ideas/archive/2021/04/we-are-constantly-reproducing-anti-asian-racism/618647/.

Nguyen, Jane. "Author Việt Thanh Nguyễn Discusses Asian American Representation in the Media." *Daily Bruin*, 23 February 2020, https://dailybruin.com/2020/02/23/author-vit-thanh-nguyn-discusses-asian-american-representation-in-the-media/.

Ninh, erin Khuê. *Ingratitude: The Debt-Bound Daughter in Asian American Literature*. New York University Press, 2011.

Oh, Stella. "Ethical Spectatorship in Adrian Tomine's *Shortcomings*." *Mosaic*, vol. 49, no. 4, December 2016, pp. 107–27.

Park, Jane Chi Hyun. *Yellow Future: Oriental Style in Hollywood Cinema*. University of Minnesota Press, 2010.

Petersen, Robert S. *Comics, Manga, and Graphic Novels: A History of Graphic Narratives*. Praeger, 2011.

Postema, Barbara. *Narrative Structure in Comics: Making Sense of Fragments*. RIT Press, 2013.

Pratt, Henry John. "Narrative in Comics." *The Journal of Aesthetics and Art Criticism*, vol. 67, no. 1, Winter 2009, pp. 107–17.

Reja, Mishal. "Trump's 'Chinese Virus' Tweet Helped Lead to Rise in Racist Anti-Asian Twitter Content: Study." *ABC News*, 18 March 2021, https://abcnews.go.com/Health/trumps-chinese-virus-tweet-helped-lead-rise-racist/story?id=76530148.

Royal, Derek Parker. "Introduction: Coloring America: Multi-Ethnic Engagements with Graphic Narrative." *MELUS: Multi-Ethnic Literature of the United States*, vol. 32, no. 2, September 2007, pp. 7–22.

Salkowitz, Rob. "New Sales Data Reveals How Covid-19 Impacted the Comics Industry." *Forbes*, 30 October 2020, https://www.forbes.com/sites/robsalkowitz/2020/10/30/new-sales-data-reveals-how-covid-19-impacted-the-comics-industry/?sh=79a3e0dbc9c9.

Saltman, Judith. Review of *Skim*. *Quill & Quire*, March 2008, https://quillandquire.com/review/skim/.

Shimizu, Celine Parreñas. *The Hypersexuality of Race: Performing Asian/American Women on Screen and Scene*. Duke University Press, 2007.

Smith, Sidonie. *The Poetics of Women's Autobiography: Marginality and the Fictions of Self-Representation*. Indiana University Press, 1987.

Song, Min Hyoung. *The Children of 1965: On Writing, and Not Writing, as an Asian American*. Duke University Press, 2013.

———. "'How Good It Is to Be a Monkey': Comics, Racial Formation, and *American Born Chinese*." *Mosaic*, vol. 43, no. 1, March 2010, pp. 73–92.

Tamaki, Mariko, and Gillian Tamaki. *Skim*. Groundwood Books, 2008.

Tomine, Adrian. *Shortcomings*. Drawn & Quarterly, 2007.

Ty, Eleanor. *Asianfail: Narratives of Disenchantment and the Model Minority*. University of Illinois Press, 2017.

UCLA First Year Experience. "UCLA's Common Book Program." https://firstyearexperience.ucla.edu/commonexperience/program-overview. Accessed 21 March 2022.

Villano, Alexa. "Author Viet Thanh Nguyen Talks Asian Representation, Life after a Pulitzer." *Rappler.com*, 26 August 2019, https://www.rappler.com/life-and-style/arts-and-culture/237707-lessons-from-author-viet-thanh-nguyen-vietnam-war-asian-representation.

Whitlock, Gillian. "Autographics: The Seeing 'I' of the Comics." *Modern Fiction Studies*, vol. 52, no. 4, Winter 2006, pp. 965–79.

Wolfe, Cary. *What Is Posthumanism?* University of Minnesota Press, 2010.

Yam, Kimmy. "Anti-Asian Hate Incident Reports Nearly Doubled in March, New Data Says." *NBC News*, 11 May 2021, https://www.nbcnews.com/news/asian-america/anti-asian-hate-incident-reports-nearly-doubled-march-new-data-n1266980.

Yang, Gene Luen. *American Born Chinese*. First Second, 2006.

PART 1

RETELLING HISTORY

Countervisualizing Barbed Wire, Guard Towers, and Latrines in George Takei and Harmony Becker's *They Called Us Enemy*

MONICA CHIU

Rea Tajiri's experimental film *History and Memory: For Akiko and Takashige* (1991) documents notions of absence, in both imagery and information, surrounding her parents' Japanese American internment. She wonders if the inexplicable gaps in her parents' narration of their time in camp speak to their waning trauma-induced memory or to how history is visualized and recorded. She narrates, "There were things which happened in the world while there were cameras watching, things we have images for," such as footage of the bombing of Pearl Harbor, taken by captured Japanese soldiers (Ono 142). "There are other things which have happened while there were no cameras watching which we restage in front of cameras to have images of," she continues, embedding clips from films such as Fred Zinneman's 1953 *From Here to Eternity,* which recreates how the navy might have acted at the moment of the bombing. Tajiri proposes two types of visualization: that captured by a camera at the event itself and that recreated in the absence of such a recording of this so-called real image. In Nicholas Mirzoeff's study on the power of visualization about which images are socially validated, *The Right to Look: A Counterhistory of Visuality,* his Visuality 1 and Visuality 2 work in concert with Tajiri's visual documentation of the seen and the unseen. Visuality 1, according to Mirzoeff, preserves capital, "safeguard[s] the authority of leadership" (23). For Tajiri, these images nationally and collectively "remember" only what actual witnesses saw or what they choose to recreate to boost national, patriotic value. Tajiri's narration approaches another type of image, one that accords with Mirzoeff's Visuality 2, defined as a "picturing of the self or collective that exceeds or precedes that subjugation to centralized authority" (Mirzoeff 23–24).[1] Tajiri's narration limns this excess when she states, "There are things which have happened for which the only images that exist are in the minds of the observers present at the time. While there are things which have happened for which there have been no observers, except for the spirits of the dead." The removal of her parents' house, after their evacuation to camp, is such an instance that occurred without a single witness. "All of a sudden, the house wasn't there anymore," says Tajiri's father in her interview with him, a former soldier in the celebrated all-Japanese American 442nd regiment who was denied permission to see his house when it was commissioned by the government for navy use. Tajiri creates a narrative from the spirits of the dead, who relate the removal of the structure from "100 feet above the ground," raised by hydraulic jacks, loaded onto a truck, and driven off. How does a structure so large simply disappear?, implicitly asks *History and Memory*. Did it not concern those, like neighbors, who witnessed its removal? Tajiri expresses what Mirzoeff defines as "countervisuality," the subtitle of his study and borrowed for the title of this chapter, wherein the powerless Japanese American evacuees claim a "right to look," to see and be seen amid the structures of authority—such as the military, Hollywood, and history itself—that retell it as they saw it.

Like the entities of visuality and countervisuality, those of history and memory are at odds in Tajiri's documentary—a film genre documenting factual occurrences—as the film ironically records the absence of information about how a group of people and their homes suddenly recede from view. The facts of Japanese American evacuation to internment camps is recorded in official military venues in the vein of Visuality 1: Japanese Americans were removed to remote locations; they did not disappear; their houses were repossessed or repurposed; after the war, they returned to successfully rebuild. These facts tell one story. How and what Japanese Americans felt at

---

1. Mirzoeff is working from Dipesh Chakrabarty's History 1 and History 2, the former "predicated by capital for itself 'as a precondition' to its own existence"; History 2 is that which is excluded from History 1 but continues to interrupt "the totalizing thrusts" of the former (22). I thank Jin Lee for this (personal correspondence, 24 January 2020).

their own disappearance and that of their material goods, at their successful return from camp, however, is undocumented in official venues. Under
Visuality 2, Japanese Americans in psychological and emotional presence
reappear in works like Tajiri's and, in this chapter, in the graphic narrative
The Called Us Enemy (2019), about former child internee, young adult activist, and later *Star Trek* actor George Takei. His cowriters are Justine Eisinger
and Steven Scott. Harmony Becker is the graphic memoir's artist. When discussing the narrative, I will cite primary author Takei, with the unstated
understanding of Eisinger's and Scott's contributions, and when discussing
images, sequencing, and other graphic narrative modalities, I will cite artist
Becker.

Because Visuality 2 exists in relationship to Visuality 1 (Mirzoeff 24),
Takei and Becker's re-visioning of three camp icons that appear with regularity in internment literature, film, and photography—barbed wire fences,
guard towers, and latrines—chafes against the War Relocation Authority's
(WRA's) authoritative images of camp. US media representations, created
for non-Japanese Americans, often were strategically devoid of images of
these objects because they suggested imprisonment and humiliation, the
"wrong" image to project to the wider public. Their visual reprisal in works
by Japanese Americans generates a defiant rejoinder to the military's former
sanitized evocations of camp. Their retaliations are different and oppositional visual play.

In *They Called Us Enemy*, the meanings of foundational objects of incarceration often are reversed and contrasted through the basal perspective of
young George, Takei's comics avatar.[2] George's child's-eye view disturbs the
WRA's typical top-down perspective. The visual turns afforded by Takei and
Becker's verbal-visual coordination powerfully connect readers to George
and the internees, distancing them from the WRA. In my reading of *They
Called Us Enemy*, I pay attention to three items prevalent in every camp:
barbed wire, sentry towers, and latrines. I am interested in how they accrue
meanings in the hands of the WRA until reattached to connotations created
by Japanese Americans.[3] In *They Called Us Enemy*, barbed wire encircling

2. He is to be distinguished from author Takei and from the narrator, who filters
camp through George's immature gaze. Becker's monstration, the visual equivalent to a
prose novel's narrator, also presents a view.

3. In "Happy Objects," Ahmed explores how "objects accumulate positive affective
value as they are passed around," in which affect is regarded as "sticky" or as "what
sticks, or what sustains or preserves the connection between ideas, values, and objects"
(29). The objects in my essay collect negative affect under Visuality 1.

camps and wooden guard towers that were occupied twenty-four hours a day by soldiers with rifles are two seminal systems of incarceration whose denotations and connotations become differently meaningful across populations of both non-Japanese Americans and so-called enemy aliens. They reassure those outside the fence of their safety while reminding internees of their confinement. Non-Japanese Americans rarely acknowledged camp latrines because they were not points of interest for the well-accommodated majority, but they resonated deeply with internees as harbingers of humiliation. Hastily assembled toilets were either long boards into which holes were cut, secured over a pit, each "seat" lacking privacy separations, or sometimes porcelain toilets initially unenclosed by individual stalls. In *They Called Us Enemy*, detention and indignity created by these material items find revision through innovative depictions.

Camp photography was visually curated by the military, allowing only limited images of internment interiors. Initially, only commissioned military and hired photographers, such as Dorothea Lange and Ansel Adams, were permitted to take photographs of camps. Prohibited images included those of barbed wire and guard towers, objects that would project camp as an imprisoning space.[4] The goal of restricting photographers from circulating certain images from relocation centers and internment camps to a wider non-Japanese American population secured the WRA's curated camp representations as safe spaces, protecting and adequately accommodating Japanese Americans, as WRA footage projects in Tajiri's work above. This "campaign of visual censorship," argues Elena Creef, whose scholarly work *Imaging Japanese America* explores the lives and legacies of camp photography (17), left the nation bereft of camp "image-icons," a term used by Marita Sturken (qtd. in Creef 17).[5] Military-issued aerial views, for example, depicted the orderly arrangement of barracks—seemingly empty of inhabitants when viewed from thousands of feet above ground—in a kind of topo-

---

4. In Mamoru Inouye and Grace Schaub's *The Heart Mountain Story: Photographs by Hansel Mieth and Otto Hagel of the World War II Internment of Japanese Americans*, author Schaub relates descriptions of "army-style rows of toilets and showers that lacked partitions" (360); when internees in Heart Mountain were given permission to take photos, this excluded photos of guard towers (32). Alinder also argues that Ansel Adams and other government-sponsored photographers were not allowed to photograph guard towers (98).

5. According to Alinder, photographs serve several purposes, including documentation, aesthetic exposition, restraint, and even control (19). In Toyo Miyatake's well-known photograph called "Boys behind Barbed Wire," the boys pictured were not actually behind the wire in the camp but went outside of it for the photos (Alinder 92).

graphical map.[6] The "empty" paths between barracks intimate a false sense of ease of navigation and cleanliness.[7] Becker first imitates such images when internees vacate a relocation facility for "a more permanent residence" (35), making the evacuated camp seem easily traversable. However, when crowded with thousands of internees, the scene is not only wildly chaotic, but also its numerous identical barracks and the unmarked paths between them create confusion. Miné Okubo's *Citizen 13660*, considered the first collection of camp drawings assembled into a narrative, and to be discussed below, demonstrates this in a drawing of a disoriented person at the crossroads of identical barracks. The caption reads, "All residential blocks looked alike; people were lost all the time" (136). For the majority of the American population who wondered where their Japanese American neighbors might have disappeared to, government-disseminated images provided them a sense of calm while, on the ground, anger, anxiety, depression, and fear ran high among internees.[8] *They Called Us Enemy* manages these established visuals through its own set of images.

---

6. See Creef 33. I borrow the idea of a topographical view from Jeff Adams's *Documentary Graphic Novels and Social Realism*, but he discusses how cartoonist and journalist Joe Sacco relied on "photographs taken at ground level" to create "imaginary [aerial] viewpoints" of the Jabalia refugee camps in his graphic narrative *Palestine*, because the area above camp's surveillance towers was "forbidden" space (127). Sacco's panels are packed with groups of people in what Adams calls the manner of Pieter Bruegel, "each of which offers an anecdotal narrative" (128); Sacco's maplike terrain from its "elevated viewpoint" permits readers to "navigate" among buildings as if they possess intimate knowledge of them (128). In contrast, government-issued aerial photography of internment camps lacks inhabitants, making the locations' empty remoteness neither conducive to readerly curiosity nor indicative of intimate, familiar spaces. Two camps, two creative approaches to readerly affect.

7. See Chiu's *Scrutinized! Surveillance in Asian North American Literature*, specifically pages 105–10 in her chapter "Intimate Details: Scrutiny and Evidentiary Photographs in Kerri Sakamoto's *Electrical Field*," for a discussion of photographs taken by the Canadian government of Japanese Canadian camps in British Columbia. Canada followed the US lead on internment.

8. It is well documented that first-generation Japanese Americans remained stoically unemotional before, during, and after internment. Aunt Emily of Joy Kogawa's *Obasan* is as stoic in the face of her daughter's impassioned and vocal call for justice as the "stone bread" she bakes. Such substantial bread is a metaphor that enlightens the reading audience on what she has internalized from Japanese culture about remaining impassionate in the face of injustice and how she continues to recreate this intractability, to pass it along for others, like her niece Nomi, to ingest.

Whose Domestic Unrest at the Bombing of Pearl Harbor? Anticipatory Threats and Affective Replies

Takei and Becker undermine perspectives that have been defined as foundations for internment. In what I find an inordinately valuable use of Visuality 2, Becker illustrates a prewar sequence by commencing with a domestic scene set in the Takeis' living room. This establishing panel focuses on Japanese Americans whose private, domiciliary calm is interrupted by the public chaos of war. In contrast, readers may be accustomed to understanding how World War II's US-based eruption interrupted the majority population, most of whom found new enemies in the minority. Through Becker's hand, the minority are busy anticipating Christmas before Japan's attack. On the left-hand side of a double-page sequence, the Takeis are trimming a Christmas tree. The radio plays "Silent Night," the lyrics written in a loopy, dreamy cursive, where vowels and consonants are doubled—as in "Allll is calm . . . Alllll is Briiiight" (14). The spellings visually resemble the elongation of a sung note (despite the fact that vowels, not consonants such as "l" in "all," are typically held in music) (fig. 1.1a).

In the panels of this page, Fumiko/Mama (George's mother) rocks his newborn sister Nancy to sleep while Takekuma Norman/Daddy (George's father) strings lights on the Christmas tree; George's younger brother Henry and George himself assist in the holiday preparations. The final panel on the left-hand page fixates on the radio. Square speech balloons with sharp tails pointing to a radio indicate the announcer's "voice" as it declares, in commensurate sharp tones, the bombing of Pearl Harbor. The broadcast interrupts the Christmas carol's phrase "sleep in heavenly peace," splicing "peace" at "p," followed by an image that represents a visual representation of the sound "pop." The letters forming the broadcast's narrative are evenly spaced capital letters that contrast with the aforementioned loopy cursive of the ballad's lyrics, the former strident in the face of Christmas calm. The report's interruption and its contents are surprising and urgent, suggest Takei and Becker, because they *pop*. As readers absorb the entirety of the spread as a whole—wherein we often understand sequentialism and/ as simultaneity[9]—they recognize how images of domestic tranquility on the left side of the double-page sequence literally battle with images of Japanese fighter planes bombing US Navy ships that dominate the right-hand side of the sequence.[10] That George's parents hail from Japan ironically and pain-

---

9. See Groensteen on "co-presence" (7).
10. Groensteen might view this as images that "rhyme" (7).

COUNTERVISUALIZING BARBED WIRE • 35

fully pits Japanese Americans against the Japanese in this scene and, as we know, the former against non-Japanese Americans.

At the bottom of the first page, the attack merely hovers in the Takeis' living space by way of radio announcement, but its consequences will soon drastically upend the Takeis' domestic existence through evacuation. As the reader's eye moves from the top left of the double-page sequence to the bottom right, she notices that the dark, upright Christmas tree in the first panel is mirrored, by shape and color, in the elongated, somewhat triangular black cloud issuing forth from a smoking US battleship in the final panel (on the second page) of the sequence. Additionally, the father/son/Christmas tree grouping adjacent to the so-called Madonna and child (Mama nursing Nancy) in the very first panel of the sequence recurs compositionally in the final panel through the shapes of exploding ships. The visual connections between domesticity and war anticipate how the Japanese American household will be incontrovertibly changed by Pearl Harbor.

Becker's double-page spread invokes Mirzoeff's Visuality 2 as a discussion around affect, not as emotion, but as implied in a network of power and impression. Read through cultural theorist Brian Massumi's "The Future Birth of the Affective Fact: The Political Ontology of Threat," the bombing of Pearl Harbor on December 7, 1941, immediately generated what Massumi might call the "future birth of [an] affective fact" (52). The documented occurrence of Japan's aggressions against the United States became a precondition for the protection of American citizens against possible future Japanese assaults.[11] "Threat is from the future," he explains, which can engender precautionary measures in the present (53). For example, the US invasion of Iraq was a "future superlative" (52) in which an incursion occurred even without clear evidence that Iraq possessed weapons of mass destruction (53). In my understanding of Massumi's future superlative, it is the anticipation of future violence; it is the implementation of (often) misguided caution; or it also can be insurance against future destruction.[12] If a threat engenders sufficient fear and uncertainty, or provokes an "anticipa-

---

11. In Silvan Tomkins's *Shame and Its Sisters: A Silvan Tomkins Reader*, he writes, "Anticipation is in part postication, the linking of the past with the future" (52), using the example of a child who burns herself on a flame, and even when the pain has passed, "the child may well have already learned that the object is something to cry about before its second encounter," which Tomkins calls "anticipatory learning" and "anticipatory avoidance," in this case relating flame and pain (53).

12. I thank Stephen Roxburgh for offering this clarifying terminology, a reading roping exploding ships and the Madonna-child image later in the essay, and for information about half-tone printing near the essay's conclusion (personal correspondence, 23 January 2020).

FIGURES 1.1A AND B (FACING). Juxtaposed images from *They Called Us Enemy* (14–15). © George Takei. Courtesy of Top Shelf Productions

15

tory reality," its upshot is affective: "Threat passes through linear time, but does not belong to it. . . . If we feel a threat, there was a threat. Threat is affectively self-causing" (Massumi 54). After the bombing of Pearl Harbor, the anticipated threat of Japanese American espionage (one that might have concluded in the future deaths of more Americans) resulted in the mass internment of Japanese Americans, many of whom were citizens, living in what General John L. DeWitt called a West Coast military zone.[13]

Becker's sequence is an affective reply to what was an anticipatory threat. When she commences this sequence in the Takeis' living room and concludes it with the bombing, when she conjures up images of domestic settings sequestered quite privately in Japanese Americans' family albums or memories and then draws images of smoking American battleships, she addresses the event in an atypical order, homing in on Japanese American affect and encouraging the countervision of Visuality 2 to reply to the authority of Visuality 1. The assault already has occurred at the bottom of the first page as announced: "A Japanese attack upon Pearl Harbor *naturally* would mean war. Such an attack would *naturally* bring a counter-attack" (Takei 15; emphasis added). On the following page, however, Becker depicts incoming Japanese planes approaching a peaceful harbor; the bombing is yet to happen in this drawing despite its already former occurrence only panels beforehand. Japanese Imperial aircraft fly from right to left as if heading into the Takei's living room, where "Allll is calm." Readers identify with the "enemy," rendering "we" as viewers invaders into their living room before the family becomes subjected to (and subjects of) an anticipatory reality. The nonsequential order of a sequence about a "natural" response to Japanese aggression—a sequence that imagines the impact of the bombing through views other than official ones—delineates the gravity of the incident: As a

---

13. The hastily assembled War Relocation Authority, charged with managing internment camps, used Executive Order 9066 to legalize and militarize the anticipatory reality of a possible future attack on the US by Japan, and even more particularly, the threat of violence by Japanese Americans on non-Japanese Americans. Narratives and later images of camp promoted by this government authority first focused on implications of anticipatory retaliation as they may play out on the majority, which was bound up in the possibility that some Japanese Americans might be spies for Japan. Hence "enemy aliens," a term erasing Japanese American humanity, required removal to militarized camps enclosed by barbed wire to secure the safety of Americans beyond the fence. If such rationale explained incarceration as a protection for *non*-Japanese Americans, another rationale argued camps as a safeguard *for* Japanese Americans, safeguarding them from the racism and anger (potential violence) of those outside the fence, beyond camp. Each report attempted to quell the anxiety of the opposing group, both by arguing for the efficacy of internment camps. As a counter version to the anticipatory violence, no Japanese American was ever found to be a spy for Japan.

traumatic event, it is lived over and over again. The bombings' afterlives for the authorities behind Mirzoeff's Visuality 1 are the future under which Japanese Americans become enemy aliens.

Behind the Fence

In Julie Otsuka's short but powerfully evocative novel about internment, *When the Emperor Was Divine*, a caged macaw metaphorizes the Berkeley, California, location of a Japanese American family. The unnamed character in the novel that is called simply "mother" releases the family's macaw—not a native Californian nor an American bird species—from its cage and into the freedom of the outdoors shortly before evacuation, else who would take care of it, we assume she reasons to herself. Unaccustomed to surviving without human protection (released from its familiar cage), it returns to tap on the family's window, as if imploring to be confined again, the only state of existence it understands (19–20). In a reverse metaphor, internment removed so-called foreign Japanese Americans, who were assimilated into American culture, from their freedom and into imprisonment.

On the day that the Takei family empties its suitcases into Block 6 of Camp Rohwer, Arkansas, after spending time beforehand in a temporary relocation center, *They Called Us Enemy* uses birdsong to indicate the imprisoned status of internees. From the woods that grow beyond the camp's barbed wire, the two Takei brothers, George and Henry, hear "Ca-caw!" floating from the surrounding trees (59). The trajectory of this sequence creates a viewpoint that shifts from an aerial (topographical) perspective that diminishes these two internees to one that swoops down to the children's eye level, asking readers to consider the boys' viewpoint (opinions) and their sight line. Our eye is drawn from the sky-high "Ca-caw!" at the top of the panel that first catches the eye, as it is positioned in the privileged upper third of an initial panel in the sequence, the space from which a typical Western acculturated top-to-bottom reading practice occurs (59). The eye instinctively moves down the panel to rest on the small boys in the lower left-hand corner, who are dwarfed by the trees and barbed wire fence. The viewpoint pans from the sky to view the children at their level, to see and eventually to hear the child internees' perspective. An older and ostensibly wiser boy—"wiser" according to George and Henry's perspective—informs them that the "Ca-caw" is really from a dinosaur and that the barbed wire fence was erected to keep these ancient lizards "caged in" (61). The boy employs a logic about the status of a wandering dinosaur that mimics the government's explanation for interning Japanese Americans: The latter will be safe from national anger (a monstrous anger) from behind the fence.[14] When the segment concludes with four strands of enlarged barbed wire before us (61)—as if we are looking through the fence and into the sky from George's eyes—Becker's perspective demands these questions: Are we on the inside of the fence looking out at the "caged-in" dinosaurs, or are we on the outside looking in at the children? "The rules about the fence were simple," writes Otsuka of the barbed wire in *When the Emperor Was Divine*. "You could not go over it, you could not go under it, you could not go around it, you could not go through it" (61). Those who tried were shot; those who breached it either froze in the night or starved to death. And so, according to Visuality 1, internees are "cared for" by the WRA.[15] From Becker's drawn perspective, we might be inside, outside, or through the fence, rendering us an authority, an internee, a dinosaur. But given her affiliation to promoting the outsider's view—that of the Japanese Americans—readers are ironically given an insider's view.

In Becker's other re-visions of barbed wire, in another panel sequence, the horizontality of three of its strands serves as gutters and as a representation of emotional divisions. Three rows of fencing run across a long top panel, severing the view of mountains in the background and serving as containers for internees (126) (fig. 1.2). In the panel immediately below this establishing image, Becker adds a soldier's boot to the scene, visually shrinking the seemingly extensive landscape through an object that puts the vast background into a different perspective (126) (also in fig. 1.2).

Soldiers who represent the stability and preservation of the state of confinement loom larger than the sweeping panoramic view.[16] In an aesthetic move, Becker uses the same horizontal line—here manifested in what comics scholar Thierry Groensteen calls an "intericonic gutter"—in the final horizontal panel running across the bottom of the facing page (Takei 127). This gutter forges a "dialectic interaction" between the images above and below, but always with the reader's "participation" (Groensteen 115). Becker's

---

14. The older boy's final, disembodied speech bubble containing the phrase "to keep them caged in" floats between two of the fence's barbs (61). The speech balloon is small enough to sneak through, but if not careful, it is in danger of exploding on a barb, visually demonstrating the dangers of possible escape from being caged in.

15. See Otsuka 101, 88.

16. See Creef's critique of Ansel Adams's photographs of internees in which "internees are ennobled by their rough environment rather than angered by their own imprisonment" (36). In Becker's enlarged boot, the ennobling mountains (the rough environment) are subjugated by the boot.

FIGURE 1.2. Horizontal barbed wire physically separates the internees from freedom in *They Called Us Enemy* (126). © George Takei. Courtesy of Top Shelf Productions.

gutter cuts across, or is laid over, the bodies of parents and their children. It visually severs the grown-ups in Tule Lake, the internment camp notorious for housing "No-Nos,"[17] from the children standing in front of them. Through visual analogies, Becker suggests that the camps divided parents from their children—generations of Issei (first-generation Japanese immigrants from Japan) from Nisei (second-generation Japanese Americans born in the United States) when they disagreed over the loyalty questionnaire, the No-Nos being sent to Tule Lake. Similarly, the barbed wire segregates Japanese Americans from their American citizenship and the majority population. Becker's depiction also visualizes the separation between depictions of internees as entire bodies and soldiers as a mere boot: The synecdochal relationship between the boot standing in for the soldier suggests that only a part of Visuality 1 is needed to incite notions of outrage, fear, or betrayal within internees. The fear incited by the boot, the gun, the tower, or the barbed wire was often greater than the empathy evoked for internees.

While the majority population was affected but not emotionally moved by internment, the Takeis understand and acknowledge the similar suffering they witness given their own recent hardships. When they are allowed to return to California, their "first [post-internment] home . . . was on skid row" (167). Formerly homeless themselves in camp, sleeping on hay-filled mattresses, the Takei family now observes some of Los Angeles's majority population sleeping on the streets. These unfortunate city dwellers prop their drunk or drugged slack bodies against a wooden fence whose many slats conjure up the horizontal lines of camp's barbed wire. But that the former are vertical and not horizontal, skid row visually announces a role reversal wherein white, unemployed, and vulnerable men sleep outside on tattered mattresses no better than the internees' bags of hay while the Takeis move temporarily into the Alta Hotel. It was "a horrible experience," not the least because of the human suffering they encounter each time they leave the premises (167).

---

17. "No-Nos" were those who replied "no" to two key questions on the War Relocation Authority's 1943 loyalty questionnaire for young Nisei men: "Are you willing to serve in the Armed Forces of the United States on combat duty, wherever ordered?" and "Will you swear unqualified allegiance to the United States of America . . . and foreswear any form of allegiance or obedience to the Japanese emperor, or any other foreign government, power, or organization?" The No-Nos were sent to the Tule Lake internment facility in California to separate them from other so-called more patriotic Nisei (http://encyclopedia.densho.org/No-no_boys/).

Guarding the Towers

If sentry towers are rare in photographs, their presence in Japanese American internment literature reminds characters of the armed and vigilant soldiers on guard in their elevated platforms. But even if an internee escaped, to where might he run in a desert, as many camps were erected in arid locations that could plunge into frigid winter temperatures at night, and how long would he survive without food and water in the infernos of summer temperatures? Mirzoeff outlines how vision and authority are and have been synonymous in overseeing, as they are enmeshed with biopolitical power (7), such as on slave plantations, in Nazi Germany's Holocaust camps, and more recently in America's fight against terrorism. He then explains how countervisuality implies the claim to a "right to be seen" (Mirzoeff 27), a right to reject "visuality's authority" (27). Internment guard towers operate as a Mirzoeffian mechanism by which internees operated (obediently) under surveillance and by which one contingent of (white) bodies controlled another (that of Japanese Americans). Interned children in *They Called Us Enemy* assert and recuperate some of their subjectivity under surveillance by taunting tower guards and interrupting their vigilance. In a three-page sequence (Takei 87–89), the perspective originates from above, as if readers are positioned on the sentry's tower, looking down at four boys. Three of them instruct Henry, George's young brother, to first ask the soldiers, who are hanging out on the dais at the tower's base, for goodies, like bubble gum and popsicles. But only by shouting the "magic word"—"'Sakana Beach' real fast" (86)—will he receive all the sweets for which he asks. As the older boys know, the sentry will hear Henry's "Sakana Beach" as "son of a bitch" and become angry (91).[18] As Henry approaches the soldiers, Becker's framing positions the reader at Henry's eye level or below, rendering Henry, in the foreground, at equal height to the guards in the background. In the last two panels at the bottom of the second page of the sequence, when the guards misunderstand "Sakana Beach" as the insult the older boys intended, Henry's face and theirs are at our eye level, equalized by Becker's perspective (88). In the panel immediately following and at the top of the next page, she lowers the perspective again, allowing Henry to loom large as he repeats, "Sakana Beach," but with more gusto, at the increasingly irri-

---

18. Joy Kogawa references "ripe pidgin English phrases" in which "sonuva bitch" is converted by Canadian Japanese to "sakana fish," for "sakana" is the word for "fish" in Japanese, and saying "sakana fish" to somebody who lobs a rock at your car, as in this scene, would be understood by Japanese Canadian Stephen, but not by the non–Japanese Canadian who throws it (218).

tated men (89). They eventually pelt Henry's retreating back with pebbles, shouting "You little snot!" Using the powerful position of a top-down view, Becker first establishes the guards' visual prominence until the child brings them "down" to his level, drawing his retreating figure from below (89).

Sara Ahmed on affect and in her essay "Embodying Strangers" might suggest how such surprising encounters "shift the boundaries of the familiar, of that which is already recognizable or known" (87).[19] Ahmed retells an encounter from Audre Lorde's *Sister Outsider* between a young Audre and a white woman who refuses to sit next to her on the subway: Was it a roach on the seat?, the child thinks to herself. Was it dirt on her snowsuit? When she finally understands, years later, that the white woman regarded young Audre as a "dirty" black child whose body the woman refused to brush against, Lorde must redefine her "social as well as bodily integrity" (86), what Ahmed calls a "dialogic production" first experienced by Lorde, then recalled, written about, and finally taken up by Ahmed (87). These various "encounters" that unite past and present, public and private reflect Takei's prose and Becker's images as they reanimate encounters between formerly silenced guards—who are "loud" only in their gun-toting presence—and interned children, the latter of whom provoke the soldiers to anger, without retaliation, in ways the adults cannot. They bring to life stoic and silent guards while also lowering them metaphorically to the children's level by infantilizing them, for they resort to throwing rocks and calling the children "snots." In recalling and reanimating encounters from new perspectives, the representations of the interned children "shift the boundaries of the familiar," from the methodical, somber, and reserved guards to their sudden unrestrained and undignified response. Public WRA depictions chafe against Takei's private ones; his memories of playing in camp contaminate, in a sort of reverse representation, the integrity of the soldier's public, authoritative, and dignified demeanor when reduced to verbally tussling with children. Like Ahmed, "touched" by Lorde's work, *They Called Us Enemy* invites "a meeting between bodies and texts" ("Embodying Strangers" 87).

Latrines and Canteens: A Sordid Combination

In Joy Kogawa's *Obasan*, the author's semi-autobiographical account of living in a Japanese Canadian internment camp, the protagonist's Aunt Emily

---

19. In "Embodying Strangers," Ahmed argues that bodies "take form through and against other bodily forms" (in my reading that of adult non-Japanese American guards vis-à-vis Japanese American interned children), allowing "bodies [to be] . . . both deformed and reformed" (86).

equates the evacuation to being "just *plopped* here [from Vancouver] in the wilderness" of Slocan, British Columbia (118; emphasis added). She conjures up terms that relate relocation to bodily evacuation, wherein Japanese Canadians were "flushed out of Vancouver. Like dung drops. Maggot bait" (118). Camp itself is a pit, a dusty, dirty place where many Japanese North Americans died (or one might even say that they were left to die), overwhelmed by stress and trauma or overcome by illness.[20] Other characters who also detest the filth and humiliation of camp in general, of public lavatories and other camp facilities in particular, but reference them with humor, are women internees in Okubo's *Citizen 13660* (1946). It is considered the first graphic narrative about internment, loosely defined as such because the drawings she created while incarcerated with her brother in Minidoka, which were not necessarily meant for binding, later were collected, sequenced chronologically, and captioned by Okubo.[21] Japanese American women in Okubo's images refute and often outwardly mock the rules and regulations of Poston, where Okubo and her brother were interned, in defiance of the sordid conditions created by camp guards in the name of sanitation. Women step over, not into, the chlorine foot baths at the entrance to camp's public showers—the only kind of shower available—because bathers were "afraid" of what lurked in the foot baths themselves (77). If chlorinated water sanitized their feet, the women's "acrobatic stunts" to avoid them make subtle mockery of officials' attempts at camp hygiene (77). Both *Citizen 13660* and *They Called Us Enemy* create sketches and panels that speak back to expected camp images—cohorts of Visuality 2—using the comics form to ironize, humor, or subvert camp icons and situations against their military-defined decree.

Despite, or perhaps because of, intolerable camp conditions, *They Called Us Enemy* uses explicit humor to "shift boundaries," in Ahmed's term, to not only counter authority but also to expose unacceptable conditions. In the upper left-hand panel of a page outlining "problems and complaints," women internees find "unacceptable" rows of toilets that are not separated by privacy stalls (78). In a panel immediately below the pictured toilets, Becker draws a plate of canteen fare that looks like a pile of shit. "I **cannot** eat this!" exclaims an internee (78). Their explicit visual proximity and order—toilet bowls placed above a plate of "shit"—deliberately draw our

20. In Stephen Okazaki's documentary *Days of Waiting: The Life and Art of Estelle Ishigo*, he records Ishigo's memory of a Japanese American woman who dies of a heart attack, from stress, as she awaits trucks to remove her to a relocation center.

21. As an array of images that recorded Okubo's first to last days in camp, they map sequential events, but were not intended as a sequential graphic narrative. *Citizen 13660* might better be called a memoir in captioned pictures, but nevertheless it is and can be considered a graphic narrative, as I have done myself in past articles. See Chiu, "Sequencing."

attention to the relationship between canteen food and excrement, the latter exemplifying a natural bodily movement, more significant after the ingestion of unacceptable fare.

According to Kogawa's aunt in *Obasan*, Japanese Canadians and Japanese Americans were "defined and identified by the way we were seen . . . a stench in the nostrils of the people of Canada" (118). Similarly, George Takei and his family eat what the nation thinks they are. This compounds questions of the efficacy of camp. If the WRA thought imprisonment would not only protect the dominant population but also improve the status of Japanese Americans—create loyal citizens of them—instead it poisoned family relations, pitting Issei against Nisei and often breaking the structure of the nuclear family so appealing to the American majority. Anthropologist Mary Douglas defines dirt as matter out of place; Japanese Americans as "matter," then, in a place of possible rectification and sanitation, ironically recycle the shit they are fed. Kogawa's image in *Obasan* of a kitten trapped in a camp latrine metaphorizes the situation of internees: "The kitten cries day after day, not quite dead, unable to climb out and trapped in the outhouse" (158).

Becker's visuals do not haunt the reader as Kogawa's do, but rather strike them with the heavy hand of silence. In the third and final row of panels on the page discussed above, flush (if I may) with the left-hand margin and the last in a column of three left-hand-side panels, Takei's father looks off to the left, not at the reader and not at anything that we can see. A plate of untouched "crap" sits before him, and George, seated to his right, pushes his own plate away, sticking out his tongue in disgust. Mr. Takei is unmoved and unmoving, his stillness and silence a beat, like the necessary pause between a joke and its well-delivered punchline. Is the food like shit? We contemplate with Mr. Takei as his son acts out his father's and other internees' agreement that yes, indeed, it is. Becker's timing through panels and images is exquisite. Her humorous sequencing adds levity to a grim and tasteless aspect of camp life.

Calling Us Enemy / Calling US the Enemy

Such relevant optic play that manages emotions about camp converge on the jacket of the graphic narrative's 2019 Top Shelf Productions publication. The background features barracks, barbed wire, a guard tower, and a soldier with a gun. In the foreground stands George, suitcase in hand, waiting to enter camp with his family and other evacuees. While all Japanese Americans in the queue turn their backs to the reader to face the camp gates (to face their bleak future and move toward it), George turns back as if to look at us. In the immediate foreground, his face dwarfs both the soldier and the guard tower in the distance, as if imploring us to see from his view, from Mirzoeff's Visuality 2, as we move forward with him. He is a Japanese American boy moving against—or turning back from—the forced forward-flow toward authority.

Moreover, the four words of the narrative's title—*They Called Us Enemy*—are bound together by barbed wire; the capital "A" in the word "Called" is drawn as a guard tower. The words are indexical semantically and symbolically, exemplifying just the kind of play we see throughout the graphic narrative. Take the pronoun "us" in the title, in all capitals: It also can wittily be read as "US," allowing Japanese American post-internees as a collective "us" to accuse the US as being its enemy. Thus, the title can be read in two ways: "They Called Us Enemy" and "They [Japanese Americans] Called US [United States] Enemy."[22] When the front and back jacket flaps are folded out, they depict images of Japanese Americans packing up to leave for camp and their arrival at camp, respectively, in purple halftones. This printing technique was used in the early twentieth century to mass-produce comics at an affordable rate, as the halftones used less ink while still providing enough color for readers to imagine the complete image. The process is a bit like an impressionist painting, in which a canvas viewed close up seems covered with many disconnected paintbrush strokes, while moving away from the image brings its figures into focus. The farther away you are, the better you are able to see the whole rather than the pieces that make up its parts. Takei and his collaborators invite us, then, to step in, to take a closer (often a child's) look. But they remind us that *They Called Us Enemy* is only one current version among others—a single contribution to Visuality 2—of how Japanese Americans affect Visuality 1, now seventy-five years in the past. The graphic narrative suggests that to understand "they" and "enemy," "camps" and "resistance," we should read beyond this contribution (this singular ink "dot" among many others) to assemble a full-tone picture. Guard towers, barbed wire, and latrines are less obstacles provoking fear and loathing than tools for an affective re-visioning of camp icons. In Takei's and Becker's hands, these items create what Silvan Tomkins, a psychologist and theorist of affect studies, calls "positive possibility," rather than a negative future superlative as defined by Massumi, or "the prospect of a [better] possible future state of affairs" (53–54).

---

22. I thank Jin Lee for this extremely insightful reading, a fascinating play on how "us" can also be the initials for the United States: US (personal correspondence, 24 January 2020).

Works Cited

Adams, Jeff. *Documentary Graphic Novels and Social Realism.* Peter Lang, 2008.

Ahmed, Sara. "Embodying Strangers." *Body Matters: Feminism, Textuality, Corporeality,* edited by Avril Horner and Angela Keane, Manchester University Press, 2000, pp. 85–96.

———. "Happy Objects" *The Affect Theory Reader,* edited by Melissa Gregg and Gregory J. Seigworth. Duke University Press, pp. 29–51.

Alinder, Jasmine. *Moving Images: Photography and the Japanese American Incarceration.* University of Illinois Press, 2009.

Chiu, Monica. "Intimate Details: Scrutiny and Evidentiary Photographs in Kerri Sakamoto's *Electrical Field.*" *Scrutinized! Surveillance in Asian North American Literature,* University of Hawai'i Press, 2014, pp. 96–111.

———. "Sequencing and Contingent Individualism in the Graphic, Postcolonial Spaces of Satrapi's *Persepolis* and Okubo's *Citizen 13660.*" *English Language Notes,* vol. 26, no. 2, 2009, pp. 99–114.

Creef, Elena Tajima. *Imaging Japanese America: The Visual Construction of Citizenship, Nation, and the Body.* New York University Press, 2004.

Groensteen, Thierry. *The System of Comics.* Translated by Bart Beaty and Nick Nguyen, University Press of Mississippi, 2007.

Inouye, Mamoru, photographer, and Grace Schaub, writer. *The Heart Mountain Story: Photographs by Hansel Mieth and Otto Hagel of the World War II Internment of Japanese Americans.* Cummings Printing, 1997.

Kogawa, Joy. *Obasan.* Reprint, Anchor, 1994.

Lee, Jin. Personal correspondence. 24 January 2020.

Massumi, Brian. "The Future Birth of the Affective Fact: The Political Ontology of Threat." *The Affect Theory Reader,* edited by Melissa Gregg and Gregory J. Seigworth, Duke University Press, 2010, pp. 52–70.

Mirzoeff, Nicholas. *The Right to Look: A Counterhistory of Visuality.* Duke University Press, 2011.

Okazaki, Stephen, director. *Days of Waiting: The Life and Art of Estelle Ishigo.* National Asian American Telecommunications Association, 1990.

Okubo, Miné. *Citizen 13660.* 1946. University of Washington Press, 1983.

Ono, Kent. "Re/Membering Spectators: Meditations on Japanese American Cinema." *Countervisions,* edited by Darrell Y. Hamamoto and Sandra Liu, Temple University Press, 2000, pp. 129–49.

Otsuka, Julie. *When the Emperor Was Divine.* Alfred A. Knopf, 2002.

Roxburgh, Stephen. Personal correspondence. 23 January 2020.

Tajiri, Rea, director. *History and Memory: For Akiko and Takashige.* Women Make Movies, 1991.

Takei, George, et al. *They Called Us Enemy.* Top Shelf Productions, 2019.

Tomkins, Silvan. *Shame and Its Sisters: A Silvan Tomkins Reader.* Edited by Eve Kosofsky Sedgwick and Adam Frank, Duke University Press, 1995.

CHAPTER 2

Ethics of Storytelling

Teaching Thi Bui's *The Best We Could Do*

STELLA OH AND ERIN KHUÊ NINH

The authors of this chapter teach *The Best We Could Do: An Illustrated Memoir* (2017) in thematically disparate courses with very different student compositions. Pedagogically, the authors prompt students to engage with the ethics of Thi Bui's storytelling and to appreciate and grapple with the difficult truths of war and refugee experiences. This chapter begins with an outline of the ways Bui counters representations of the Vietnam War in popular imagination by focusing on intergenerational trauma, discusses how Bui's storytelling methods can be used to talk about loss and memory in two different classroom settings, and concludes with remarks about the problematic depiction of the good refugee.

The Vietnam War is one of the most iconic wars in American history and is the subject of several books, comics, documentaries, films, and television shows.[1] Often the focus of these representations is a white male American soldier who encounters physical, political, and psychological trauma.

---

1. Images of the Vietnam War were constructed through prose fiction such as Michael Herr's *Dispatches* (1977), Bobbie Ann Mason's *In Country* (1985), and Tim O'Brien's *The Things They Carried* (1990), as well as Hollywood blockbusters including *The Deer Hunter* (1978), *Apocalypse Now* (1979), *Platoon* (1986), and *Full Metal Jacket* (1987). Don Lomax published sixteen issues of the comic *Vietnam Journals* from 1987 to 1991.

Such stories of white masculine struggle and bravado applaud American exceptionalism and reinforce racial and gendered anxieties. Contrary to such popular films and literature of the Vietnam War, Thi Bui's *The Best We Could Do* narrates stories about the Vietnam War through memories of her family members. Bui recounts the Vietnam War from memories of her mother and father as well as her own experiences to create a more palpable reality of the material and affective consequences of war. The focal point of Bui's narrative is not war but the traumatic effects of war on individuals. Such ethical storytelling signals to individual experiences anchored in national history and its exclusions.

The Best We Could Do offers a different lens through which to view the larger historical context of colonization, war, and imperialism. Bui engages in narrating alternative memories that represent diasporic subjectivity that "is derived from the need to re-inscribe nationalism into individual perspectives" (Shih 147). *The Best We Can Do* illustrates memories and stories of women and families often disregarded as unimportant and affirms their importance in understanding history and identities shaped by such exclusions. In *The Best We Could Do*, births of children are narrated vis-à-vis nationhood as the family moves through the turbulent spaces of war as refugees and later immigrants. Central to Bui's narrative is the strained relationships between children and parents and the devastating effects that displacement and war have on subsequent generations.

Bui writes that "though my parents took us far away from the site of their grief," "certain shadows stretched far, casting a gray stillness over our childhood" (59).[2] According to Marianne Hirsch, "postmemory is the relationship that the 'generation after' bears to the personal, collective, and cultural trauma of those who came before" (*Generation* 5). In this case, the ethics in telling "stories and memories of the previous Vietnamese generation act as a silent scrim for the second generation" (McWilliams 319). Bui writes of a "darkness we did not understand . . . but could always FEEL" that continues to haunt her and family long after the war (60). The visuality of the graphic novel can lend itself to rendering trauma, which often congeals as an "indelible image"; too much for the mind to process, traumatic memory imprints as "fragmentary sensation, [or] image without context" (Herman 38). The compositional placement of panels and images in *The Best We Could Do* evoke this: Creating a fragmented and besieged state very similar to those experienced by victims of trauma, Bui jumps from different geographic, temporal, and spatial locations for a jarring effect. Yet referring to how the

2. Unless otherwise stated, all quotes from Thi Bui are from *The Best We Could Do*.

legacy of her father's trauma affects her in the contemporary moment Bui also writes, "I had no idea that the terror I felt was only the long shadow of his own" (128, 129). Rather than direct connection to trauma, postmemory mediates though imaginative creation often by textual and visual narratives. As an illustrator technically of second-order or intergenerational trauma— that which was never experienced firsthand—Bui raises intriguing questions regarding the visuality of postmemory and the ethics of storytelling.

In one particular scene, Bui illustrates the haunting legacy of trauma and postmemory through the use of long vertical panels that resemble prison bars. The vertical paneling allows for visual comparisons of both Bui as a young girl and her father as a young boy. The long rectangular frames "inform the way text reads" and elongate the affective states of fear and loneliness felt by both figures (Miodrag 66). Here, we can visualize trauma and see the father's feelings of fear and loss traverse temporal and geographic spaces intersecting with Bui's own postmemory of trauma. Addressing affect, spatiality, and temporality, *The Best We Could Do* addresses the ruptures of trauma as memories and postmemories emerge in "affects, states, somatic sensation or visual images" (Caruth 159). The ability to go back and forth in time connecting the past to the present and vice versa through textual, visual, and haptic ways is an essential part of narrating trauma and engaging in an ethical form of storytelling.

Discursive understandings of trauma can be limited in recalling memory. While empirical knowledge privileges what is visible, the concrete and the verifiable, Bui's work welcomes and expands upon what Avery Gordon calls "sensuous knowledge," which is "a different kind of materialism, neither idealistic nor alienated, but an active practice or passion for the lived reality" (205). Reflecting on Gordon's "sensuous knowledge," *The Best We Could Do* engages in a form of ethical storytelling. Contending with established thought that regards history as irrelevant to the workings of individual dislocation, ethical storytelling takes into consideration the personal and often embodied states of memory. Rather than a detached and objective recounting of history, Bui engages in a personal ethics of memory that is visual, visceral, emotive, and reflective.

Offering new perspectives of the Vietnam War through the lens of family and motherhood, Bui's graphic narrative addresses the intersections of history, memory, trauma, and their dislocating effects. Capturing feelings of depression and precarity, Bui's work addresses the fissures of memory and the generational trauma that is manifest in a sensuous and embodied knowledge. *The Best We Could Do* speaks to what Cvetkovich refers to as an archive of emotions, that "refuses to silence either colonialism's destructiveness or masculine hetero-patriarchal terror" (McWilliams 323). Memories are retraced and illustrated; alternative histories emerge from silence and are articulated.

The following individual sections walk through our pedagogical approaches, as they are tailored to meet our respective students at their interests, but also as they are equally directed by questions of ethical storytelling. The chapter will resume an integrated discussion thereafter about this memoir's circulation in current public discourse around refugee crises, and will conclude with ethical considerations for exercising care around that usefulness.

"Solving the Storytelling Problem": Student Graphic Narrative Projects (Stella Oh)

I teach Thi Bui's *The Best We Could Do* in a women's and gender studies upper-division course titled "Gender, Race, and Graphic Narratives: Displacement, Loss, and Ethical Optics." Although it is a course offered by the Department of Women's and Gender Studies, it also fulfills the Creative Experience category of the university core curriculum where I teach. As a result, students who take the course are very diverse; their majors range across gender studies, animation, Asian American studies, literature, biology, and business. Students read Bui's graphic memoir along with other texts such as Mine Okubo's *Citizen 13660*, Art Spiegelman's *Maus*, Lynda Barry's *One! Hundred! Demons!*, and Marjorie Liu and Sana Tanaka's *Monstress*, exploring the ethics of memory and storytelling as it pertains to displacement and loss. During fall 2019, students had the opportunity to read *The Best We Could Do* and meet with Thi Bui.

I teach Bui's graphic narrative in a way that students can grapple with the complicated historical terrain of the Vietnam War but also connect with larger questions of migration, displacement, belonging, and ethical storytelling. Bui articulates her frustration of trying to "solve the storytelling problem of how to present history in a way that is human and relatable and not oversimplified" (Preface). She gestures to the inability of language to accurately articulate trauma. As Marianne Hirsh notes, images have a "unique ability to represent the impossible demands of trauma, memory and narration" ("Editor's Column" 1212). The use of images and color expresses heightened states of pain that exceed linguistic frames of reference. Graphic narratives like Bui's engage in an ethical storytelling that bears witness to discarded memories, and in its recalling of personal histories engages in the essential process of constructing a post-traumatic narrative of identity. Reframing the discourse of the Vietnam War, Bui makes the collective national loss intimate and casts the political as personal and vice versa.

In a provocative panel, Bui illustrates a mirrored image of Việt Nam carved onto the naked back of a female figure. This mirrored image of Việt Nam gestures to the ways in which war has physically, emotionally, and mentally etched its violence and trauma upon the backs of women.[3] *The Best We Could Do* is a corporeal narrative that speaks to the material ramifications of the violence of war on individual bodies and minds, particularly those who are marginalized. Slightly above the image of the naked woman with the mirrored image of Việt Nam is an image of a correct outline of Việt Nam. This proper image of Việt Nam bleeds into a panel that depicts Bui writing (see fig. 2.1). As she writes, Bui ponders if she can fill the missing carved piece on her back and can see both "Việt Nam as a real place, and not a symbol of something lost" and her "parents as real people" (36). Addressing the haunting legacy of the Vietnam War as the war that America lost and "loved because it lost," Bui's graphic narrative strives to addresses the gaps and fissures and "fill the void between my parents and me" through her memory and postmemory (36). She recognizes that feelings of loss, fear, and anxiety will always be there but hopes that in visualizing trauma she will not "pass along some gene for sorrow" (327).

By centering *The Best We Could Do* around family, Bui creates an important link to current debates on refugees and migration. In a talk entitled "Now That We're Here" given at Loyola Marymount University on November 19, 2019, Thi Bui framed her lecture by connecting her graphic memoir with the migrant situation at the US-Mexico border and the global refugee crisis. One of the major aspects of immigration politics today has been the separation of children from their families. The ACLU estimates that approximately 5,500 migrant children were separated from their parents under the Trump administration.[4] Through deeply personal memories and the articulation of embodied histories, *The Best We Could Do* inserts itself into the

---

3. Sally McWilliams notes that the mother figure of Hang in *The Best We Could Do* "becomes a potential symbol of the exploitive power of globalization to take advantage of migrant and refugee women" (326).

4. After public outrage, President Trump signed the executive order "Affording Congress an Opportunity to Address Family Separation" on June 20, 2018. However, the executive order did not account for how and when separated children would be reunited with their parents. Jasmine Aguilera, "Here's What to Know about the Status of Family Separation at the US Border, Which Isn't Nearly Over," *Time Magazine*, 21 September 2019.

FIGURE 2.1. Mapping bodies in Thi Bui's *The Best We Could Do: An Illustrated Memoir.*
Used with permission from Abrams Comic Arts. ® an imprint of ABRAMS, New York.
All rights reserved.

political dialogue about migration and family separation. Bui began her talk by discussing her short graphic narrative "Precious Time" (2017), which connects her family's experience as refugees fleeing the Vietnam War with the experiences of other families struggling with similar plights in the contemporary moment. "Precious Time" was commissioned as part of the *Illustrated PEN*'s State of Emergency feature with the goal of articulating stories of communities who may be at highest risk. Bui ends "Precious Time" with an illustrated image of the death of Alan Kurdi, a three-year-old child who drowned in the Mediterranean Sea while his family was trying to flee Syria. Photographs of the boy washed ashore made headlines on the cover of several news outlets, including *Time* magazine, revealing the horrors of war and the apathy of the global community to address the current refugee crisis. Reminding us that war does not discriminate and political decisions have real consequences that affect human lives, Bui focuses on narrating war in a way that helps readers relate to the human casualties of war. The illustrated image of Alan Kurdi washed ashore, his back toward the audience, mirrors the naked female figure in *The Best We Could Do* who has a mirror image of Việt Nam etched on her back. Both figures are young, vulnerable, marginalized, and often regarded as disposable. Their backs are literally and figuratively engraved with a reversal of ethical responsibility in which the global audience remains apathetic to war and the growing plight of refugees and migrants who are displaced.

After listening to Bui's talk and engaging in deep extended discussion with the author, students had an assignment in which they were required to create a short comic that illustrates how a personal memory of displacement speaks to and adds to a larger historical memory of an event. How are autobiographical memories of a personal experience reflective of a larger collective memory? How do personal memories usher in new histories? The results were fantastic mini-graphic narratives dealing with depression and post-traumatic stress syndrome after serving in the Afghanistan war, living with bipolar disorder, and wrestling with interracial adoption, to name a few. The assignment called for a focused plot development over the course of eight to ten panels. The narrative arc of the project needed to incorporate different panel sizes, shading, gutters, frames, and other comic architecture to communicate ideas of emotional, temporal, and spatial displacement. Students were encouraged to use different digital platforms such as Comic Life, Photoshop, or Illustrator to create their graphic narratives.

Here, I'd like to focus specifically on two examples of student graphic narrative projects. The first project, "War Is a Racket," was written by Anderson Marin, who had served in the Afghanistan war. The graphic narrative addressed the post-traumatic stress syndrome that he struggled with and the lack of sufficient resources for returning veterans. Displacement during and after the war, temporal dislocation, and the difficulty of coping and returning to civilian life were some of the powerful issues this graphic narrative addressed. The title of this project, "War Is a Racket," was taken a from a speech by Major General Smedley Butler, who argued that war benefits very few at the expense of the many. The student illustrated his own personal experience as a war veteran whose self-reflexive guilt was indicative of the larger social and psychological effects of the war. Contrasting the two years of training he received for combat with the one week of training that was provided upon return to civilian life, Marin critiques the lack of training skills and placement veterans are offered once they return from war. In the graphic narrative, loyalty to country is emphasized and symbolized through the image of soldiers who are depicted as bulldogs. Rather than meaningful training and good-paying jobs, many veterans face an empty rhetoric of gratefulness for their service.

The second student project, by Jolie Brownell, explored feelings of displacement as an adoptee from Haiti. "The Ungrateful Orphan" addressed complex external and internal pressures to feel grateful for being adopted by white American parents. The student remarked that Bui's focus on family, separation, and displacement prompted and inspired her to create her own story about belonging, gratefulness, and geopolitical displacement. In *The Best We Could Do*, Bui notes her desires to "turn a little more American" by walking along streets named after American presidents (65). A panel that depicts Bui and her sisters reciting the Pledge of Allegiance, "one nation under GOD indivisible," is sharply contrasted with another panel in which Bui and her father are accosted by strangers spewing racial slurs, "You stupid Gook" and spitting on them (67). Attempting to embrace the United States as her new home and become a "little more American" runs counter to the xenophobic violence and policies like Prop 187 that deliberately attempt to deport migrants. In *The Best We Could Do*, Bui depicts the constant tension involved in negotiating between her displacement from Việt Nam, gratefulness for her new home in America, and deep frustrations toward America's anti-immigrant policies.

Similarly, as a black child adopted by white parents, Brownell struggles to find meaning and belonging. As she poignantly illustrates in "The Ungrateful Orphan," the pressure to "be grateful for not being really seen" negates part of her identity as a black Haitian woman who is adopted by white parents. A few months after taking the class, Brownell had an opportunity to give a TED Talk on the same topic. Similar to questions of displacement and trauma she explored in "The Ungrateful Orphan," her TED Talk addressed the compelling question of why her birth mother in Haiti put her up for adoption. Brownell states, "Dear mother, did you fail me or was it the world that failed you?" Like Bui, Brownell connected her own feelings of trauma and separation with mothers who cross borders into foreign lands to bring their children to a safer place. The traumatic effects of losing a child or losing a mother, by individual choice or by the powers of colonization, imperialism, and neoliberalism that lurk behind such semblance of choice, are illustrated in this project. If "to be traumatized is precisely to be possessed by an image or an event," then the medium of the graphic novel intervenes in the difficulty of representing trauma (Caruth, *Unclaimed* 4–5). As Brownell writes, "What do you do when both blessing and grief are at war inside your bones?" Graphic narratives offer a productive medium to engage in an ethical storytelling of the hidden violence of transnational adoption. The tensions that are present in and through our reading practices actively engage in a process of retelling and recreating history.

Postmemory at Work:
Proceed with Caution (erin Khuê Ninh)

I teach *The Best We Could Do* in an upper-division class on Vietnamese American experience at UC Santa Barbara. In this course in particular, students who are children or grandchildren of Vietnamese refugees or immigrants form a near hegemony. They may arrive bearing just an inkling of their families' histories, but with an implicit expectation that this course help *explain* things.

In the syllabus, Thi Bui's memoir comes near the end, preceded by ground laid with some of the history of Việt Nam and its contact with the West, but especially with criticism regarding how history is told: slanted per Vietnamese North or South, US conservative or liberal or ethnic studies, public or familial interests. Class exercises and writing assignments ask students to navigate these conflicting accounts, and have them experience for themselves when to counterbalance and when to choose, given truths that will not reconcile. I prime students to appreciate, then, the ethics of Bui's storytelling.

That Bui does this well is partly a matter of authorial persona, which acts as metadata a text transmits from the very first page. The full-page panel that opens Bui's narrative is a view of her pregnant belly, with legs and feet astraddle as for a delivery table. Captions accompanying this image immediately establish the story's focalization, that is, "the consciousness through which the narrative is filtered" (Kunka 63):

> New York / Methodist Hospital / November 28, 2005
> I'm in labor.
> The pain comes in twenty-foot waves and Má has disappeared. (Bui 1)

Approximating her literal point of view, this "ocularization" localizes Bui's perspective in time, place, and emotional context. That specificity is an authorial practice throughout the book: a regular pinging of location that enables and even reminds the reader to gauge the relationship between the narrator and the information being relayed. This perspective could certainly be seen as maternal—motherly, daughterly—but of course to understand it as feminist is more salient: It is a fundament of feminist storytelling, whether literary or ethnographic, to own up to one's point of view. In terms of technique, this means to "[foreground] the fact that" all narratives, including the present one, are "created by an individual moved by her whims, biases, and general subjectivity" (Kunka 77).

Of course, ocularization is a technique mundane to comics and film—in the latter known as subjective camera (Mulvey)—and not inherently ethical (though certainly always ideological). Bui's use stands out, however, given that normally an image "contain[ing] the view as seen through the eyes of the narrator" would mean "the narrator could not be seen in the panel, except perhaps through a mirror" (Kunka 63). But her opening frame is so emblematic precisely because it arranges for us to see *as she sees* and also to see *her, as she is positioned,* in the how and why of the story's telling.

What this will mean is a conscientiousness about disclosing as the writer exercises her authority over the story, and over the people who figure in it. After all, we hear of them, from them, only through whatever filter Bui has put in place. I see her being careful with her power in moments like these:

> Lacking memories of my own, I do research.
> Lots of research. (Bui 183)

> The [ideological] contradiction in my father's stories troubled me for a long time.
> But so did the oversimplifications and stereotypes in American versions of the Vietnam War. (207)

> I'd like to tell this as a happy story, in which a young man, my father, meets a young woman, my mother.

They fall in love and marry and several years later, have me.
But my mother's version of the story foils it. (190)

The sorts of things these self-reflexive moments acknowledge are her epistemological limits and methods, the choices duly made in synthesizing (multiple hi)stories into plot, and the complexity of portraying her interview/narrative subjects given the competing uses to which a story can be put. What Bui models is a combination of scrupulousness and agency that I hope for my Vietnamese American students.

Along with that opening panel, I find Bui's use of color emblematic of her storytelling. Throughout she uses just one: a rust-orange/red in different concentrations, varying suffusions of the page. Granted, this was necessity mothering invention: In an interview, Bui freely admitted that keeping to one color was cheaper to print. But she added that as an artist, this turned out to be a richly useful parameter, forcing her to be extremely judicious or thoughtful in its application—especially since something with red tones can easily become overwhelming (Skype interview, 6 December 2017).

Aesthetically, then, this color keeps her circumspect—to manifold ethical effect. Her war-storying avoids sensationalism, and her family history eschews melodrama. There *is* feeling, but it can't be sloppy or self-indulgent. This resonates even with her personification, which is refreshingly free of self-aggrandizing: That view of her belly and feet does not flatter her as the scion or culmination of wars and ancestors.

I especially appreciate the monochrome for granting such visual consistency to all the chronotopes (Bakhtin) of Bui's family history: Past and present, here and there, they bleed the same. This commensurability is particularly important because it countervails a tendency in second-generation Vietnamese American narratives, even and especially in students' Vietnamese Culture Night productions, across campuses and decades. The classic plot goes like this: A selfish or clueless or disobedient refugee's child travels back through time and/or space to rediscover his ancestral history; what he sees there explains the troubles in his family's present, unlocks their conflicts, and makes him a better person/child. He finally recognizes the magnitude of his parents' sacrifices and is convinced of his enormous debt to them. In conclusion, his life and so-called problems end up looking pale and trivial against the blood and gore of his parents' suffering.

So that is one sense in which I wish Bui had modeled something different. Aside from her even-handed colorizing, the memoir capitulates to that stock moral suasion. She presents the project that becomes this book as being about "bridging the gap between past and present" so that she can "fill the void between my parents and me" (Bui 36). Fair enough, but her operating bias is debilitating. Early on she calls the second generation "lame"—"assholes," even (29)—because apparently, the familial gap is of the second generation's doing, and reconciliation a matter requiring their concessions alone.

For all of its author's critical perspicacity, the memoir recites this shibboleth at face value: "My parents escaped Việt Nam on a boat *so their children could grow up in freedom.* / You'd think I could be more *grateful*" (30; emphasis added). My students are wired to these same beliefs and attendant reflexes of guilt, self-denigration: As the generation once-removed from war and flight, they and their experiences are nothing. And so I must remind them that we have read Mimi Thi Nguyen's *The Gift of Freedom*, which invites us "to know the refugee's sorrow, and her indebtedness for its cure," in order to confront the genealogies and assumed virtue of "liberal powers that undergird the twinned concerns of . . . the gift of freedom and the debt that follows." The questions Nguyen asks of the refugee figure's scripted debt to the savior US state apply, equally and by extension, to the next generation's scripted debt to the refugee: "How is this . . . [morally extracted] thankfulness, and all that it implies about the gift and its giving, a problem of imperial remains? . . . Why are we—those of us who have received this precious, poisonous gift of freedom—obliged to thank? What powers oblige us?" (3).

And we have read Marianne Hirsch on the complicated inheritance of historical trauma, hardly innocent of harm:

> Postmemory is a powerful form of memory precisely because its connection to its object is mediated not through recollection but through an imaginative investment and creation. . . . Postmemory characterizes the experiences of those who grow up *dominated by narratives that preceded their birth, whose own belated stories are displaced by the stories of the previous generation,* shaped by traumatic events that can neither be fully understood nor re-created. ("Past Lives" 662; emphasis added)

I don't assign my monograph on debt and intergenerational conflict in any of my classes because I've not figured out how to teach my own work without imposing too much, or being redundant in lecture. But *Ingratitude: The Debt-Bound Daughter in Asian American Literature* is devoted to showing "filial obligation" for the toxic narrative it is; that analysis underlies what I see as Bui's dereliction of duty to herself, and by extension to her lame, asshole readers.

It is dangerous to buy into another's version of events so unquestioningly that it exiles one's own from the page. This is true especially when the other uses terms like "love," "freedom," "sacrifice." Bui ends by calling her life "a gift that is too great—a debt I can never repay" (325). With a moral narrative this obligating, this totalizing, no wonder she is unable to justify devoting so much as a single panel to depicting her own anger at her mother, and what it might have been about. She mentions that whole unwritten narrative only once—"How do I let go of all the anger I have put away?" (322)—a single word by way of resolving to erase it unsaid.

Imagine if she extended the same narrative to her son: *I suffered to keep you alive. I sacrificed to give you opportunities. You be grateful and repay me. There is nothing you deserve to say for yourself.* Is that freedom she'd be giving him, then?

The Good Refugee Story

A month after the release of *The Best We Could Do* in 2017, *The Guardian* published an essay by an Iranian novelist, speaking to this same moment in history when the Global North has decided it has run out of compassion for all the refugees it has created, in all these shades of brown. In "The Ungrateful Refugee: 'We Have No Debt to Repay,'" Dina Nayeri writes,

> With the rise of nativist sentiment in Europe and America, I've seen a troubling change in the way people make the case for refugees. Even those on the left talk about how immigrants make America great. They point to photographs of happy refugees turned good citizens, listing their contributions, as if that is the price of existing in the same country, on the same earth. Friends often use me as an example. They say in posts or conversations: "Look at Dina. She lived as a refugee and look how much stuff she's done." As if that's proof that letting in refugees has a good, healthy return on investment.

It is dicey work, reassuring the xenophobes and nationalists, and yet indispensable: a matter of lives and deaths. To speak a neoliberalist's language is to argue the respectability of refugees, their economic convertibility to workers and taxpayers; to speak a racist's language is to assure them that our families love like their families, that our toddlers drowned on a seashore look like their own. It is dicey work that *The Best We Could Do* does well, and not naively: When Bui speaks at universities and libraries up and down state lines, the talks are an extension of her activism. She leads with the memoir that landed the invitation, and leaves audiences with the comic art she has done since:

> Now that she's written a story about her own refugee experience, Thi is writing stories about people whose refugee experiences do not match hers. She wants to challenge the "model minority" stereotype that Asian Americans are often painted with—the notion that Asian immigrants to America are always successful and perfect. Thi tells stories of people who are in prison, in detention centers, who are waiting to be deported, people who didn't have nice, neat, successful immigrant stories. ("Cartoonist")

These are narratives more in the spirit of Nayeri's piece, and they do not reassure.

You could say that Bui teaches her own memoir with a sense of the dangers attendant to the Good Refugee story. In an especially extradiegetic maneuver, she reframes *The Best We Could Do* inside activism that critiques rationales of deportation and the logic of public charge,[5] rejecting demands that refugee lives be weighed and owed in productivity and gratitude. Rather, this critique insists,

> what America did was a basic human obligation. It is the obligation of every person born in a safer room to open the door when someone in danger knocks. It is your duty to answer us, even if we don't give you sugary success stories. (Nayeri)

But however true it is that the protection of the vulnerable is a basic obligation for nations—the provision of food, clothing, and shelter a rudimentary duty not to be mistaken for sainthood or brandished later in debt collection—it is all the more true of parents.

For Asian American studies, teaching Bui's memoir well in this political moment must also mean teaching that footnote: that a "good" refugee story need not be one of telos and reconciliation. This is important ethical work to do with a general readership; it is imperative with one composed of the children and grandchildren of refugees, whom we cannot leave with such a dangerous definition of freedom.

---

5. See https://thenib.com/refugee-to-detainee-how-the-u-s-is-deporting-those-seeking-a-safe-haven/ and https://www.kqed.org/arts/13865075/illustrating-the-opposition-to-trumps-public-charge-rule.

Works Cited

Bakhtin, M. M. "Forms of Time and of the Chronotope in the Novel." *The Dialogic Imagination: Four Essays,* edited by Michael Holquist, University of Texas Press, 1981, pp. 84–258.

Bui, Thi. *The Best We Could Do: An Illustrated Memoir.* Harry N. Abrams, 2017.

——. "Cartoonist and Refugee Rights Activist." *Bippity Bricks,* https://www.bippity-bricks.com/refugee-thi-bui.

——. "Now That We're Here." November 19, 2019. Loyola Marymount University, Los Angeles. Lecture.

——. Skype interview with AsAm 100EE, University of California, Santa Barbara. 6 December 2017.

Brown, Jolie. "Call Me By My Name, Not My Stereotype." *TED,* January 2020. www.ted.com/talks/jolie_brownell_call_me_by_my_name_not_my_stereotype.

Caruth, Cathy. "The Body Keeps the Score: An Interview with Bessel van der Kolk." *Listening to Trauma: Conversations with Leaders in the Theory and Treatment of Catastrophic Experience,* Johns Hopkins University Press, 2014, pp. 153–78.

——. *Unclaimed Experience: Trauma, Narrative, and History.* Johns Hopkins Press, 1996.

Gordon, Avery. *Ghostly Matters: Haunting and the Sociological Imagination.* University of Minnesota Press, 2008.

Herman, Judith. *Trauma and Recovery.* Basic Books, 1992.

Hirsh, Marianne. "Editor's Column: Collateral Damage." *PMLA,* vol. 119, no. 5, 2004, pp. 1209–15.

——. *The Generation of Postmemory: Writing and Visual Culture after the Holocaust.* Columbia University Press, 2012.

——. "Past Lives: Postmemories in Exile." *Poetics Today,* vol. 17, no. 4, 1996, pp. 659–86.

Kunka, Andrew. *Autobiographical Comics.* Bloomsbury Academic, 2018.

McWilliams, Sally. "Precarious Memories and Affective Relationships in Thi Bui's *The Best We Could Do.*" *Journal of Asian American Studies,* vol. 22, no. 3, October 2019, pp. 315–48.

Miodrag, Hannah. *Comics and Language: Reimagining Critical Discourse on the Form.* University Press of Mississippi, 2013.

Mulvey, Laura. "Visual Pleasure and Narrative Cinema." *Screen,* vol. 16, no. 3, Autumn 1975, pp. 6–18.

Nayeri, Dina. "The Ungrateful Refugee: 'We Have No Debt to Repay.'" *The Guardian,* 4 April 2017, https://www.theguardian.com/world/2017/apr/04/dina-nayeri-ungrateful-refugee.

Nguyen, Mimi Thi. *The Gift of Freedom: War, Debt, and Other Refugee Passages.* Duke University Press, 2012.

Ninh, erin Khuê. *Ingratitude: The Debt-Bound Daughter in Asian American Literature.* New York University Press, 2011.

Shih, Shu-mei. *Visuality and Identity: Sinophone Articulations across the Pacific.* University of California Press, 1997.

PART 2

SUBVERTING STEREOTYPES

CHAPTER 3

Bitch Planet's Meiko Maki Is Down for Justice!

JEANETTE ROAN

In 2012 writer Kelly Sue DeConnick, along with artist Dexter Soy, introduced Carol Danvers as Captain Marvel to the world in *Captain Marvel* #1. This relaunch of the superhero formerly known as Ms. Marvel was inspired by the history of women in aviation and DeConnick's own experiences growing up on U.S. Air Force bases, and it included a redesign by artist Jamie McKelvie of Ms. Marvel's stereotypically revealing costume to something more befitting a fighter pilot.[1] While the title was generally well received, especially by the community of ardent fans known as the Carol Corps, there were also negative reactions to DeConnick's purported "feminist agenda." DeConnick was taken aback by this response: "I was just kind of like floored by that reaction and pissed off by it, and I thought, you know, this is *not* 'angry feminist.' This is a very uplifting, very kind of light superhero fare. If you want to see 'angry feminist,' *I will show it to you*. And so there was 'Bitch Planet'" (Saraiya).

The Image Comics series *Bitch Planet*, written by DeConnick with art by Valentine De Landro, colors by Kelly Fitzpatrick, and letters by Clayton

---

1. Of course, there is a new Ms. Marvel now, Kamala Khan. See chapter 6 of this volume for an analysis of Kamala Khan as Ms. Marvel.

Cowles, critiques patriarchy through an intersectional feminist lens upon a dystopian world. *Bitch Planet* features African American women at the center of its narrative and includes a diverse cast of characters, including two significant Asian American characters.[2] The title references the off-world prison at the center of the comic, the Auxiliary Compliance Outpost, or A.C.O., colloquially known as Bitch Planet. The world in which the narrative occurs is disconcertingly familiar. The world is run by the Protectorate, and the Protectorate is run by men such as Father John Johnson, the High Father, and Father Edward Josephson, the Father of Media. Women are subjected to a litany of expectations and constraints familiar to women in the contemporary moment but raised to the level of law. Violation of these expectations and constraints results in severe punishment, the most extreme of which is banishment to the off-world prison. While some infractions parallel those in our world, such as assault or murder, others speak to the ways the world of the comic is rigidly determined by the wants, needs, and perspectives of men, as women are imprisoned for such crimes as seduction and disappointment, emotional manipulation, patrilineal dishonor, disrespect, and being a bad mother.

In her introduction to the anthology *Drawing New Color Lines: Transnational Asian American Graphic Narratives*, Monica Chiu writes that the essays in the book

> acknowledge an historical gallery of visual representations of Asians and Asian Americans—visual imperatives—produced from public fantasies about them that have been shaped by material history and popular culture, politics, social science and economics. The discussions collected here reference these enduring representations, sometimes overtly and sometimes surreptitiously, subsequently conjuring new ones. There exists provocative imagining in comics' imaging. (3)

Bitch Planet's satirical intertextual engagement with popular visual culture similarly highlights, challenges, and overturns hegemonic representations of, among others, Asian American and African American women. My focus in this chapter will be upon the characters Meiko Maki and Penny Rolle, the only two from the series to have entire issues devoted to their backstories. The cover of issue #3, titled "The Secret Origin of Penny Rolle," foregrounds Penny in a defiant stance as the text "Bold, Beautiful and . . .

---

2. Although *Bitch Planet* does not specify that the narrative takes place within the US (or some future version of it), the context of the comic and the signifiers assigned to the Maki family make them legible as Asian Americans.

Baaaaaad!" is stamped across the front. Issue #6, "Meiko Maki is an Extraordinary Machine!," with art by Taki Soma, shows a kneeling woman from the side with her hands bound behind her back. The text of the cover reads "Bound by Law . . . Down for Justice . . ." While both covers utilize the visual conventions of exploitation film posters, they also suggest very different stories. Taken together, the backstories of Meiko Maki and Penny Rolle demonstrate the ways in which racialized gender operates differently for Asian American and African American women as well as what resistance in each circumstance might look like, while their relationship to each other on Bitch Planet offers a vision of interracial collaboration and intimacy.

Caged and Enraged: Women-in-Prison Films

DeConnick has been clear about her "genuine affection" for women-in-prison exploitation films: "I like this stuff so much, and it's so terrible, it's so deeply awful and delicious, like those candies that are bad for you. So I wanted to see if there was a way that I could play with the things about it that I love and also the things about it that make me wildly uncomfortable" (Hero Complex). These films are indeed disturbing in their misogynist display of women and the often brutal punishments they endure, but also compelling in terms of a space filled almost entirely by women who are often sexually aggressive, physically violent, and critical of the system that has oppressed them. Bev Zalcock celebrates women-in-prison films as a genre that features active, dangerous women, often from marginalized groups (36). A chapter about women-in-prison films in an edited anthology about violent women in film similarly appreciates the alternative vision of a women's world that the films provide: "Women-in-prison films—in all their strangeness, their multiple marginality—often present images of women and women's relationships rarely found in more mainstream genres" (Walters 106). Women-in-prison films have, in short, often offered more interesting images of women than many mainstream Hollywood films despite their problematic spectacles and narratives. Or as feminist film scholar Judith Mayne succinctly puts it, "There is much to love, and much to hate, about the women-in-prison film" (115).

Where film scholars have written about the regressive, progressive, and transgressive aspects of women-in-prison films, DeConnick and her collaborators attempt to weave a similar kind of appreciation but also critique of the genre in *Bitch Planet*. Thus, *Bitch Planet* is not an adaptation of a specific film, but rather a thoughtful engagement with a film genre and its conventions.

One obvious such moment is "The obligatory shower scene" in issue #4, announced as such in a banner at the top of the page. In the films, the mise-en-scène and cinematography of these scenes are orchestrated to elicit visual pleasure for an assumed heterosexual male spectator, including featuring a very narrow range of idealized female body types. In *Bitch Planet*, as Rachel Marie-Crane Williams notes, "the art within the entire book, but this set of panels in particular, lovingly portrays the bodies of realistic looking women of all shapes, colors, and sizes." Rebecca Wanzo writes of how a later scene of the character Kamau Kogo seemingly masturbating in the shower evokes and critiques pornography's fragmentation and objectification of the female body, while also being an erotic, pro-sex image of a Black woman (61). Both shower scenes, albeit in different ways, use the aesthetic strategies available to comics creators—drawing style and visual composition, panel framing, layout—to overturn the voyeuristic gaze of the film camera.[3]

The "obligatory shower scene" is but one example of *Bitch Planet*'s multiple references to yet also disruptions of the conventions of exploitation films. Another is the inclusion of a significant character of Asian descent. Women-in-prison films commonly featured a multicultural cast, and a number of scholars have analyzed the racial dynamics of these films. Mayne suggests that in this genre, "differences between women are stressed, as if to take the place usually occupied by gender" (127). She considers in particular the eroticization of racial difference, though the films she examines only represent the opposition between African American women and white women. Mia Mask focuses upon films starring Pam Grier and notes that many women-in-prison films of the 1970s were shot in the Philippines for the low cost of labor and, presumably, the "exotic" locations. Mask argues that *The Big Doll House* (Jack Hill, 1971) "presents a racialized, gendered economy of power and privilege in which white women are positioned as naturally feminine. There is a clear ethnic distinction between the butch Philippine prison guards and the mostly femme white inmates" (80). But Mask, like many other scholars, understates the effect of the fact that in many of these films, all of the prisoners aside from the main characters, all of the prison guards, and all manner of other extras are Filipinx.

Some of these films also include an Asian woman incarcerated in the same cell as the (African American and white) main characters, such as Teresa (Sofia Moran) in *Women in Cages* (Gerardo de Leon, 1971) and Rina (Marissa Delgado) in *The Big Bird Cage* (Jack Hill, 1972). However, Rina barely speaks a single word in the film. Teresa has more to say, yet she

---

3. For a useful and thorough overview of aesthetic strategies in comics, see Postema. For a specifically semiotic analysis of comics, see Groensteen.

remains in the background compared to the African American and white characters. The attention to the Black-white racial dynamics of the main characters without a full account of the racialized backdrop of these films, including their landscape, sizable cast of Filipinx extras, and occasional references to lambanóg, neglects a significant aspect of these films.

Unlike the films, as well as much of the scholarship about them, *Bitch Planet* foregrounds an important woman of Asian descent, Meiko Maki.[4] Meiko's role in this story of rebellious "Non-Compliant" women not only emphatically inserts Asians into a narrative of resistance against oppression, but it also speaks to the distinctive racialized gendering of Asian women in a multiracial context, along with the possibilities of coalition building (and perhaps more) among women with very different identities, social locations, and experiences. By making Meiko one of the main characters of the narrative, *Bitch Planet* underlines the ways in which the scores of Asian women who have appeared in women-in-prison films of the 1970s have so often been silent and uncredited, but omnipresent all the same. While Meiko cannot and does not represent the Filipina extras in the films, not least because of the historical relationship between Japan, the Philippines, and the US, whereas Asian women were merely background in the films, in *Bitch Planet* one is front and center, and she changes the calculus of difference.

Seeing Racialized Gender

Meiko's backstory in issue #6 compared to Penny's backstory in issue #3 offers insight into the ways in which racialized gender operates differently for Asian American women and African American women, particularly under the disciplinary white heterosexual patriarchal gaze. Anne Anlin Cheng's *Ornamentalism* proposes a theory of the "yellow woman," an effort to think through the specificity of "Asiatic femininity." Cheng argues, "While primitivism rehearses the rhetoric of ineluctable flesh, Orientalism, by contrast, relies on a decorative grammar, a phantasmatic corporeal syntax that is artificial and layered" (5–6). She further elaborates, "To put it crudely, our models for understanding racialized gender have been predominantly influenced by a particular view of bodies of African origins that has led us to think in a certain way about raced female bodies, when there has been in fact something of a bifurcation within the racial imaginary between bare

---

4. Viewers of the Netflix series *Orange Is the New Black* (2013–19) may recall that this relatively recent iteration of the women-in-prison film genre, in streaming television series format, features two Asian American inmates, Mei Chang (Lori Tan Chinn) and Brook Soso (Kimiko Glenn). For a critical analysis of these two characters, see Kim.

flesh and artificial ornament" (6). In devoting one issue entirely to Penny Rolle's origin story, and another to Meiko Maki's, *Bitch Planet* highlights the distinctive ways in which African American women and Asian American women are seen and subjected. Furthermore, the particularities of these scenes of subjection also frame the possibilities for resistance and rebellion.

We first meet Penny Rolle in the opening pages of *Bitch Planet*, as she arrives among a group of new transports. The two-page spread features a series of small rectangular panels on the top tier with a vaguely religious voiceover narration, and a corresponding series of tall, rectangular, and very pink panels on the bottom tier, each featuring one naked prisoner in suspended animation for the interstellar trip. From the very beginning, Penny's ample girth is a point of visual emphasis. Her body extends beyond the frame, suggesting that she is too large to be contained by the panel. Each inmate has a "sin" associated with her, as highlighted in a narrative caption. Penny's is "gluttony." Even her very name suggests her size. As Wanzo writes, "Her nomenclature, in the way of exploitation films, references her rolls of fat, black flesh" (57). After the inmates arrive, when Penny takes out her assigned uniform, she immediately bristles at its inadequacy: "Where'm I supposed to put my other tit?" she demands, as she holds the too-small jumpsuit up. Her "born BIG" tattoo, the words framed by two trumpeting elephants, is visible on her left bicep and highlighted in a panel of her upper body in profile. Although the guard insists that the uniforms are "constructed for your specific measurements," Penny is certain hers will not fit. The confrontation then escalates to a full-scale fight.

Penny Rolle's backstory centers upon her challenge to the aesthetic and behavioral ideals of proper femininity. At the beginning of the issue, a man reels off a list of offenses that Penny has been charged with, including assault, "aesthetic offenses," and "wanton obesity." In a large panel that takes up half of the page, Penny faces a grid of male faces, each contorted into an expression of disgust as they gaze upon her. Yet her resistance is evident in a small inset panel featuring a close-up of one eye, narrowed in anger. Most of the issue is devoted to flashbacks to moments in Penny's life. At school, Mother Siebertling insists that Penny must learn to see herself "through the Father's eyes" as she prepares to "fix" Penny's supposedly unruly hair. In the incident that leads to her imprisonment, Penny explodes in anger as male customers at her muffin shop denigrate her appearance in racist, sexist terms while a news anchor promotes the use of gastrointestinal parasites for weight loss.

Following her arrest, the presiding Fathers attempt to use a "Cerebral Action-Potential Integration and Extrapolation Matrix" to extract Penny's "ideal self" from her mind in order to aid in her rehabilitation. Penny thinks to herself, "I wish you could see me . . . the way I see myself." She seems to succeed, as the men learn that Penny's ideal self (as reflected in a mirror-like contraption) aligns perfectly with her actually existing self, much to their surprise. In the end, Penny has the last laugh, as she repeats her grandmother's statement "If it ain't broke, don't fix it," thereby refusing the notion that there is anything wrong with her at all. The Fathers are so taken aback by this discovery that they sentence her to imprisonment on Bitch Planet, deeming her a lost cause. "In the tradition of women's prison narratives and blaxploitation flicks," Wanzo writes, "the fat black woman's body is treated as a sign of the grotesque. But the creators suggest that it is the gaze that categorizes the body as grotesque, not the body in itself" (57). Another way of seeing this scene is through Nicole Fleetwood's concept of excess flesh, which she defines as *"a performative that doubles visibility: to see the codes of visuality operating on the (hyper)visible body that is its object.* Excess flesh does not destabilize the dominant gaze or its system of visibility. Instead, it refracts the gaze back upon itself" (112). Despite society's, that is, the Father's, best efforts to discipline Penny to see herself as they see her, she is able to force them to see her as she sees herself, as someone who was "born big," and is perfect just the way she is.

For Meiko as for Penny, ideal femininity is a terrain of contestation. However, whereas Penny challenges what the Fathers of *Bitch Planet* define as desirable, explicitly rejecting their narrow definition of "ideal," Meiko fits it all too well, or at least one version of it. Yet Meiko's more normative body is hardly an advantage, as it subjects her to the predations of the same gaze that dismisses Penny. And in these contrasting relationships to the gaze, the series touches upon the ways in which racialized gender operates differently for different women. We initially encounter Meiko in the second issue of the series. However, it is in issue #6 that we learn Meiko's backstory and are introduced to the entire Maki family—Meiko and her younger sister Mirai, their mother Yume and their father Makoto.[5]

---

5. Some readers, however, may choose not to engage with this story at all; it begins with a content warning, informing readers that the material to come deals with sexual assault, and that those who choose not to read the issue/chapter may skip ahead to the next one to continue with the main narrative. This is the only time in the series that such a warning appears. In an unsettling real-life connection to the subject matter of the issue, comics creator Taki Soma, guest artist for this issue of *Bitch Planet,* accused the executive director of the Comic Book Legal Defense Fund (CBLDF), Charles Brownstein, of sexual assault in 2005. Although a police report was filed, ultimately the charges were dropped although the incident was reported and discussed in the comics press and led to the Friends of Lulu creating a fund for victims of sexual assault or harassment in the comics industry. In June 2020 Brownstein resigned as executive director of the CBLDF following a resurfacing of Soma's allegations alongside additional accusations of misconduct.

From the very beginning, Meiko's body as desirable ideal is apparent. Following the cover, credits page, and a content warning page, the issue begins with a splash page consisting of a background of musical notation, with a large unframed image on the right of Meiko, unclothed, seated, and seen from the back, with two f-stops drawn upon her lower back in a visual echo of the quartet of human-sized violins on the page. The drawing of Meiko references Man Ray's well-known photograph *Le Violon d'Ingres* (*Ingres's Violin*) from 1924, a famous objectification of the female form. The Orientalism of the original is signaled in the turban wrapped around the model's head and the title's reference to nineteenth-century French Orientalist painter Jean-Auguste-Dominique Ingres. *Bitch Planet* literalizes the concept by removing the prop and the art historical nod, that is, collapsing what Cheng calls "ornamental artifice" and "Asiatic femininity" in Euro-American visual culture (7) onto the body of an Asian woman. A series of small rectangular panels cascades down the left side of the page with fragmented images of Meiko's upper body as she is being groped and caressed against her will by an unnamed man. The narration of the page makes explicit its visual analogies by speaking of how men compare the hourglass shape of a violin to that of a woman's body. The idealization and objectification implied by the reference to the famous photograph are thus juxtaposed with the ongoing assault. Meiko's desirable femininity as well as vulnerability are therefore highlighted at the outset in a series of images that are perhaps the closest to those of exploitation films in the entire series. She appears conventionally beautiful, helpless, alone, and under assault. Although she represents all women in this misogynist musical analogy, she is also racialized as an Asian woman, and this apparent reinforcement of Asian women as a certain type of idealized femininity is deeply disturbing. However, how Meiko responds to such perceptions is what distinguishes her from scores of others in popular visual culture.

Whereas Penny was taken away from her beloved grandmother when she was eight, and news of the arrest of her parent for "gender terrorism" and miscegenation plays on the feed during her angry outburst at the muffin shop, Meiko is raised in what appears to be a model heterosexual, cisgendered, racially homogeneous nuclear family, a family of model minorities. Makoto, who goes by Mack, is a rising star architect within the Protectorate. Yume teaches violin lessons to girls. Meiko and Mirai are cheerful, obedient young teenagers. But they are not entirely what they seem. Behind closed blinds, Meiko has been secretly working with her father on his latest high-profile project, and he tells her that in a better world, her name would be listed alongside his as the creator. Behind a locked door and with a musical recording playing in the background, Yume teaches physics and calculus, not music, to girls.

The subversive efforts of the Maki family to contravene the patriarchy begin to fall apart with the appearance of Doug Braxton, Mack's coworker. Doug notices a potentially fatal yet seemingly purposeful flaw in the design of Mack's (and Meiko's) latest project, and he threatens to expose Mack if Mack does not offer one of his daughters to him. "I'm lonely," Doug complains. He adds, "I'm no good at meeting people. You have two daughters, Makoto. You can't already have plans for them both." Mack is predictably outraged and kicks Doug out of the house, then deciding to turn himself in and plead incompetence. What Mack doesn't know is that his daughters have been listening to the entire exchange, hidden around the corner in the stairwell. Meiko decides to take matters into her own hands to save her family.

Bitch Planet satirically engages with various popular cultural representations of women throughout the series, but the staging of the home of blond, blue-eyed Doug Braxton, which is decorated with swords on display on the wall, images of geisha, Japanese-style furniture and lighting, and a rising sun flag, takes aim at a different figure within popular culture, the white man who has a fascination with Asia and Asian women, seen in well-known films like *The Teahouse of the August Moon* (Daniel Mann, 1956), *Sayonara* (Joshua Logan, 1957), and *The World of Suzie Wong* (Richard Quine, 1960), as well as countless other films, television shows, and other cultural texts.[6] Cheng's theory of ornamentalism, a hybrid of the Oriental and the ornamental that challenges the distinction between persons and things, helps us understand that Doug sees Asian women as decorative objects, akin to his home furnishings. The fact that he is indifferent to which daughter is offered to him speaks to their interchangeability as objects rather than their individuality as subjects.

Doug assumes he understands the situation when Meiko arrives at his home, perhaps because he, as well as we, have seen similar scenarios play out so many times on-screen. Homi Bhabha famously wrote of the stereotype as "a form of knowledge and identification that vacillates between what is always 'in place,' already known, and something that must be anxiously repeated" (66). Yet in this instance, despite looking the part, Meiko refuses to stick to the script. Doug's inability to see beyond the stereotype, his misperception of Meiko, leads to quite an unexpected twist. Meiko begins by proposing to play a piece on her violin for him first, an action that fits easily

---

6. For critiques of these types of films, see Soe; Marchetti. For a study of the hypersexualization of Asian women, see Shimizu.

FIGURE 3.1. The end of Doug, *Bitch Planet* #6. Courtesy of Kelly Sue DeConnick, Valentine De Landro, and Taki Soma.

within Doug's image of her.[7] When a string breaks Doug remains unconcerned, but this rupture leads to a series of violent actions that take place on the next page, across five equally sized and shaped horizontal panels, each the width of the page. Although the composition of the panels pushes the violence into the gutters, leaving the reader to imagine what Meiko does to Doug, the bloody effects are unavoidable.

The fifth and final panel of the page is astounding (see fig. 3.1). Seen from above, Doug lies inert in his own blood while Meiko stands off to the side looking down, her smiling face reflected in a large pool of red. This spectacular act of violence leads to a complicated set of emotions, heightened by the stylized and suspenseful way in which it was presented: shock at the cold-blooded murder, satisfaction that Doug's stereotypical perceptions were turned against him, horror in seeing a young girl capable of such an act, relief that Doug can no longer threaten Meiko or her family. The character of Doug Braxton references a long line of men with fetishistic racialized desires who received exactly what they expected from their exotic, erotic Oriental women. In seeing Meiko as a beautiful, decorative object, Doug no more anticipated that she would harm him than that the swords on display on his wall would somehow turn their blades against his flesh. The pleasure of this scenario, for the reader, lies in the way that Meiko upends all expectations.

However, Doug's death is not what lands Meiko on Bitch Planet. Instead, the issue ends with a much older Meiko in prison, a continuation of the first page of the comic where, as we see now, the man who is assaulting her is a prison guard. In the last two pages of the comic she fights back against

7. See Yoshihara for an in-depth study of Asians and Asian Americans in classical music.

him, grabbing his baton and holding it to his neck. The unseen, nameless authorities determine "Subject had intent to kill!" while the guard, on his knees and trying to catch his breath, threatens, "I was just lonely 'kaff' you fucking 'kaff' bitch! You'll go 'kaff' to the A.C.O. for this!!" But on the last page Meiko has the last word, as she plays the world's tiniest violin in a mock gesture of sympathy while word balloons filled with the various rationales used to justify racialized fetishes—"It's not racist, everybody has a type"—or sexual harassment—"It was a compliment"—float on the page, unattributed to any particular speaker, just a part of the larger cultural context. The last panel of the page shows Meiko as if from the perspective of a security camera looking down. Although her hands are held behind her back and there is a prison guard to each side of her, she is fully clothed again and has a look of resolve as she exits with the statement that "the sound of the world's tiniest violin" is "the only song I'll ever play for you." Although much less dramatic than the earlier murder, the issue ends with a critique of the fetishization of Asian women as well as an unrepentant Meiko who refuses to feel sympathy for the lonely men who seek comfort from her. Penny's resistance takes the form of refusing the judgments of the dominant gaze and defiantly embracing her existing self as ideal, while Meiko plays against type, knowing how she appears to others but acting contrary to expectations.

On Bitch Planet: Penny + Meiko

Penny's and Meiko's backstories both feature a key moment of violence and end with a gesture of resistance. Penny assaults a man in her muffin shop and smashes the screen playing "the feed" with her rolling pin. Meiko carries out a cold-blooded murder of a man. Penny gets the last laugh while Meiko has the last word. In each instance, they rebel against the tyranny of the patriarchal gaze and racialized and gendered expectations, even if the two women are subject to very different visions. On Bitch Planet, although they are still under the authority of the Fathers, as in the women-in-prison films, "women in this world live together, love together, fight each other, and most centrally, fight back against the largely male systems of brutal domination that keep them all down" (Walters 106). In this other world, where they are imprisoned and surveilled yet also in some ways less subject to the dominant gaze than they were on the "outside," Penny and Meiko have the opportunity to embody their identities in relation to each other and to other women, rather than to the white, heterosexual patriarchy.

In Meiko's first appearance in *Bitch Planet*, she is shown alongside Kamau Kogo, an African American woman who is reminiscent of the characters Pam Grier often played in women-in-prison films. They are depicted side by side in a series of seven horizontal rectangular panels over two pages, making their physical differences apparent. Meiko is petite—she barely comes to Kam's shoulders—while Kam has the muscular build befitting a former professional athlete. When Meiko tries to persuade Kam to form a Megaton team at the prison, saying, "Put me on the team, pick the players that I tell you and I'll make it worth your while," Kam replies dismissively, "You're a hundred pounds sopping wet!" Meiko responds, "So what? Put Penny on and we'll balance each other out."[8] When Kam initially appraises Meiko, she sees a small Asian woman with a slight physique who could do little in a brutally physical sport, but Meiko's suggestion of pairing her with Penny recognizes different roles in the game for different women. Thus begins a partnership between two physically contrasting figures who find a way to make the most of their respective advantages; Penny's size and Meiko's speed turn out to be a winning combination.

In their first scrimmage of inmates against inmates, Penny blocks several opposing players through her sheer size and strength, wrapping her arms around three women and lifting them up off the ground (even though the rules of the game dictate only one-on-one matchups). Penny's blocking allows Meiko to run past "like a cheetah," Kam remarks from the sideline. The final four panels of the page show Meiko streaking past an opposing player yelling, "Suck it, chumps," and then scoring in the next panel. The two last panels on the page show a close-up of Penny's face, laughing, and then a close-up of Meiko's face, with her tongue sticking out and with the words "And that is how it's done, muthafuckaaaaaaas!" Although the very idea of a Megaton team made up of Bitch Planet inmates is an exploitative one, dreamed up by the Father of Media to boost television ratings and profits, training for and participating in the sport allows the women to use their bodies and express their personalities in ways that supersede appearance. Meiko's shit-talking spirit, her pleasure in besting their opponents, and her bond with Penny are evident in this sequence. Their exuberance at their vic-

---

8. In the world of *Bitch Planet*, Megaton is a version of the sixteenth-century Italian sport of calcio fiorentino, a sort of combination of football and rugby. In Megaton, there are two teams with any number of players, but their combined weight cannot be more than two thousand pounds. They compete to score using a ball filled with twelve pounds of sand, and any kind of grappling between players is allowed as long as it remains one-on-one.

FIGURE 3.2. Penny and Meiko celebrating, *Bitch Planet* #4. Courtesy of Kelly Sue DeConnick and Valentine De Landro.

tory is also apparent on the next page, which shows several of the women, with Penny and Meiko in the foreground, celebrating in the showers. In an especially joyful moment, Penny wraps her arms around Meiko and lifts her up into the air as she exults, "Who's gon' show them mother fuckers how it's done, huh? Who is?" Meiko yells out in response, "WE IS!!" (see fig. 3.2). As in the shower scenes discussed earlier, the women in these panels are entirely unclothed, yet the way in which they are drawn works against prurience or voyeurism.

Valentine De Landro has said that for this series he needed to consciously reconsider his habitual methods of representing the female form: "I had to step back and think about just drawing the form as the form, and not trying to extend the male gaze. . . . They're naked, yes, but they're still just bodies" (Santori). De Landro's drawings on this page use outlines to indicate the contours of the bodies, with relatively minimal lines to show the curve of a spine, the bend of a leg, breasts, hair, and so on, with a bit of shading for three-dimensionality. This somewhat abstract drawing style contrasts with the cinematographic voyeurism of the women-in-prison films, with their photographic fetishization of skin, hair, breasts, and buttocks. The image of Meiko wrapped in Penny's arms and enveloped by her ample flesh does highlight their differences in size, build, and skin color, but also serves as a vision of complementarity and cooperation, not to mention affection, an alliance between women from contrasting backgrounds who have been perceived and treated very differently by society, but find a connection, common ground, and maybe more in the confines of the prison.[9] We see that they are naked, yes, but what we are shown above all is one woman embracing another in a moment of joy and affection. In these brief moments, competing on the field and celebrating in the showers, Penny and Meiko appear relatively free of the racialized and gendered discursive framings that were responsible in very real ways for their imprisonment.

Their next scrimmage is against the prison guards, which offers players the welcome opportunity to fight the guards without repercussion. Penny's size is again effective in blocking competing players from stopping Meiko from scoring. Unfortunately, she is unable to help when Meiko's taunting scoring celebration—"Ha ha ha muthafucker!"—angers the guard nearest her. He retorts, "Keep laughing, little girl," then grabs a handful of her hair and slams her head to the ground, breaking her neck and killing her. The first volume of the trade paperback of *Bitch Planet*, issue #5 in the single issues, ends with the prisoners on the field gathered around Meiko's body, in shock at her sudden and violent murder. However, Meiko's death is not the end of the story. Her father, who in the intervening years has become one of the Protectorate's most well-known architects, is asked to build a sports stadium on Bitch Planet. He accepts because he is promised the opportunity to see his daughter again. The authorities choose not to inform him of his daughter's death so that he will travel to the planet and oversee the construction. After he arrives, when he asks to see her, they try to cover over her death by creating a fake hologram of her, saying that she cannot meet him in person.

Once again, Meiko appears as the image that others have of her. The projection that the authorities present to Mack, of a demure, respectful young woman dressed in a kimono with an obi imprinted with the prison's "NC" logo, hair styled in a perfect updo and with an ingratiating smile, couldn't be further from the daughter Mack knew and loved, as the puzzled expression on the close-up of his face suggests. Her promise to come home "better than I was" further arouses his suspicions. As a test, he asks her to play an extremely difficult piece on the violin. Once again, Meiko is placed against a backdrop of musical notation, this time as she performs for her father, the very picture of a dutiful daughter and a talented musician conforming to expectations of middle-class Asian femininity. When she plays the piece successfully, Mack knows that his daughter is gone, as the real Meiko was

---

9. I thank Qiana Whitted for inviting me to reflect upon *Bitch Planet* in the virtual roundtable on the series hosted by Osvaldo Oyola on his *The Middle Spaces* blog, and for pointing out the possibility of a more intimate relationship between Meiko Maki and Penny Rolle in the series.

never very talented at the violin since the music lessons were only a cover for instruction in physics and math. In life, Meiko never did fit the image she presented to the world, so the seamless congruence between the image and her actions is a dead giveaway.

When Mack realizes Meiko is no longer alive, he takes over the prison and releases all the prisoners. He shares with them over the loudspeaker that he is Meiko's father, but that she is gone now. He tells them, "I have taken the automation center in her honor. All operations are under manual control. Under my control. I don't . . . I don't know what comes next. It's almost funny. Meiko . . . Meiko would have had a plan. She had a way . . . Me? No, I'm not sure . . . But for now, the locks on your cells are disabled." His actions are what lead to the conclusion (thus far) of *Bitch Planet.* Like Meiko, Mack uses his appearance to his advantage. No one could have anticipated that the celebrated architect and model (minority) citizen would commit such an act, but Mack, in honor of the memory of Meiko, offers one last lesson on the perils of not seeing beyond the stereotype.

Works Cited

Bhabha, Homi. "The Other Question: Stereotype, Discrimination, and the Discourse of Colonialism." *The Location of Culture,* Routledge, 1994, pp. 66–84.

Cheng, Anne Anlin. *Ornamentalism.* Oxford University Press, 2019.

Chiu, Monica. "Introduction: Visual Realities of Race." *Drawing New Color Lines: Transnational Asian American Graphic Narratives,* edited by Monica Chiu, Hong Kong University Press, 2015, pp. 1–26.

Fleetwood, Nicole. *Troubling Vision: Performance, Visuality, Blackness.* University of Chicago Press, 2011.

Groensteen, Thierry. *The System of Comics.* Translated by Bart Beaty and Nick Nguyen, University of Mississippi Press, 2007.

Hero Complex. "Kelly Sue DeConnick Tackles Exploitation Tropes in 'Bitch Planet." *Los Angeles Times,* 24 January 2014, https://web.archive.org/web/20180705180335/ http://herocomplex.latimes.com/comics/kelly-sue-deconnick-charts-a-course-to-bitch-planet/#/0.

Kim, Minjeong. "'You Don't Look Full . . . Asia': The Invisible and Ambiguous Bodies of Chang and Soso." *Feminist Perspectives on* Orange Is the New Black*: Thirteen Critical Essays,* edited by April Kalogeropoulos Householder and Adrienne Trier-Bieniek, McFarland, 2016, pp. 61–76.

Marchetti, Gina. *Romance and the Yellow Peril: Race, Sex, and Discursive Strategies in Hollywood Fiction.* University of California Press, 1994.

Mask, Mia. *Divas on Screen: Black Women in American Film.* University of Illinois Press, 2009.

Mayne, Judith. *Framed: Lesbians, Feminist, and Media Culture.* University of Minnesota Press, 2000.

Postema, Barbara. *Narrative Structure in Comics: Making Sense of Fragments.* RIT Press, 2013.

Santori, Matt. "Game Changers: Valentine De Landro on *Bitch Planet*." *Comicosity,* 28 April 2015, http://www.comicosity.com/game-changers-valentine-de-landro-on-bitch-planet/.

Saraiya, Sonia. "'If You Want to See Angry Feminist I Will Show It to You': *Captain Marvel* Writer Opens Up about the Backlash against Carol Danvers." *Salon,* 18 November 2015, https://www.salon.com/2015/11/18/if_you_want_to_see_angry_feminist_i_will_show_it_to_you_captain_marvel_writer_opens_up_about_the_backlash_against_the_new_carol_danvers/.

Shimizu, Celine Parreñas. *The Hypersexuality of Race: Performing Asian/American Women in Screen and Scene.* Duke University Press, 2007.

Soe, Valerie. *Picturing Oriental Girls: A (Re)Educational Videotape.* Oxygen Productions, 1992.

Walters, Suzanna Danuta. "Caged Heat: The (R)evolution of Women-in-Prison Films." *Reel Knockouts: Violent Women in Film,* edited by Martha McCaughey and Neal King, University of Texas Press, 2001, pp. 106–23.a

Wanzo, Rebecca. *The Content of Our Caricature: African American Comic Art and Political Belonging.* New York University Press, 2020.

Williams, Rachel Marie-Crane. "How Does *Bitch Planet* Deconstruct the Stereotypes of Black Women in Prison?" *Bound By Law: Bitch Planet Comics Studies Roundtable Part Two,* edited by Qiana Whitted, *The Middle Spaces,* 8 March 2018, https://themiddlespaces.com/2018/03/08/bitch-planet-2.

Yoshihara, Mari. *Musicians from a Different Shore: Asians and Asian Americans in Classical Music.* Temple University Press, 2007.

Zalcock, Bev. *Renegade Sisters: Girl Gangs on Film.* New and updated edition, Creation Books, 2001.

CHAPTER 4

Anachronistic Figures and Counternarratives

Comics as a Subversive Form in
American Born Chinese and *Johnny Hiro*

JIN LEE

Both Gene Luen Yang's *American Born Chinese* and Fred Chao's *Johnny Hiro* make use of anachronistic figures who visit their present-day protagonists to highlight the ways the characters explicitly or implicitly suffer racism. In *American Born Chinese*, a character, whose manner and physical appearance resemble those of Chinese coolies in nineteenth-century magazines, returns annually to stay with a high school boy. In *Johnny Hiro*, samurais (medieval and early modern Japanese warriors) and a monster that evokes Godzilla, whose appearance in films dates back to 1950s, attack the main characters. These figures from history who visit contemporary characters represent the continuity of "outdated" stereotypes—"outdated" because they carry more than half-a-century-old racist histories that should not exist in our time. As mentioned in the introduction, the "outdated" stereotypes in *American Born Chinese* have been addressed in terms of the historical racist representations of Asians in popular media (Song, "'How Good'"; Dong). Building on and departing from these enlightening discussions on how Yang repurposes such persistently stereotyped images, this chapter turns its attention to the medium of comics, especially the medium's visual potential as a subversive form. That is, Yang and Chao effectively communicate the anachronistic presence of racist stereotypes through such figures by their choice of the comics medium. In this essay, I argue that Yang and Chao use comics as a subversive form to remind us of the legacies of racialized histories in America. I begin by first discussing an oft-cited postcolonial theory that peculiarly treats time and space as commensurable, and that explains how narrative stereotypes are structured. Then, I analyze how the postcolonial theory explains Yang's and Chao's use of comics space to ultimately present counternarratives against the stereotyped ones.

In *Location of Culture*, Homi Bhabha opposes essentialist cultural or group identities attached to imagined communities in the postcolonial, global cosmopolitan context. He reveals the nuts and bolts of the strategies signifying a people or a nation, and illustrates the fictiveness of the unity or homogeneity of those identities (212–13). The signifying process in narrating a people or a nation entails the temporality of the narrative and implies that identities given to the people or the nation are neither eternal nor natural, but constructed over time. (As Bhabha's discussion is not limited to a specific nation, or the concept of "nation," I will use the term "nation" in a more inclusive sense to address race and ethnicity too.) His emphasis on "a temporality of representation" in the narrative of the nation spatializes the time of writing/narrating the nation (i.e., constructing essentialist identities) as he explains how a temporality of representation "*moves* between cultural formations and social processes" (202; emphasis added).[1] More specifically, in his observation about narrating the nation/the people (or "stereotyping," for the purpose of this chapter), temporality and spatiality become commensurable as he notes, "The difference of space returns as the Sameness of time, turning Territory into Tradition, turning the People into One" (213).[2] That is, in "stereotyping" narratives, spatial differences (territories), although arbitrarily defined by jurisdictions, are tied with and responsible for traditions, which are often considered to be inherently and eternally attached to a cultural or national group but are actually man-made customs and beliefs, subject to change over time. Those affiliated with Territory tend to be perceived as bound to Tradition, thereby being homogenized as if they (the People) were but One individual.

Bhabha's point on the homogenizing process can be visualized in comics due to the medium's unique features. First, as scholars note, temporality is portrayed by means of spatiality in comics in that the medium compart-

---

1. Bhabha discusses "the *spatialization* of historical *time*" in Bakhtin's reading of "Goethe's vision of the microscopic, elementary, perhaps random, tolling of everyday life in Italy" (205; emphasis added).

2. While the Western nation is Bhabha's focus, his explanation on the Harlem Renaissance and "an Afro-American nation" suggests that his theory can be applicable to other nations too. See Bhabha 207–8.

mentalizes pages into differentials in space to communicate the passage of time.[3] As comics spatialize temporality, comics artists can take advantage of the medium's capability to portray different temporalities, spatialities, and/or people as one. For instance, Hilary Chute celebrates Art Spiegelman's groundbreaking use of the medium to represent the continuing presence of the Holocaust, as in the often-discussed panel in *Maus* that co-presents mouse corpses (Holocaust victims) from Nazi Germany with the artist himself in his 1980s SoHo studio as if they were contemporaneous ("The Shadow" 213). In another instance, LeiLani Nishime explains how the co-presence of noncontemporaneous, "anachronistic" characters in Asian American graphic narratives, including *Johnny Hiro*, can trouble "the stereotype of a multiracial bridging figure" (196, 198). Such use of comics form, according to Nishime, challenges "a teleological narrative of racial progress toward assimilation or a post-racial future" wherein mixed-race characters exist only to bridge between cultures (198). In this context, to discuss transnational figures in graphic narratives that overlay multiple temporalities/spatialities/people to present a counternarrative of the national narrative, Bhabha's explanation of the signification of "the nation" and "the people" can be helpful. Reading Bhabha and those graphic narratives together suggests that the comics medium can provide an effective form that is postcolonial, liberating, and subversive.

In Asian American history, essentialist ideas of culture and identity are often given to people according to their race, as well as their nationality, although people of Asian descent are not, as the term "Asian American" seems to suggest, a homogenous group. Some of them do not see themselves as American at all, or they believe they belong to multiple nations (Duncan 5). However, Asian Americans have often been viewed as homogenous, and as a result, they are discriminated against, which is emblematized in Asian American stereotypes. Against this Asian American history, Gene Luen Yang's *American Born Chinese* and Fred Chao's *Johnny Hiro* take advantage of the comics form to effectively visualize such homogenized identities, as reflected in stereotypes, and to produce their counternarratives.[4] As Bhabha

---

3. As Hilary Chute notes, "'Time as space' is a description we hear again and again from theorists of comics" ("The Shadow" 202). Just to name a few: Most notably, Scott McCloud points out, "In learning to read comics we all learned to perceive time *spatially*, for in the world of comics, *time and space are one and the same*" (100); see Charles Hatfield for his discussion on "synchronism" (52–58); see Lawrence L. Abbott for "the power of the panel text to establish a time duration" (162–65). Based on this unique feature of comics, Thierry Groensteen explores "the rhythms of comics" (133–57).

4. According to Nicholas Mirzoeff "visuality" is the nineteenth-century historian Thomas Carlyle's term, for "the visualization of history" that "sustain[s]" and legitimizes autocratic authority, by making it seem "self-evident" (2–3). Visualizing enables

might put it, the aforementioned anachronistic figures "evoke and erase [the] totalizing boundaries" of the nation and "disturb" essentialist identities (213).[5] Despite Sau-ling C. Wong's skepticism on taking a postcolonial approach to read Asian America, Asian American studies has been open to such an approach, especially to describe diasporic Asian experiences.[6] For instance, Lingyan Yang points out the close connection between Asian America and postcoloniality: "The racial marginalization of people of color within the American political and legal systems as well as the economic exploitation of multiracial and multiethnic migrant and immigrant cheap labor within the American political economy lies on a continuum created by the centuries-long Western colonial racial and economic subjection of subalterns 'in Other Worlds'" (144).[7] Bhabha's postcolonial theory can be illuminating to understand the graphic narratives' transnational figures affected by both Western and Eastern colonialisms. Chin-Kee in *American Born Chinese* evokes Chinese coolies from the nineteenth century whose migration was propelled by Western imperialist expansion and whose labor was exploited by American capitalism.[8] Gozadilla in *Johnny Hiro* recalls Godzilla that arose from the

---

authority to perceive "the processes of 'history'" (3), while excluding those visualized by various means, including separation and segregation. For instance, in the colonial slave plantations, slaves were defined as "a species," and "the spatializing of mapping . . . separated and defined slave space and 'free space'" (10). Keeping in mind that Mirzoeff is critical of Carlyle for his antidemocratic vision in visuality, which can be used authoritatively to control the circulation of information, and suggests countervisuality to confront visuality's exclusive access to histories, I use the word "visualize" to specifically explain the comics medium's potential as a subversive form for countervisuality.

5. For Bhabha, "counter-narratives of the nation that continually evoke and erase its totalizing boundaries . . . disturb those ideological manoeuvres through which 'imagined communities' are given essentialist identities" (213).

6. See Sau-ling C. Wong, "Denationalization Reconsidered: Asian American Cultural Criticism as a Theoretical Crossroads," *Amerasia*, vol. 21, no. 1–2, 1995, pp. 1–27; Nerissa B. Balce's "Laughter against the State: On Humor, Postcolonial Satire, and Asian American Short Fiction," *Journal of Asian American Studies*, vol. 19, no. 1, Feb. 2016, pp. 47–73; Kavita Daiya's "Provincializing America: Engaging Postcolonial Critique and Asian American Studies in a Transnational Mode," *South Asian Review*, vol. 26, no. 2, 2005, pp. 265–75; and L. Yang; among others.

7. Yang refers to the title of Gayatri Chakravorty Spivak's book, *In Other Worlds: Essays in Cultural Politics* (Routledge, 1988).

8. Sucheng Chan notes, "Asian international migrations of this period [between the end of the Opium War in 1842 and the beginning of World War II] were an integral part of Western economic development and imperialist expansion. Chinese emigrants left to escape poverty in China, which resulted from insufficient land and overpopulation but was exacerbated by the political, economic, and social disruptions caused by Western activities" (16). *This Bittersweet Soil: The Chinese in California Agriculture, 1860–1910*, University of California Press, 1986.

atomic bombings of Japan, preceded by the Japanese colonial aggression on Pearl Harbor. Before I move on to my main argument, I will first briefly introduce the two graphic narratives.

American Born Chinese and *Johnny Hiro*

American Born Chinese alternates between the stories of three main characters: a Chinese mythical character, Monkey King, who struggles with his identity as a monkey and finally overcomes his identity crisis by accepting it; American born Chinese Jin Wang, who experiences racism at school and transforms into a boy with blond hair and blue eyes; and a white American boy named Danny who suffers from racism caused by his Chinese cousin Chin-Kee's annual visit to him. The stories culminate in the last chapter, which reveals the relationships among these characters. Chin-Kee turns out to be the legendary Monkey King, and Danny, who is actually Jin, transforms back to his Chinese American body.

In *Johnny Hiro*, a monster named Gozadilla (a derivative of Godzilla) comes from Tokyo to kidnap Mayumi, the eponymous protagonist's girlfriend, from their apartment in New York. Gozadilla is after Mayumi for a long-awaited revenge on her mother, who defeated him a few decades ago. However, he suddenly falls asleep due to jet lag and consequently is taken away by New York City mayor Michael Bloomberg's team. After cleaning up the monster's mess, Bloomberg asks Hiro and Mayumi to not tell anyone about the monster because he wants to keep the city's property values high and, ultimately, to win the upcoming election. Bloomberg's request causes the couple's landlord to sue them for the monster's damage, and Bloomberg comes to court to help the couple. Along with the Gozadilla attack, the zany episode of the samurai attack interrupts the otherwise realist depiction of the couple's life in the city, where Hiro works as a busboy and Mayumi an editor.

Anachronistic Figures

Graphically positioned in grids and panels of graphic narratives, Asian/ American figures can be literally and figure-atively located in "the interstitial, disjunctive spaces and signs" that Bhabha views as "crucial for the emergence of the new historical subjects of the transnational phase of late capitalism" (311). Drawing on Fredric Jameson's reading of a poem, "China,"

Bhabha's new historical subjects are postcolonial: an emergent "collectivity . . . after the long subjection of feudalism and imperialism" (Jameson 29; qtd. in Bhabha 308). In the context of globalization, these new historical subjects include "minorities and migrants within the West" (306). For Bhabha, the new historical subjects comprise at least "two temporally succeeding selves," the image of which Charles Taylor considers as "overdramatized" or "quite false" for "the structural features of a self" (qtd. in Bhabha 305; Taylor 51).[9] Bhabha views Taylor's point as "set[ting] temporal limits to the problem of personhood" and argues that "such 'overdramatized' images are precisely [his] concern" in consideration of the "double lives" of migrants and diasporas in the postcolonial world (305–6). Importantly, "it is only through a structure of splitting and displacement—'the fragmented and schizophrenic decentring of the self'—that the architecture of the new historical subject emerges at the limits of representation itself" (310). Here, the architecture of the new historical subject emerging through a structure of splitting and displacement can explain the anachronistic figures in *American Born Chinese* and *Johnny Hiro*, as their "fragmented and schizophrenic" selves in comics' interstitial, disjunctive spaces reveal the makeup of their subjectivity. In *American Born Chinese*, Chin-Kee turns out to be the Monkey King while Danny is revealed to be Jin. Further, Chin-Kee/the Monkey King visits Danny/Jin to "serve as [his] conscience—as a sign post to [his] soul" (221). Thus, Chin-Kee/the Monkey King and Danny/Jin can be considered a person's fragmented and schizophrenic selves, vacillating between how he is perceived, how he wants to be socially accepted, and (if problematically) who he really is. In *Johnny Hiro*, the ex-employees in samurai armor, whose Japanese company recently went bankrupt, chase after Hiro and his friend Toshi. If the samurais/ ex-employees, as I argue later, can be viewed as an old stereotype that follows people of Japanese descent, including Hiro, the samurai characters can be understood as Hiro's fragmented and schizophrenic selves *in* the narrative of the nation, which views the samurainess/ the stereotype as consisting in Hiro's self. And these fragmented and schizophrenic selves "evoke and erase the totalizing boundaries of the nation" (Bhabha 213), pointing to "the nation split within itself, articulating the heterogeneity of its population" (Bhabha 212). The visual representations of Danny and Hiro are white, if not ambiguous in Hiro's case, and their association with the old Asian stereotypes suggests the nation (white America)

---

9. In his book *Sources of the Self*, Charles Taylor claims that unlike other cultures "in our world, the supposition that I could be two temporally succeeding selves is either an overdramatized image, or quite false. It runs against the structural features of a self as a being who exists in a space of concerns" (51).

split within itself and the heterogeneity of its population.[10] Thus, Yang's and Chao's anachronistic figures "disturb those ideological manoeuvres through which 'imagined communities' are given essentialist identities" and present "counter-narratives of the nation" (Bhabha 213).

American Born Chinese and the Return of the Repressed

Chin-Kee and Jin/Danny in *American Born Chinese* reveal such "two temporally succeeding selves." If Bhabha's new historical subjects comprising "two temporally succeeding selves" ultimately point to the fictiveness of the homogeneity of the colonizer (i.e., "the heterogeneity of its population"), Yang's anachronistic figures consist of "two temporally succeeding selves" that correspond to and eventually counter stereotypes.[11] First, Chin-Kee embodies the two stereotypes: the nineteenth-century Chinese coolie (for his manner and physical appearance) and the twenty-first-century model minority (for his perfect answers to all his teachers' questions).[12] Second, Danny is gradually associated with Chin-Kee (and stereotyped), and finally returns to his old self, Jin. Highlighting the anachronistic homogenizing force of those stereotypes, the makeup or "architecture" of Chin-Kee's and Jin/Danny's selves shows Bhabha's formula for signifying the nation/people. In the stereotypes, "the difference of space returns as the Sameness of time": Jin/Danny is American born Chinese living in contemporary California but is treated as a "Chinese," the concept of which includes the

---

10. Nishime notes, "There seems to be no overt making of racial difference between characters whose race we know textually. Hiro, the 'half-Asian' hero of the title, Mayumi, his Japanese girlfriend, and even David Byrne, the white pop singer, are not visually differentiated by race" (202).

11. I call both Chin-Kee and Jin/Danny anachronistic figures because the anachronistic figure, Chin-Kee, becomes part of Jin/Danny's identity in that Jin/Danny is remembered as "Chin-Kee's cousin." I also do so because Chin-Kee is part of Jin/Danny's selves, as the former tells the latter, "I came to serve as your conscience" (221).

12. Scholars point out the model minority myth that Chin-Kee embodies. See, among others, Davis; Song, "Comics" and "'How Good.'" Robert G. Lee notes, "The Yellowface coolie and model minority, despite their apparent contradiction, not only coexist but, in fact, can become mutually reinforcing at critical junctures because neither is created by the actual lives of Asians in America" (12). For recent scholarly discussions on the model minority myth, see Eleanor Ty's *Asianfail: Narratives of Disenchantment and the Model Minority* (University of Illinois Press, 2017) and Yoonmee Chang's "Asian Americans, Disability, and the Model Minority Myth" in *Flashpoints for Asian American Studies,* edited by Cathy J. Schlund-Vials (Fordham University, 2018) among others.

nineteenth-century imaginations of Chinese people. Regardless of where Jin/Danny comes from (California), he is perceived as the same as those from China.[13] Thus, stereotypes turn territory into tradition: China's (Territory's) history includes many dynasties and their different borders, but anyone of Chinese descent is essentially and inherently perceived to have "Chinese-ness" (Tradition) despite the arbitrariness of such association. As a result, despite their individuality, a person of Chinese ancestry (the People, including American born Chinese Jin/Danny) turns into stereotypes (One, as represented in Chin-Kee). At his elementary school, Jin encounters a racist comment that presupposes that all Asians (Territory) eat dogs (Tradition), and therefore being Chinese American (the People), he eats them (One) too (33). By showing how stereotypes operate, Yang shows the absurdity of this homogenization of Territory and the People. His work stages and performs the problematic continuity (the Sameness of time) of the racist stereotypes of the Chinese in the contemporary American society.

Thus, Yang presents a counternarrative of the nation by employing the nineteenth-century racist stereotypical figure. Chin-Kee "is the grotesque stereotype of the Chinese as racially alien that first appeared in the nineteenth century, as Western imperial countries chipped away at China's sovereignty and as Chinese workers began to populate California and the rest of the American West in visibly large numbers" (Song, "Comics" 137). Yang relocates to the contemporary American high school, a denigrated depiction of a Chinese character, Chin-Kee (the phonetic equivalent to the racist slur "chink"). Chin-Kee highlights the signifying process in the racist stereotypes of Asian Americans. As Bhabha might put, the difference of the over-a-century-old space, which the archetypes of Fu Manchu and Charlie Chan are supposed to securely inhabit, "*returns* as the sameness of time, turning Territory into Tradition, turning the People into One" (Bhabha 213; emphasis added). In Chin-Kee, the differences in time, space, and individualities between the old racist stereotypes and real Chinese/Americans are homogenized. Yet, this synchronicity of Chin-Kee's presence in a twenty-first-century American high school troubles itself due to its blatant absurdity, a "caffeine comic" moment, in Spiegelman's terms, that awakens us to the racist reality (qtd. in Chute, "The Shadow" 202). This seeming anachronism (what Chin-Kee stands for is supposed to be too old to be synchronous) is a double-edged sword. It reveals the signification process of depicting Asian Americans as if a different species, as well as racist sensibilities disturbingly

---

13. Similarly, Jin's friends, Wei-Chen and Suzy Nakamura, also suffer from racism when their classmates indirectly call them "chink" and "nippy" for being Taiwanese and Japanese (96).

still lingering in the present.[14] Thus, Yang counters the narrative by showing how its racist sensibilities are ideologically structured.

Chin-Kee's anachronistic presence in a contemporary American high school, or "Territory-turned-into-Tradition" and "the-People-turned-into-One" in Chin-Kee, suggests that we may not have a nineteenth-century Chinese coolie in this present time and space, but some of us might have experienced racism as if being that Chinaman. After learning that Danny is Chin-Kee's cousin, Melanie (Danny's love interest and classmate) suddenly notices Danny's buck teeth (which are not recognizable to readers) and recommends an orthodontist. Readers may remember how this incident peculiarly echoes an earlier one where Jin as a transfer student at May-flower Elementary School was called "Bucktooth" (33). Later, readers learn that Danny is Jin (American born Chinese) who magically transformed into a high school boy with blond hair and blue eyes. This episode—how Chin-Kee's visit affects the way Danny is perceived by his peers—illustrates how some Asian Americans may be assimilated enough that they are considered, viewed, and treated as (almost) white, whereas some others may fail in perfect assimilation: After Chin-Kee's visit, he is not Danny ("honorary white," if you will) anymore but Chin-Kee's cousin.

If reality is, as Slavoj Žižek argues, "a fantasy-construction which enables us to mask the Real of our desire" (323), Yang exposes that fantasy construction and the Real of "our" desire by means of the anachronistic character Chin-Kee. Conglomerating historical stereotypes of Asians, Chin-Kee's larger-than-life images and behaviors reveal the fantasy construction that people of Asian descent are more or less like Chin-Kee. And this fantasy construction enables "us" to mask the Real of "our" desire that wants to exclude Asians from "us," as Žižek might put it, serving as a support for the social reality—the discriminations or microaggressions against Asians and Asian Americans.[15] While Chin-Kee's grotesqueness and mischief may justify his schoolmates' avoidance of him, such ostracism (or "unpopularity" ["'How Good'" 78], as Min Hyoung Song calls it) recalls the systemic exclusion of Asians in US history through the exclusionary immigration laws and the denigrated depictions of Asians in popular culture. Importantly, the hatred and anxiety toward Chin-Kee at school are automatically transferred to Danny, as the latter, although seemingly white, turns out to be Chin-Kee's

---

14. See Robert Lee for his discussion on how Asian Americans "have been made into a race of aliens" (xi). This process seems to echo a strategy, as Mirzoeff identifies, that visualizers take to legitimize their authority.

15. Žižek argues that ideology is "a fantasy-construction which serves as a support for our 'reality' itself" (323).

cousin. By portraying Danny as white and revealing later that he is Chinese American, Yang refers to the Asian American history, where race has been more perception than physiognomy or even "blood."[16] Narrating Danny's true identity as Chinese American, Yang seems to question readers: If it does not seem fair for Danny to deal with his peers' hatred and anxiety because of Chin-Kee, is it fair for people of Asian descent, including Jin? In this way, Yang exposes and challenges the uncomfortable orientalist/racist ideology, the fantasy construction. Žižek points out that "the function of ideology [i.e., a fantasy construction in its basic dimension] is not to offer us a point of escape from our reality but to offer us the social reality itself as an escape from some traumatic, real kernel" (323). In *American Born Chinese,* Chin-Kee shows not only "the quiet, 'socially acceptable' faces of racism" but also "the hidden truth—the figure that's too embarrassing and too upsetting for most folks to want to look at directly or talk about" (qtd. in Dong 241). Although "too embarrassing and too upsetting," Chin-Kee provides "us" with "an escape from some traumatic, real kernel," an excuse/alibi for the racialized histories in the US, as well as offering "us" that social reality itself. By situating a character whose features largely embody the old racist stereotypes in the present time and space, Yang troubles the stereotypes. Chin-Kee's presence not only points out the anachronistic continuation of racism but also evokes that history of segregation and separation—while it may be uncomfortable (as Danny's schoolmates feel) to see Chin-Kee in the American high school, Asian students were historically segregated from attending schools in the late nineteenth and early twentieth centuries.

Chin-Kee's anachronistic presence may remind readers of the iconic panels in *Maus,* where Spiegelman jam-packs multiple temporalities. However, the multiple temporalities/spatialities/people in Chin-Kee push Spiegelman's economic use of comics space further. If in *Maus,* the aforementioned victims' corpses function like the background or foreground of Spiegelman's iconic scene, the image of the nineteenth-century Asian American stereotypes becomes a person (Chin-Kee) and returns to a contemporary Chinese American boy (Danny) as his cousin. Not only does Chin-Kee reflect the Chinese coolie in the nineteenth-century popular magazines, he also embodies

---

16. Robert Lee points out race as "a product of popular ideology": "In *Ozawa v. United States,* the court had ruled that no matter what the actual color of his skin, nor how much he could prove himself culturally assimilated, [Takao] Ozawa's Japanese 'blood' made him 'unamalgamable' by marriage into the American national family. In *United States v. Thind,* despite the ethnological evidence presented by [Bhagat Singh] Thind that he, a high-caste Hindu, was a descendent of Aryans and hence white by 'blood,' the court ruled that he was not, holding that race was not a scientific category but a social one, and upheld the revocation of Thind's citizenship" (3–4).

the contemporary model minority myth, an updated stereotype. In addition, Chin-Kee is a more dynamic character than *Maus*'s corpses—literally, the former is alive, but the latter are dead. Whereas "concentration-camp corpses wordlessly invade a present-day SoHo studio" in *Maus* (Chute, "Comics" 459), the victims of Chinese descent from the nineteenth century and onward seem to arise from the dead to visit the Chinese American boy. If *Maus* is about, as Chute puts it, "inheriting the past" ("The Shadow" 206), *American Born Chinese* is about interacting with and counteracting the past, which the narrative of the nation presents as an essential identity of people of Chinese descent. Indeed, Yang explains how he reworks and counternarrates the past through the scene where Danny (who is also Jin) fistfights Chin-Kee for all the troubles the latter made: "For me, Chin-Kee was an exorcism of sorts. He was my chance to gather many of the little pains, annoyances, and embarrassments I experienced as a child; put them into a single character; and behead him" (qtd. in Dong 241). In this vein, Yang's use of comics space is more liberating and subversive, as well as more dynamic.

Furthermore, Chin-Kee is more than "Territory-turned-into-Tradition" and "the-People-turned-into-One" in that as the narrative unfolds, he turns out to be a complex character, embodying Asian stereotypes since the nineteenth century, from a Chinese coolie and Fu Manchu to model minority and William Hung.[17] Thus, while he may be "Territory-turned-into-Tradition" and "the-People-turned-into-One" in each frame, his character as a whole ends up exceeding Bhabha's formula, being both Territory and Tradition, the People and One. Indeed, the full-fledged character, Chin-Kee-who-is-also-the Monkey-King, takes advantage of an essentialist identity, which Bhabha's theory works against. Near the end, Chin-Kee/the Monkey King does so to help Jin overcome self- and racial hatreds and reconcile himself with Wei-Chen, who used to be his only friend at school from Taiwan. When Jin meets Wei-Chen a long time after their falling out, Wei-Chen does not soften up a bit toward Jin until Jin tells him, "I met your father [the Monkey King]" (89). Then, Jin momentarily sees Wei-Chen's true self as a monkey. While it "points directly to the need to confront a painful visual history of racial disparagement" (Song, "'How Good,'" 90), Jin's perception of Wei-Chen as a monkey and reconciliation with him after accepting the lesson of the Monkey King ("how good it is to be a monkey" [223]) can suggest Yang's strategic use of an essentialist identity. It is an instance of turning the People (Chinese and Taiwanese) into One (the simian), a homogenizing process. However problematic it is, the simian here is used as a catalyst for

---

17. See Song, "'How Good'" 82.

Jin and Wei-Chen to bond over, in contrast to how they become estranged earlier in the narrative: Wei-Chen breaks with Jin after the latter disagrees on their relation, saying "We're nothing alike," and calls him an F.O.B. (190–91).

Of course, Yang's turning around an essentialist identity to counter another does not come without a cost. In particular, the fact that Chin-Kee is revealed to be the Monkey King, whose advice for Jin is to be comfortable in his own skin ("how good it is to be a monkey" [223]), troubles scholars like Song in consideration of the history of racial representation. As Song astutely points out, "the image of the monkey has historically been deployed as a racial diminutive, a way to picture Asians as subhuman or beyond" ("'How Good'" 85). Song further makes an important, valid point on the Monkey King's lesson that Yang seems to present "finding social acceptance" as "a lack of conscience" (Song, "'How Good'" 83). But, what needs also to be considered is Jin's *way* of "finding social acceptance." Jin does so at the cost of self- and racial hatreds: To become Danny (i.e., to be "socially accepted" [Song, "'How Good'" 83]), he breaks with Wei-Chen, with whom he is made fun of—"Hey, I *chink* it's getting a little nippy out here" (96; emphasis added)—as well as erases "racial characteristics" from his body.[18] In contrast, after Jin accepts who he is, as the Monkey King advises, Jin reconciles himself with Wei-Chen, which suggests Jin's overcoming of self- and racial hatreds. Being a social construct, race provides, even if problematic, vocabulary useful in articulating and countering racist Asian stereotypes. In *American Born Chinese*, Yang uses comics space to criticize the homogenizing processes that construct essentialist identities, by turning Territory into Tradition, the People into One. At the same time, he strategically uses an essentialist identity, although problematically embodied as the simian, for racial solidarity.

Johnny Hiro and Samurais

Fred Chao's *Johnny Hiro: Half Asian, All Hero* has been nominated for four Eisner Awards and has been included in *The Best American Comics 2010*. Despite the remarkable recognition, *Johnny Hiro* has not received much scholarly attention apart from Shan Mu Zhao's and Nishime's illuminating works. The seemingly nonsensical or fantastic elements in Chao's book tend to divert readers' attention from his political commentary to his humor.

---

18. I put the phrase "racial characteristics" in quotation marks to recognize that race is a social construct.

FIGURE 4.1. Samurai attack in *Johnny Hiro*. © and used with permission from Fred Chao.

However, the nonsensical and fantastical are deeply intertwined with Asian American history, as in *American Born Chinese*. For instance, Chao depicts Japanese and Japanese American characters, as well as a Godzilla, a King Kong, and samurai warriors in magical realist scenes to portray the "fantasy-construction" (Žižek 323) of the contemporary racial experiences. That is, the fantastical moments reveal what people of Asian descent might encounter in twenty-first-century New York City. On the one hand, such moments can come across as "nonsensical," which I explore elsewhere in terms of the ways in which Chao's book prompts readers to recognize historical traumas (see J. Lee). On the other hand, they effectively portray "the fantasy-construction" (Žižek 323): The nonsensical or fantastic scenes capture the signification process of "Territory-turned-into-Tradition" and "the People-turned-into-One," in Bhabha's terms. Thus, Chao lays bare "the fantasy-construction," the inner working of the outdated but continuing presence of Asian stereotypes in contemporary society. If Lynda Barry compresses time and space to "stage dialogues among versions of self" (Chute, *Graphic Women* 5), so too does Chao stage dialogues among versions of marginalized subjects. They turn out to be transpacific figures (a Godzilla and samurais come to New York City from Japan) or transracial (Chao's Godzilla recalls King Kong, whose fate is often viewed as an analogy for that of blacks caused by the transatlantic slave trades). In this vein, *Johnny Hiro* can be a critical text for the "black Pacific" where the transpacific finds itself entangled with the transatlantic.[19]

While Yang repurposes the racist stereotypical figure from nineteenth-century magazines, Chao employs the anachronistic figure—samurais from the medieval and early-modern Japan—to portray twenty-first-century Asian/American experiences. While attending an opera at the Metropolitan Opera House, the half-Japanese half-white protagonist Hiro unexpectedly encounters his Japanese friend Toshi. The two are suddenly visited by a group of samurais who magically appear from the top of the bathroom stalls (see fig. 4.1). These samurais turn out to be the employees of a Japanese company, TokyoFind.co.jp, which recently went bankrupt, fatally affected by the great success of Toshi's internet search engine company. Omigoshi. com was so successful that it closed down "almost all of Japan's competitor sites" (89). Following the Japanese tradition, the ex-employees of Tokyo-Find.co.jp came to the US to take revenge on Toshi (89). Toshi happens to be on a business trip from Japan, and Hiro has just met him by chance in the Opera House. This episode's ending is quite telling: While Toshi is running away from the vengeful samurais, he accidentally enters and destroys the stage with the samurais and ruins the opera, whose performance "could . . . have opened opportunities for Asians in mainstream theatre" (108) who have been "completely overlooked in popular American theatre" (90). Chao's overlaying samurais, Japanese (Toshi) and Japanese American (Hiro) characters, and the failure of the Asian opera does not seem merely playful or humorous. Like Chin-Kee, the Japanese-employees-as-samurais reveal Bhabha's homogenizing process: The contemporary "loyal" ex-employees from Japan (difference of space) return as samurais from centuries-old Japan (the Sameness of time, as they are depicted in the same space with contem-

---

19. The term "black Pacific" has various meanings among scholars, but two meanings relevant to my discussion are as follows. Vince Schleitwiler uses King Kong to explain the "black Pacific" in his book, *Strange Fruit of the Black Pacific*. For him, the "black Pacific is "a *historical nonentity*, for it never actually existed except as speculative fantasy, yet its material consequences persist—a paradoxical condition, to be sure, but one that should hardly be unfamiliar to scholars of race. The black pacific . . . is the indispensable blank or blind spot on the map; the empirically observable terrain, within which it makes its absence felt, is a *transpacific* field, charted by imperial competition and by the black and Asian movements and migrations shadowing the imperial powers" (2). For Heather Smyth, the term "indicate[s] black diasporic culture that is shaped by a Pacific location such that it looks not just East in the imagination to Africa—across the Atlantic and the Middle Passage—but also West to Asia and the Pacific rim, and is shaped by the geography of the Pacific as well as the confluence, friction, and sometimes coalition of African, Asian, South Asian, First Nations, and European cultures in British Columbia" (390).

porary characters), turning people from Japan (Territory/the People) into "Samurainess" (Tradition/One). This episode seems to be an analogy of an old stereotype that follows people of Japanese descent: Toshi's global business success brings him to New York City, but samurais from Japan (a synecdoche of Japanese stereotypes, if you will) follow him wherever he goes. Of course, samurai is not *the* Japanese stereotype, but a letter to the *Guardian* suggests the Japanese are still associated with samurai. Yoko Yamashita asserts, "Western people's favorite stereotypes about Japan," such as "samurai, seppuku, and harakiri," were mentioned in the *Guardian* in 2018 to attribute Japan's current high suicide rates to the samurai spirit instead of other sociocultural factors.[20]

Similarly and significantly, the failure of the Asian opera in *Johnny Hiro* suggests how an Asian opera can be overshadowed by an Asian stereotype or an imagined homogeneity in Chinese opera. The episode is loosely based on a true story of the first China-made opera at the Met, which was "panned in the critics' eye" (Chao, personal interview, 22 and 23 June 2021). In response to the comparisons to Puccini in "almost every review," the composer and conductor of the opera, Tan Dun, retorted, "Because Puccini used Chinese melody, no Chinese composer can use Chinese melody without being compared to Puccini!" (Melvin). Chao said, "I just read the article [on the opera failing] and used it as inspiration. . . . But that [the opera failing] has nothing really to do with [*Johnny Hiro*] . . . [as] the Chinese opera failed for a completely different reason" (personal interview). Yet, the substitution of the samurai attack for the critical reviews in *Johnny Hiro* suggests a peculiar parallel between the two as the cause of the Chinese opera failing: While Puccini's "Chinese-inspired 'Turandot'" as a "standard of the Western opera repertoire" (Melvin) can still haunt a China-made opera almost a century later, the samurai stereotype can follow people of Japanese descent.

Further, the samurai attack in *Johnny Hiro* curiously echoes, if loosely, how Asian Americans could be followed by "outdated" stereotypes and become "the People-turned-into-One." In 1996, Gunner Lindberg and Dominic Christopher murdered Thien Minh Ly in Tustin, an hour away from San Diego. Thien was rollerblading in his hometown, and they killed him for being "a jap" although he was not "a jap" but "a twenty-four-year-old Vietnamese American who . . . had just returned home after finishing a master's degree in biophysics and physiology at Georgetown" (Robert Lee x). The word "jap" could have a longer history, but it became derogatory particu-

---

20. Yoko Yamashita, "Too Much Emphasis on the Samurai Spirit," *The Guardian*, 5 June 2018, https://www.theguardian.com/world/2018/jun/05/too-much-emphasis-on-the-samurai-spirit. Accessed 27 January 2020.

larly during World War II. Considering the hatred against "a jap"—"Thien ... had been stabbed more than forty times" (Robert Lee x)—this stereotype of "a jap" in the murderers' minds dates back to the 1940s, when Japanese and Japanese Americans were interned after the bombing of Pearl Harbor. Even after decades, the word and the hostility attached to the word persistently (and fatally) followed an Asian American. The fact that Thien was not "a jap" is also illuminating: Toshi is Japanese, but Hiro is half-Japanese and half-white. However coincidental it may seem, the samurais now chase after Hiro, too, with their homogenizing force. Chao does not make a close connection between Hiro's current job and racism: Hiro is a college dropout, and it is unclear whether or not he would get a better job than a busboy in a sushi restaurant. However, in a world where samurais from medieval and early-modern Japan can follow him, and a customer can falsely accuse Mayumi of cheating, for which her colleague blames her English, the racism—of the "bamboo ceiling" people of Asian descent experience, comparable to the "glass ceiling"—might have played a role in preventing Hiro from getting a better job.[21]

The samurai episode has further resonance in Asian American history. Reflecting the federal government's instruction to portray national unity during the war, the World War II combat film *Bataan* (1943) "depicts Japan as an enemy that is even more racist to black Americans than white Americans, transferring the mark of racism from white to Asian" (Locke 155).[22] For such purposes, *Bataan* uses the samurai sword to draw a new color line between Japan and the US, thereby evoking the boundaries of the latter: The first African American equal to white characters in American film history is killed by a Japanese solider with a samurai sword, which functions to

21. The term "bamboo ceiling" was coined by Jane Hyun, who wrote *Breaking the Bamboo Ceiling* (Harper Collins, 2005), to explain why Asian Americans are "often significantly under-represented in the executive suite" despite the model minority myth, as well as their number in the workforce and achievements (Chen). Liza Mundy notes, "According to a 2011 study by the Center for Talent Innovation, Asian Americans are far more likely to have a college degree than the average person, and while they make up just 5 percent of the population, they constitute 18 percent of the student body at Harvard and 24 percent at Stanford. They have little trouble getting hired, but the picture changes as they move toward senior management; despite their numbers and achievement level, Asian Americans account for just 1.4 percent of *Fortune* 500 CEOs and 1.9 percent of corporate officers overall."

22. White mistreatment of blacks led some African Americans to "side with the Japanese enemy on the common ground of nonwhite status" during World War II (Locke 20). To such disunity, "the federal government began to enforce systematically the theme of national unity within the film industry in June 1942" (Locke 20).

"displac[e] antiblack racism from whites onto the Japanese" (Locke 29).[23] As Brian Locke notes, "The samurai sword is distinctively Japanese, an icon of essential national character signifying Japan's archaic military aggression" (31). Emblematized in the samurai sword, the Japanese "barbaric" ways of killing "sets the Japanese apart from the American and Allied heroes" (Locke 31). Due, in part, to such governmental war efforts, white racism "in an overtly antiblack fashion," including lynching, became un-American and unacceptable (Locke 34). The way Hollywood films helped white and black Americans bond at the expense of the Japanese still continues, even if differently. As Locke points out, "The 2008 remake of Robert Wise's 1951 science fiction classic, *The Day the Earth Stood Still* . . . features a white mother (Jennifer Connelly) and her black stepson (Jaden Smith) who bond when [Chinese-speaking] aliens . . . invade Earth" (157). Apparently, the Japanese in the past, and the Asians (aliens speaking in Chinese) in 2008 are used to define "the boundaries of the nation," to narrate the unity and homogeneity of the US. These Asian characters in the films constitute fantasy constructions, which serve as a support for the social reality in which people of Asian descent are completely other than, and alien to the nation.

Ensconced in the frame story of a Godzilla figure (i.e., Gozadilla), the samurai attack can not only "evoke [but also] erase the totalizing boundaries of the nation" (Bhabha 213). The first Godzilla film (1954) was released almost ten years after the atomic bombings of Hiroshima and Nagasaki in 1945. As Chon Noriega highlights, the US military occupation of Japan followed the bombings, which "dismantled and rebuilt the Japanese family and society in such a way as to ensure that Japan never again become a *military* threat to the Allies" (65). This kind of socioeconomic and political reform involved "repression," and "the repressed had returned" in the form of the Godzilla film, catalyzed by the tests of H-bombs near Japan by the US and the Soviet Union (Noriega 66–67). In this context, Godzilla partially "comes to symbolize . . . Japan in 1954" (Noriega 68). If the samurais and Gozadilla are the "two temporally succeeding selves" of the Other—the formidable foe and the victim of the atomic bombings—their presence in New York City after 9/11 can generate different meanings about the "boundaries" of the nation. Those boundaries are rather whimsical: While the WWII combat film *Bataan* (the first of its kind) portrays the Japanese as the enemy, the post-9/11 Japan is now an important ally after her generous support of the

---

23. Bhabha argues, "Counter-narratives of the nation that continually evoke and erase its totalizing boundaries—both actual and conceptual—disturb those ideological manoeuvres through which 'imagined communities' are given essentialist identities" (213).

US with $10 million. Yet, Peter Vallone, who accepted Japanese aid for New York City as council speaker, said the memories of 9/11 would overshadow those of the attack on Pearl Harbor (Locke 156). Later in 2001, commemorating the Pearl Harbor attack, "George W. Bush echoed Vallone's assessment" (Locke 156). Despite Japan's alliance with the US for the war on terror, Pearl Harbor apparently haunts the US, threatening to overshadow Japan's generous donation. Even in their favorable comments, Vallone and Bush ironically evoked the boundaries of the nation (i.e., the Japanese assault on Pearl Harbor) to erase them as they "drew parallels between the Japanese assault on Pearl Harbor and the events of 9/11" (Locke 156). Interestingly, evoking and erasing the totalizing boundaries of the nation is, according to Bhabha, what counternarratives of the nation constantly do, "disturb[ing] th[e] ideological manoeuvres through which 'imagined communities' are given essentialist identities" (213). Situated in the post 9/11 New York City, Gozadilla and the samurais counter the national narrative of Vallone and Bush, while constituting the narrative.

In this vein, the last chapter of *Johnny Hiro* peculiarly echoes Japan's ambivalent position after 9/11. If the Godzilla figure—especially the one in the Hollywood reedited film in the 1950s—contributes to constitute those boundaries like Japan during World War II, Hiro and Mayumi, who find themselves responsible for the monster damage while helping Bloomberg erase the monster's footprint in the city, parallel the post-9/11 Japan who recalls their own guilt in American conscious, while helping the US reconstruct the city after the terrorist attacks.[24] Better yet, while Hiro and Mayumi's situation highlights the contradictory logic of the "boundaries" of the nation, the Godzilla figure functions as a counternarrative because the monster symbolizes not only Japan, but also the US, and now the US is Other in him (Noriega 68). In this way, Chao uses comics space to its maximum capacity, by overlaying anachronistic characters—Gozadilla and samurais—whose appearance evokes, questions, and erases the boundaries of the nation, thereby countering narratives that define the people of Japanese descent as the Other and an ally.

Thus, the anachronistic figures in *Johnny Hiro*, like those in *American Born Chinese*, effectively counter stereotyping narratives by visualizing their "fantasy-construction" (Žižek 323), and show the potential of comics as a subversive form. Unlike Yang, however, Chao does not provide "a narrative

---

24. According to Noriega, "Embassy Pictures reedited the [first Godzilla] film" so that Godzilla became totally otherized: In the reedited film, "an American sense of guilt toward the Japanese . . . is . . . projected onto the monster" as in "other American radioactive-monster films" (69–70).

that can bring them all together" (Nishime 199). In *American Born Chinese*, chapters on the Monkey King, Jin, and Danny converge at the end, with an essential identity to integrate and reconcile the characters, who turn out to be the fragmented selves of a person, Jin. In *Johnny Hiro*, different cultures, histories, and perspectives do not fuse into a single, coherent narrative. For instance, Chao does not explain how Gozadilla's abduction of Mayumi and the samurai attack are related, nor does he provide a character like the Monkey King to help Hiro with an essential identity to fend off stereotyping narratives, which are less explicitly suggested than in Yang's work. Chao's take is slightly different. Instead, multiple temporalities, spatialities, and people, which often carry racialized histories and discourses, challenge Hiro, who ends up emerging unscathed by their homogenizing forces that could have transformed him into "Territory-turned-into-Tradition" and "the People-turned-into-One." Thus, as the title *Johnny Hiro: Half Asian, All Hero* suggests, Chao's otherwise ordinary Hiro becomes a *real* hero.

Works Cited

Abbott, Lawrence L. "Comic Art: Characteristics and Potentialities of a Narrative Medium." *Journal of Popular Culture,* vol. 19, no. 4, Spring 1986, pp. 155–76.

Bhabha, Homi K. *The Location of Culture.* Routledge, 1994.

Chao, Fred. *Johnny Hiro: Half Asian, All Hero.* Tor, 2012.

———. Personal interview. 22 and 23 June 2021.

Chen, Liyan. "How Asian Americans Can Break through the Bamboo Ceiling." *Forbes,* 20 January 2016, https://www.forbes.com/sites/liyanchen/2016/01/20/how-asian-americans-can-break-through-the-bamboo-ceiling/#2bd89fdc1e43. Accessed 17 February 2020.

Chute, Hillary. "Comics as Literature? Reading Graphic Narrative." *PMLA,* vol. 123, no. 2, October 2008, pp. 452–65.

———. *Graphic Women: Life Narrative and Contemporary Comics.* Duke University Press, 2010.

———. "'The Shadow of a Past Time': History and Graphic Representation in 'Maus.'" *Twentieth Century Literature,* vol. 52, no. 2, Summer 2006, pp. 199–230.

Davis, Rocio G. "American Born Chinese: Challenging the Stereotype." *Graphic Subjects: Critical Essays on Autobiography and Graphic Novels,* edited by Michael A. Chaney, University of Wisconsin Press, 2011, pp. 279–81.

Dong, Lan. "Reimagining the Monkey King in Comics: Gene Luen Yang's *American Born Chinese.*" *The Oxford Handbook of Children's Literature,* edited by Julia L. Mickenberg and Lynne Vallone, Oxford University Press, 2011, pp. 231–51.

Duncan, Patti. *Tell This Silence: Asian American Women Writers and the Politics of Speech.* University of Iowa Press, 2004.

Groensteen, Thierry. *Comics and Narration.* Translated by Ann Miller, University Press of Mississippi, 2011.

Hatfield, Charles. *Alternative Comics: An Emerging Literature*. University Press of Mississippi, 2005.

Jameson, Fredric. *Postmodernism or, The Cultural Logic of Late Capitalism*. Duke University Press, 1991.

Lee, Jin. "Graphic Nonsense and Historical Trauma in Fred Chao's *Johnny Hiro*." *CLC-WEB: Comparative Literature and Culture*, vol. 23, no.3, 2021, https://doi.org/10.7771/1481-4374.3496.

Lee, Robert G. *Orientals: Asian Americans in Popular Culture*. Temple University Press, 1999.

Locke, Brian. *Racial Stigma on the Hollywood Screen from World War II to the Present: The Orientalist Buddy Film*. Palgrave Macmillan, 2009.

McCloud, Scott. *Understanding Comics: The Invisible Art*. William Morrow, 1994.

Melvin, Sheila. "'The First Emperor,' and a Flutter of Chinese Fans—in New York." *The New York Times*, 5 February 2007, https://www.nytimes.com/2007/02/05/arts/05iht-tandun.html. Accessed 25 June 2021.

Mirzoeff, Nicholas. *The Right to Look*. Duke University Press, 2011.

Mundy, Liza. "Cracking the Bamboo Ceiling: Can Asian American Men Learn from *Lean In*?" *The Atlantic*, November 2014, https://www.theatlantic.com/magazine/archive/2014/11/cracking-the-bamboo-ceiling/380800/. Accessed 17 February 2020.

Nishime, LeiLani. "Manga or Marvel?: Multiracial Japanese/American Visual Narrative in Indie Comics." *Hapa Japan*, edited by Duncan Ryuken Williams, Kaya Press, 2017, pp. 189–204.

Noriega, Chon A. "Godzilla and the Japanese Nightmare: When 'Them!' is US." *Cinema Journal*, vol. 27, no. 1, Autumn 1987, pp. 63–77. *JSTOR*, www.jstor.org/stable/1225324.

Schleitwiler, Vince. *Strange Fruit of the Black Pacific*. NYU Press, 2017.

Smyth, Heather. "The Black Atlantic Meets the Black Pacific: Multimodality in Kamau Brathwaite and Wayde Compton." *Callaloo*, vol. 37, no. 2, Spring 2014, pp. 389–403. *JSTOR*, www.jstor.org/stable/24265015.

Song, Min Hyoung. "Comics and the Changing Meaning of Race." *The Children of 1965: On Writing, and Not Writing, as an Asian American*, Duke University Press, 2013, pp. 127–51.

———. "'How Good It Is to Be a Monkey': Comics, Racial Formation, and *American Born Chinese*." *Mosaic: An Interdisciplinary Critical Journal*, vol. 43, no. 1, March 2010, pp. 73–92.

Taylor, Charles. *The Sources of the Self: The Making of the Modern Identity*. Harvard University Press, 1989.

Yang, Gene Luen. *American Born Chinese*. First Second, 2006.

Yang, Lingyan. "Theorizing Asian America: On Asian American and Postcolonial Asian Diasporic Women Intellectuals." *Journal of Asian American Studies*, vol. 5, no. 2, 2002, pp. 139–78.

Zhao, Shan Mu. "Conveying New Material Realities." *Drawing New Color Lines: Transnational Asian American Graphic Narratives*, edited by Monica Chiu, Hong Kong University Press, 2015, pp. 299–320.

Žižek, Slavoj. "How Did Marx Invent the Symptom?" *Mapping Ideology*, edited by Slavoj Žižek, Verso, 1994, pp. 296–331.

CHAPTER 5

"A Storm of a Girl Silently Gathering Force"

Peminist Girlhoods in the Comics of Trinidad Escobar and Malaka Gharib

MELINDA LUISA DE JESÚS

In the twenty-first century, Filipinx Americans constitute the third-fastest-growing Asian American ethnic group in the United States today. Likewise, the discipline of Filipino American studies itself has developed exponentially, and along with it, a heartening and pride-inducing tsunami of Filipinx American cultural production in the form of literature, spoken word and poetry, theater, hip hop, film, visual art, and graphic novels. Simultaneously, girls' studies, formerly a subset within the discipline of women's studies, has become a viable and robust field of academic study.

These three developments coincide with the explosion of graphic novels, particularly by artists of color, and the broader acceptance of graphic novels and comics for youth, especially in the genre of young adult literature.[1] With self-distribution via social media platforms like author websites and apps like Instagram, Twitter, and Facebook, as well as Web-based distributors like *The Nib* and *The Believer*, Filipinx American cartoonists like Trinidad Escobar and Malaka Gharib are finding eager audiences and inspiring budding cartoonists to create their own zines and comics.

---

1. For example, see the Comic Book Legal Defense Fund (CBLDF) handout "Panel Power," a rich resource for parents, teachers, librarians, and booksellers that describes how graphic novels and comics contribute to youth literacy and lifelong reading.

While there have always been a plethora of Pinxy poets, I have been especially heartened by the recent emergence of North America Pinay novelists and writers like Elaine Castillo, Grace Talusan, and young adult novelist Erin Entrada Kelly, as well as cartoonists Rina Ayuyang (*Blame This on the Boogie*, 2018) and Montreal-based Lorina Mapa (*Imelda Marcos, Duran Duran and Me*, 2017), in addition to Gharib and Escobar. In *Pinay Power: Peminist Critical Theory* (2005), I defined peminisms, or Filipina/American feminisms, as the gendered analysis of imperial trauma (6). Twenty-first-century Pinay writers engage with the themes of identity, family, colonial mentality, diasporic identities, sexuality, religion, education, class, and trauma. Their unflinching engagement in the peminist project of decolonization characterizes and unites this body of work.

Nevertheless, amid the current explosion of comic art by and about people of color of all genders and sexualities, there still remains a dearth of Filipinx representations. I've noted previously that one major cartoonist labored in the field for over forty years although few knew her racial identity as a Filipina mestiza (de Jesús, "Liminality" and "Of Monsters"). Lynda Barry, 2019 MacArthur Fellow and 2009 Eisner awardee, and now associate professor of interdisciplinary creativity at the University of Wisconsin, is the best-known Filipina American cartoonist, and her groundbreaking *One! Hundred! Demons!* (Drawn and Quarterly, 2003) has been an important influence on both Gharib and Escobar. Barry's delving into her myriad "demons" established a critical and crucial assertion of peminist presence in mainstream American comics, and literally delineated how comics offer the possibility of healing and decolonization to both the reader and the cartoonist.[2]

This chapter seeks to situate peminist comics within the rise of both girls' studies and Filipinx American studies. Drawing upon my previous work on Lynda Barry's *One! Hundred! Demons!*, I trace the lineage of contemporary peminist comics, focusing on the themes of decolonization, identity, family, and healing in the comics of Trinidad Escobar and Malaka Gharib. I argue that these new comics constitute an important contribution to the field of girls' studies, which, despite its efforts to center intersectionality and diversity in researching girlhoods, remains dominated by an overfocus on white and Anglo girls in the US, United Kingdom, and Australia.

---

2. See my articles "Liminality" and "Of Monsters" for more information.

Girls' Studies Today: An Overview

"Girls' Studies: What's New?," Johnson and Ginsberg's introduction to *Difficult Dialogues about Twenty-First-Century Girls* (2016), offers a concise history of the discipline, arguing convincingly that girls' studies has eclipsed women's studies as a potent site of engagement for third- and fourth-wave feminists and activists for whom intersectionality and diversity are a given, and outlining current methods and themes that characterize girls' studies inquiry today. Johnson and Ginsberg's volume is dedicated to the "difficult dialogues" girls' studies scholars must engage in to continue girls' studies growth as a discipline. Of note is the authors' emphasis on intersectionality and the dangers of cooptation of the "Intersectional Method . . . particularly as it relates to the lens of race." (5) To my mind, the pressing "difficult dialogues" American girls' studies practitioners are currently engaged in revolve around diversity and inclusion, and include the following: (1) the disruption of white feminist hegemony in American girls' studies and (2) the dismantling of "girl effect" logics in thinking about girls' lives in the Global South.

As a girls' studies scholar grounded in critical ethnic studies discourse, I have found the very recent emergence of the following symposia and research initiatives very heartening: the White House Council on Women and Girls' forum on Advancing Equity for Women and Girls of Color (November 2015); Oakland, California's "Breaking The Silence" Town Hall on Girls & Women of Color (February 2016); The Black Girls Movement Conference at Columbia University (April 2016); Know Her Truths: Advancing Justice for Women and Girls of Color Conference at the Anna Julia Cooper Center, Wake Forest University (April 2016); St. Louis's Black Girls Are Magical Conference (February 2017); Columbia, South Carolina's Every Black Girl Conference (March 2017); The Global History of Black Girlhood Conference at the University of Virginia (March 2017); and the Black Girls Lead conference at Barnard (July 2017). Clearly rooted in the urgency of the Black Lives Matter movement, these incisive projects center the voices and experiences of US girls of color and thus provide an important counternarrative to the prevailing white hegemony that continues to plague contemporary feminist and gender studies today. The research being created here will provide important contexts regarding the complexities of the lives of US girls of color, particularly in relation to the nation-state, and will set the agenda for American girls' studies into the twenty-first century.

Likewise, recent girls' studies scholarship critiques the power relations enforced by the *girl effect* or *girl factor ideology* that has dominated mainstream and popular culture understandings of Third World girls' lives.[3] For example, Skalli, Desai, and Bent and Switzer, among others, explore how girl effects logic has appropriated and co-opted girl-centric discourse around girls' education and empowerment in the service of multinational, corporate, neoliberal, capitalist, racist, and neocolonial interests; indeed, Skalli's work is notable in its indictment of girl factor as both a product and a tool of racism, militarism, and Islamophobia. Moreover, Bent and Switzer contend that girl effects logic results in the imposition of what they term "oppositional girlhoods": the flattening, simplistic logic that comprehends Western girlhoods and Global South girlhoods as forever irreconcilable, never intersecting, wherein Western girlhood is upheld as the universal model of girls' progress and empowerment.[4] Fittingly, Bent and Switzer present the concept of intersectional "relationality" as a methodology for moving beyond the limitations of oppositional girlhoods:

> As an analytic and praxis, relationality resists subsuming global girlhoods under a singular narrative of experiential sameness and oppositionality; indeed, it challenges us to consider how social location, structural violence, historical processes and inequalities integral to girls' daily lives bring about a deeper, more complex transitional understanding of "how girls' lives matter." (22–23)

Despite the recent work of Black feminist activists and scholars to highlight the experiences of African American girls, girls' studies remains overly white today, as acknowledged by the convenors of the first International Girls' Studies Association conference in the UK in 2016: "It is fair to say that we still know much more about heterosexual, able-bodied, Anglophone, white, cisgender girls that we do about any other group of girls" (Cann et al xvii–xviii). Studies by and about Latinx, Native American, Asian American, mixed-race, and queer girls are sorely needed. Indeed, the absence of Pinays in girls' studies is a challenge I have taken on personally, and I'm

---

3. "Girl Effect" is the Nike Foundation's philanthropic program for girls' education in the Global South (see http://www.girleffect.org/). Skalli defines "girl factor" as "an unprecedented interest of the international development community, policy circles, and corporate sectors in the power and potential of young women from developing countries" (1).

4. "Global girl power discourses reduce the intersectional complexity of girls' lives into opposing representations that reinforce artificial neocolonial divides between and among girlhoods, often to the explicit occlusion of the racialized, class-based and geopolitical realities and histories of girls' daily lives" (Bent and Switzer 2).

always grateful for new peminist work to incorporate into my Girl Culture class.[5]

In sum, the push for anti-racism, intersectionality and diversity in contemporary girls' studies mirrors the continuing struggle for Pinay representation in Filipinx American Studies as well as comics as a whole. It is my hope that girls' studies continues to evolve to center the experiences of girls of color, refugee and immigrant and girls in the Global South. This essay is one such tool towards that transformation.

Comics as a Tool for Peminist Decolonization

Leny Strobel, in her foundational work on decolonization, *Coming Full Circle*, writes:

> If language is the site of ideological struggle, it can also be a site for negotiation. Language can become an oppositional force and an affirmative force: it can create new ways of reading history through the reconstruction of suppressed memories. Therefore language can create new identities capable of challenging the conditions that negate the voices, desires and histories of silenced peoples. (69)

Similarly, I view comics as a potent site of ideological struggle—the melding of language and image enables decolonial imaginings, new ways of thinking about and seeing the self. I argue that comics becomes an incredibly potent space for the creation of new identities, histories, and ways of being. Indeed, the peminist comics discussed here disrupt colonizing and erasing narratives through the assertion of the Pinay's voice, history, and agency, her worldview. In short, Escobar's and Gharib's peminist comics enable the disruption of the white heteropatriarchal status quo of comics, the androcentrism of Filipinx American studies, and the Anglocentrism and racism of girls' and women's studies. They connect to the literary girlhoods of M. Evelina Galang and Erin Entrada Kelly, as well as the girl-centric peminist hip hop of Pinay icon Ruby Ibarra.

---

5. Lynda Barry's *One! Hundred! Demons!* is an important text for the Girl Culture class, and it encouraged my students to use comics to theorize their own girlhood experiences. See their class zines here: https://issuu.com/peminist/docs/girlculture2018_zine_issuu.

Moreover, E. J. R. David in his groundbreaking *Brown Skin, White Minds* notes that

> perceptions, attitudes, and beliefs about both the Filipino and American culture that are better informed, in turn, can lead to fewer instances of automatically regarding anything American as superior, desirable, or pleasant, and automatically regarding anything Filipino as inferior, undesirable, or unpleasant. In other words there will be fewer instances of CM [colonial mentality] or internalized oppression among Filipinos and Filipino Americans. (157)

This, he maintains, is the definition of "psychological decolonization." His quote deftly describes what I see all Filipinx/American cultural production accomplishing in the twenty-first century: decolonization through self-reflection and understanding one's identity as a historical process, and the continual re/creation of a culture and community grounded in knowledge, liberation, and radical love. For Filipina/Americans this translates into peminism: the gendered exploration of imperial trauma, and the creation of a distinctly Pinay comic vision that resists stereotypes and highlights peminist ways of knowing and resistance.

Many contemporary Pinay graphic novels are memoirs, or what Whitlock calls "auto-graphics," or autobiographical graphic narratives. As Susie Bright noted in the introduction to *Twisted Sisters*,

> There is literally no place beside comix where you find women speaking the truth and using their pictures to show you in vivid detail what it means to live your life outside of the stereotypes and delusions we see on television, in shopping malls and at newsstands. (7)

For Pinays, comics are a space for re-visioning oneself beyond the neo/colonialist gaze; they provide what Denise Cruz in *Transpacific Femininities: The Making of the Modern Filipina* deems "the rupture of imperial forgetting" (234). Peminist cartoonists employ talk-story, folklore, and humor to resist racist and sexist stereotypes, and to assert their own realities and visions for the future.

In what follows, I offer short readings of Malaka Gharib's and Trinidad Escobar's contributions to girls' studies and Filipinx American studies. I include the email interviews I conducted with each artist as I find their very different takes on the idea of a Pinay comic aesthetic, the role of decolonization, and how their work relates to girlhood studies to be as fascinating as their comics themselves.

Malaka Gharib's *I Was Their American Dream* (2019)

Filipina Egyptian journalist and comic artist Malaka Gharib is deputy editor and digital strategist of *Goats and Soda*, NPR's global health and development blog. During the pandemic lockdown, in addition to her regular
reporting, she has been creating zines and comics about COVID-19 health
and safety for all ages.[6] Gharib's lighthearted, colorful memoir, *I Was Their
American Dream* (Clarkson Potter, 2019), is a humorous but heartfelt exploration of her mixed-race identity. Reminiscent of *One! Hundred! Demons!*'s dis-
armingly naive explorations of the seemingly mundane, the memoir begins
with Gharib's parents' immigration stories and youthful investments in the
promises of the American Dream, then traces her own girlhood in the "Asian
bubble"[7] of Cerritos, California, in the late '80s and '90s, and the twists and
turns of her understanding and reconciling her very unique family history
and cultural identity through high school, college, and into adulthood.

In an interview with *Asian Journal*, Gharib acknowledged that the anti-
immigrant/anti-Muslim rhetoric unleashed by then presidential candidate
Donald Trump in 2016 was an impetus for her writing her memoir:

> I never really thought much about race issues that deeply until 2016 and
> seeing all the anti-immigrant rhetoric in the news. . . . I wanted to correct
> the narrative that I was seeing and provide my own nuanced perspective
> for my readers and my generation.

In the same interview she described her comic style in the following way:

> For me, I wanted to use the least amount of information to convey the max-
> imum story. That's what I really love about the comics format in that it's
> very restrictive. It's like poetry: what are the base images, words and dia-
> logue you need to tell the most impactful story? (Oriel)

Indeed, Gharib's memoir is whimsical, childlike, simple, and spare, but
endearing and very funny. Moreover, *I Was Their American Dream* utilizes the
colors of the flag (red, white, and a variety of blues) throughout to underscore its explorations of what the American Dream is, and what it means to
be American. Chapter 1 opens with her musing that even as a young girl she

---

6. See https://www.npr.org/sections/goatsandsoda/2020/11/16/934679210/just-
for-kids-how-to-stay-safe-from-the-coronavirus and https://www.newyorker.com/
humor/daily-shouts/alternative-uses-for-face-masks.

7. "I grew up in a town that was an Asian bubble and had a lot of diversity and
people from every social class."

knew that "I had to somehow rise above my parents' life in America. But how?" Thus she sets up the major conflict explored in her memoir: her parents' and extended family's focus on becoming American via assimilation, economic stability, and professional class aspirations versus her own search for identity, and her own dreams.

One unique stylistic aspect of the book is Gharib's incorporation of different forms throughout her memoir, varying the panels within each chapter. The included quizzes, checklists, bingo cards, recipes, samples of old zines, and directions for making one's own zine provide quirky, interactive aspects for the reader, all the while encouraging them to engage more deeply in the many cultural contrasts the author strives to delineate. My favorite of these is her comparisons of Filipino and Egyptian foods, culture, language, and social customs in chapter 2, which details her younger girlhood experiences. Throughout *I Was Their American Dream* Gharib uses every opportunity to teach the reader simple words in Tagalog and Arabic: For example, in 2:13 she includes a chart of the words for egg, girl, milk, tomato, and so on. We also learn *baon* and *mabait*, and when to say *Inshallah* and *Ameen*. Similarly, the page entitled "Game Time" in this same chapter asks the reader to guess among the many activities listed the ones disallowed by her parents (she includes the answers at the bottom of the page: "hanging out after school, sleep overs, dessert, extracurricular activities, Lunchables"; allowed activities include "R rated movies, drinking soda, staying up late, drinking soda, cussing in English"). The allowed/disallowed activities are surprisingly different from expected mainstream American parenting norms, and these contradictions underscore the confusing aspects of Filipino, Egyptian, and American cultures Gharib must always navigate.

Furthermore, the negotiation of mestiza identity through Malaka's contrasting and understanding the very different customs, religions, and perspectives of her parents to forge her own unique worldview and sense of self is the major theme of this novel. I've outlined previously in "Of Monsters and Mothers" and "Liminality and Mestiza Consciousness" how mestiza-ness and mestiza consciousness are major tropes in contemporary Filipinx American cultural production. Gharib's contribution to this canon is her exploration of being both Filipina and Egyptian, Catholic and Muslim, and everything in between. Her articulation of and her insistence upon making space for her unique Pinay Egyptian identity is a crucial intervention and contribution to both Filipinx American studies and to girls' studies today.

In an email to me Gharib noted that she found my reading of the white mestiza in "Liminality and Mestiza Consciousness" "so powerful"; moreover in our interview she addressed how decolonization is central to the novel itself:

> I think the most heartbreaking part of writing the book was acknowledging that I had been trying to pass as white and minimize my cultures because I thought that's what you had to do to assimilate, to be American. It messed me up—I had succumbed to the colonial mentality without even realizing it. That's what I wanted the book to do . . . go through the emotional process of freeing oneself from the ideas of who one ought to be. (Personal interview, 31 May 2020)

Gharib addresses head-on how negative stereotypes about Filipinos from her own family and community greatly impacted her own identity:

> My whole life, we were taught that being Filipino was a bad thing. In high school, I went to school with a lot of other Asians but I quickly understood that Filipinos were at the bottom of whatever hierarchy of the Asians, with the Japanese at the top. When I would go to Egypt, my dad would tell me not to tell others that I was Filipino because, in the Middle East, Filipinos are the help. I had thought it wasn't an honorable thing to be Filipino, but now I get so excited when I see another Filipino out in the world. It's a time to celebrate each other and it has lifted my heart in so many ways. (Oriel)

In *I Was Their American Dream*, Gharib delineates through the voice of a young mestiza the differences and similarities between her two rich but very different and sometimes oppositional home cultures, and the ways she must reconcile them. Her parents divorce when she's very young, and her father moves back to Egypt when she's eleven and remarries. Her childhood is mostly spent with her extended Filipino family, grandparents and aunts and uncles who helped to raise her. For this reason, Gharib takes care to show that her specific mestiza liminality is very singular as she's the only child of her parents; her half-sister is fully Filipino, and her other stepsiblings are fully Egyptian, living with her father and stepmother in Cairo. Malaka alone has to move between these cultural spaces and make sense of, and create a self from, very differing religious, cultural, and gendered messages (see fig. 5.1). She's very aware that who she is and what she knows as her home life differs radically from what she sees on TV and for other kids around her, what her nuns and teachers understand.

Gharib's choice to have her extended Filipino and Egyptian family's skin tones represented with the color peach throughout her memoir instead of varying shades of brown is a striking contrast to Lynda Barry's representations of the white mestiza in relation to her brown Pinay mother. This choice makes one particular scene from chapter 1 at once confusing but devastating. In recalling how her father's nickname for her was "Brownie," Gharib relates how he was shocked by her appearance at birth: "Why is she so BROWN? Where's her blue eyes like her father?" (1:14). Here Gharib deftly illustrates how, at birth, her skin difference from her father is codified, and how colorism inherently drives the sense of Pinay liminality for the mestiza. Furthermore, despite sharing the peach coloring of the Filipinos throughout *I Was Their American Dream*, Malaka is always aware of how she never appears Filipina enough, like her little sister Min-Min, and how this sense of erasure affects her negatively.

As Malaka grows, she comes to an understanding of how much her immigrant parents struggle to provide a basic middle-class life for her. She acknowledges her very Filipino sense of gratitude and obligation in the hilarious "Perfect Filipino Kid" checklist of chapter 2. This section provides the launch for the subsequent chapters where the protagonist appreciates her parents' sacrifice and belief in the American Dream but struggles to define her own path as an adult. I asked Gharib what she wanted the reader to come away with from her memoir and she answered:

> The struggle in America doesn't end with our parents' generation. . . . [O]ur parents think that it will be so easy for us because we won't have to build new lives from scratch or learn a new language or culture. But we have our own struggles too—like fully accepting that we [are] Americans ourselves. Trying to balance multiple cultures. And liking ourselves. (Personal interview, 31 May 2020)

I Was Their American Dream concludes with Malaka's joyful claiming of her many inheritances and contradictions. Our last image is of Malaka and her white Southern Baptist husband, Darren, on their honeymoon in Egypt, cruising down the Nile, and her thinking about returning there with their future children: "And they'll know someday, somehow, that this is part of them too." She details how she has managed to forge her own way as a journalist and writer, and can appreciate the unique circumstances of her growing up. Like *halo-halo*, Malaka has learned to combine everything she is and all that she loves, and to mix it together into something new; in this way she truly fulfills her high school yearbook epithet of "Most Unique."

In this short reading, I have traced Malaka Gharib's unique contributions to girls' studies and Filipinx American studies through her articulation of

FIGURE 5.1. "What are you?" Reprinted from *I Was Their American Dream*. © 2019 by Malaka Gharib. Published by Clarkson Potter, an imprint of Penguin Random House LLC.

the Filipina Egyptian, Catholic, and Muslim mestiza's voice and worldview, and her journey to understand her parents' American Dreams as well as creating her own. In what follows, I will analyze Trinidad Escobar's darker and harrowing exploration of girlhood in her memoir, *Crushed: Book One*, and her stand-alone comic, "Silently Gathering Force."

Trinidad Escobar's *Crushed* and "Silently Gathering Force"

Trinidad Escobar is a queer California-based comic artist, poet, educator, and mom. She was the first graduate of the California College of the Arts (CCA) MFA in comics, and, full disclosure, as chair of diversity studies at CCA, I hired her to teach "Race and Comics" for my program at CCA from 2015 to 2018. Her forthcoming graphic novel, *Of Sea and Venom*, will be published by Farrar, Strauss and Giroux in 2021, as well as a graphic novella, *Tryst*, for Gantala Press (Philippines). She is working on a collection of short stories called "Little Corn Fields." Her graphic memoir, *Crushed: Book One*, was self-published in 2018. She describes her aesthetic in the following way:

> I would say I am most interested in pushing the boundaries of the Pinay Gothic. I am interested in telling stories that are, yes, about migration, abuse, mythology and folklore, family—the usual themes found in Pinay diasporic writing, but there [are] fine cracks and dark shadows in each of those areas of study. My interest in erotica, horror and mythology defaults my comics in the Gothic and speculative traditions in literature. (Personal interview, 14 June 2020)

Indeed, Escobar's *Crushed* exemplifies these points. Through what she deems "biomythography," this evocative and haunting work explores trauma, transnational adoption and reunification, identity, family history and inheritance, domestic violence, mental illness, and healing in a diasporic Filipina/American context. Escobar's comic style here of crisp lines in black and white complements her sinuous, poetic narrative. As she wrote in her original synopsis of the novel,

> *Crushed* is the story of trauma caused by adoption, abuse by my adoptive mother, mental illness and reunification with my birth family after 28 years of separation. . . . [It] is an intimate encounter of memory and grief people keep nearby like Lynda Barry's close examination of the difference memories attached to specific kinds of pain in *One Hundred Demons*.

Moreover, in an email interview with me, she noted the significance of Barry's invocations of girlhood:

> Lynda Barry's representations of Pinay girlhood are my favorites. She's able to capture, and not simply talk about, the grit of childhood, the creepiness and the dangers, as well as the nuanced humor. I think I don't see enough of the Pinay representation and that's why most of my characters will be girls or femme. I want to see more stories that reflect my experience and the experiences and personalities of many of my Pinay friends growing up in California, experiences that were not sweet or obedient or safe. (Personal interview, 14 June 2020)

As I've noted earlier here and elsewhere, one of the key elements of *One! Hundred! Demons!* is Barry's prompting the reader to paint her own demons, and she provides a full-color how-to at the end of the book to inspire the reader's participation. Escobar takes Barry's encouragement to heart and has created a comic that exorcises the demons of institutional racism and the international adoption industry to heal mental illness and trauma.[8] In this way, *Crushed* expands Jane Jeong Trenka's research and activism for Korean adoptees and her critique of the globalized racism and misogyny that characterizes the adoption system, particularly transcultural adoption. Escobar's critique of the adoption system in the Philippines and its roots in imperialist, sexist, and poverty-shaming ideologies is a necessary and important voice.

Crushed: Book One is a haunting *balikbayan* tale, told in stark black and white. Escobar's invocation of mythical and folkloric creatures like sirenas and aswangs is complemented by the eerie sense of ghosts and hauntings throughout the book. And *Crushed* is indeed a ghost story. Here Escobar shares that she was born amid Super Hurricane Gading in 1986 to a very humble family called the Dorognas, which means "crushed." In the aftermath of the devastation, her older sister dies of malnutrition and the measles, and her parents make the decision to allow their youngest to be adopted into an American family in the hope that she might have a chance for a better life. Originally named for her mother, Trinidad, Escobar was given the name and birthdate of "Nicole," an infant who had died during the drawn-out international adoption proceedings begun by her adoptive family. Escobar feels she is living this dead girl's life and is haunted by her presence.

To illustrate this, Escobar utilizes the image of a larger-than-life baby girl literally tethered to Niki with a rope as she arrives in the Philippines and travels the many miles to meet her birth family. In the opening scenes of Nicole's reunion with her birth family, the rope snaps, and the baby girl is left behind, sitting and smiling on like a Buddha. Escobar's gut-wrenching caption of the moment she first meets her family is simply "I learned how an open wound might experience love." This symbolic severing of Niki/Trinidad underscores the deep-seated trauma Escobar has endured to get to this moment of reclaiming her birthright and reuniting with her family, a moment very few international adoptees can ever have. The rest of *Crushed: Book One* details Escobar's bonding with her parents and siblings, trying to erase the decades of their being estranged. Amid the joy of these moments, Escobar also explores the stress the reunion places on her mental health and her marriage, and how family secrets and cycles of abuse get passed on to future generations.

---

8. In our first-ever conversation, Trinidad shared with me the story of how CCA Comics MFA chair Matt Silady handed her *One! Hundred! Demons!* in her first semester of study, saying, "You need to read this!" *Crushed* is her response to Barry.

Due to space considerations, however, I will focus on Escobar's stand-alone comic, "Silently Gathering Force," published in the *Brooklyn Review* (2016). While *Crushed* tells the story of the adult Trinidad's *balikbayan* story, "Silently Gathering Force" explores this story on a metaphorical level through the imagination of a much younger girl seeking refuge from her abusive home life.

The full-color comic opens with Escobar's invoking Einstein and Newton, and her belief in parallel, alternate realities—a reality where she was never adopted, and never left her village and birth family. Trinidad is a good older sister to her younger brother, and a good swimmer, as befits people who live by the sea: "My family is of the water. We are water people," she notes. Escobar underscores here how her older sisters teach the younger ones "how to keep safe because as poor people we knew all too well how fragile life is." All the while a storm approaches, and swelling waves grow darker and more menacing, rushing toward and crashing over Trinidad and her brother before they can react.

On page 4, Trinidad notes: "In that reality I don't freeze up in danger and my voice doesn't get stuck in my throat." As the wave hits them, Trinidad struggles to keep herself and her brother afloat. "Hold on, don't let go!" she yells, but the water is too strong and they are torn apart. Here Escobar uses a series of tight frames with white-capped waves to show the danger the children suddenly find themselves in. Page 6 begins with the caption "In that reality, I believe in angels," and the following five panels show how a sirena (mermaid) appears out of nowhere to save her little brother and bring him to her. Emphasizing the power of the storm and the sea's surge, these large swaths of blue here highlight the desperate situation, how deep the sirena must dive to save him.

Once back on land, page 7 shows Trinidad climbing a tree, carrying her brother with her to safety. She shouts for help, the caption on page 8 under-scoring the importance of her actions:

In that reality. . . . I believe that I can survive. I am not passive, but a storm of a girl silently gathering force. This version of me—she's right next door. In a land I cannot see. I can sense her standing tall, doing what I could never do when I was being hurt by a member of my new family, in my new country, in my reality. (See fig. 5.2)

Escobar powerfully reimagines herself and her history from victim to agent, unprotected to protector. She juxtaposes the story of her troubled childhood in America with what would have been her life with her birth

FIGURE 5.2. "A storm of a girl silently gathering force." Reprinted from *Silently Gathering Force* (2016). © Trinidad Escobar. Used with the artist's permission.

family in the Philippines, imagining them as simultaneously existing, and in conjuring this new reality she creates a powerful spell of wholeness and healing.

The final, devastating panel of the comic shows a small young girl, very similar to the baby girl in *Crushed*, cowering in the long shadow of a very large, imposing female figure, implying the figure's dominance and the small girl's fear. In this way she emphasizes the reality behind the idealized childhood of transcultural adoption stories as she simultaneously imagines herself as an agent of change: She is the strong savior and protector unafraid to use her voice, a "storm of a girl" equal to the storm facing her and her brother, and the storms she must face as an adoptee. This fierce brown girl (with magical helper) saves her brother and her, and accomplishes what she wishes she could have done for herself as a little girl.

In an email interview, Escobar shared the following insights about this piece:

> In a few of our pre-colonial animist belief systems (that were also influenced by other religions like Buddhism in some parts of the Philippines), we believed in different planes of reality. Multiple dimensions of existence. In *Silently Gathering Force* I was thinking about what one of my inter dimensional counterparts was doing while I struggled being hit and verbally ridiculed as a child by a family member. I thought, if there are infinite possibilities then one of those must include a version of myself who can save herself. There must be a girl who is not only strong enough to save herself but who has the strength to also help someone else. I believe in her existence. I also believe that there are only so many permutations of DNA that there must be more than one of these versions of me existing on other planes as well (just as the physicist Michio Kaku and other scientists have hypothesized that there are other versions of ourselves on other planets and possibly other universes). *Though the comic doesn't drive this point home, I hoped to show myself that if these other girls exist then I have within me everything I need to survive.* (Personal interview, 14 June 2020; emphasis added)

"Silently Gathering Force" is a such a gift to its readers. Its vision of the Filipina girl as a loving but also brave and active agent, one who confronts and overcomes great dangers, is a metaphor for all of our peminist work around decolonization. Like *One! Hundred! Demons!*, it is a wonderful example of how peminist comics offer a space both for healing trauma and for self-forgiveness for both the artist and the reader.

Lynda Barry ends *One! Hundred! Demons!* with a lesson on how to draw your own demon; similarly, Escobar begins *Crushed* with a quick lesson about how to read comics, sharing specific common forms and elements. She welcomes her readers to the nuances of comic art, and emphasizes the reader's agency and empathy in the process of making meaning in comics. Escobar's insistence here on interaction, agency, and empathy is crucial to our continuing efforts to decolonize as we explore our own complex histories and evolutions as Pinays today. I look forward to Escobar's forthcoming works that continue to limn the intricacies of Filipinx American girlhoods, in both their mystery and triumph as well as their darkness and sorrow.

Conclusion

> I think most of the Pinay work right now in comics is decolonized storytelling.
>
> —Trinidad Escobar, personal interview, June 2020

Foundational girls' studies scholar Sherrie Inness, in her introduction to *Delinquents and Debutantes,* insists that "too often girls' culture is shunted aside by scholars as less significant or less important than the study of adult women's issues, but girls' culture is what helps to create not just an individual woman but all women in our society" (7). This insight underscores the reality that socialization and culture very much shape girls into women, and begs our asking ourselves: Exactly how are we helping Filipinx girls grow into empowered Pinays today? How can we help them become "a storm of girl silently gathering force"?

Above I've outlined how the comics of Malaka Gharib and Trinidad Escobar, like those of Lynda Barry before them, are compelling examples of the incredible diversity within Filipina America. Their peminist explorations of Filipina Egyptian girlhood and the transcultural adoptee experiences are important additions to the contemporary Filipinx American canon and to literatures about girls of color. They are stories that the authors themselves wished they had growing up. In addition to providing crucial representation and validation to Pinay readers, peminist comics like *I Was Their American Dream, Crushed,* and "Silently Gathering Force" are potent tools for decolonization and healing for both the creator and her audience. Seeing ourselves and our realities included in popular culture and literature, our voices and girlhoods as central rather than peripheral, inspires us to reflect upon our own identity development and to create our own stories and art, further enabling an exponential web of peminist work and interconnection throughout the diaspora for the twenty-first century—and beyond.

Indeed, comics create a necessary space for the expansion and diversification of both girls' studies and Filipinx American studies, but most importantly, they are a conduit for peminist empowerment because confident girls grow into confident, politicized Pinays. I've seen the impact of this phenomenon with my own eyes. My daughter Malaya Lanikai, a mixed-race Pinay, has read comics by both Gharib and Escobar, and both inspired her to create her own stories and comics about her own experiences. In this way I know that the adage "If you can see it, you can be it" is very true.

In sum, comic artists Trinidad Escobar and Malaka Gharib, like Lynda Barry before them, are comix vanguards of peminist hope and resistance. Their graphic opposition to the neocolonial, imperialist, and misogynist forces of erasure and amnesia—themes that continue to dominate the Filipinx American psyche and cultural production—give us myriad tools for survival, for celebration, and for reflection. These unforgettable comics enable our seeing, our remembering, and our transformation, and it is in these collective leaps of the peminist imagination that our true liberation resides.

Coda

It has taken an inordinate amount of time to complete this chapter and I am greatly indebted to editor Eleanor Ty for her faith and patience as I attempted first to write amid the growing horror of the COVID-19 pandemic and then the aftermath of the George Floyd murder. At times it has felt like a completely useless and unimportant task, given the number of deaths in the United States and across the globe, and the reality of even more Black lives taken by police terror and racialized violence. Added to this is the reality of increasing anti-Asian hate crimes rooted in scapegoating Asians as creators and carriers of the virus itself.

Moreover, I first presented my work about Trinidad Escobar at the National Women's Studies Association conference in Montreal, Canada, in November 2016, the day after the election of 45. At that time it too felt futile and pointless to discuss the comics and healing. Never had I felt my life and my work, my family, my community, and my history so dismissed and devalued as irrelevant, unwanted. Upon reflection, I came to see that 45's espoused desire for the further erasure and oppression of all nonwhite peoples and other minorities—the literal whiting out of Filipinx life and work—has been the enduring condition we Filipinas have existed under, labored under, and resisted since the time of Spanish colonization. Then and today, amid this pandemic, I decided that for me to give up and *not* discuss Filipina comix would therefore be an act of self-erasure and denigration. As Jeff Chang notes in *Who We Be*:

> Here is where artists and those who work and play in the culture enter. They help people to see what cannot yet be seen, hear the unheard, tell the untold. They make change feel not just possible, but inevitable. Every moment of major social change requires a collective leap of imagination. Change presents itself not only in spontaneous and organized expressions of unrest and risk, but in explosions of mass creativity. So those interested in transforming society might assert: cultural change always precedes political change. Put another way, political change is the last manifestation of cultural shifts that have already occurred. (6)

Similarly, Maxine Hong Kingston exhorts us in her epilogue to *The Fifth Book of Peace*: "In a time of destruction, create something. A poem. A parade. A community. A school. A vow. A moral principle. One peaceful moment." I offer this essay and interview excerpts as one small intervention in this time of great destruction, as a testament to my sisters throughout the diaspora, and to the broader history of peminist cultural production and solidarity in the name of decolonization and healing.

MAKIBAKA!

Works Cited

Ayuyang, Rina. *Blame This on the Boogie*. Drawn and Quarterly, 2018.

Bent, Emily, and Switzer, Heather. "Oppositional Girlhoods and the Challenge of Relational Politics." *Gender Issues*, vol. 33, no. 2, 2016, pp. 122–47.

Bright, Susie. Introduction. *Twisted Sisters 2: Drawing the Line*, edited by Dianne Noomin, Kitchen Sink Press, 1995, 7–20.

Cann, Victoria, et al. "Contemporary Girls Studies: Reflections on the Inaugural Girls Studies Association Conference," *Girlhood Studies*, vol. 11, no. 3, Winter 2018, pp. vi–xxi.

Castillo, Elaine. *America Is Not in the Heart*. Atlantic Books, 2019.

Chang, Jeff. *Who We Be: A Cultural History of Race in Post-Civil Rights America*. St. Martin's Press, 2014.

Comic Book Legal Defense Fund. "Panel Power." *CBLDF*, cbldf.org/panel-power/.

Cruz, Denise. *Transpacific Femininities: The Making of the Modern Filipina*. Duke University Press, 2012.

David, E. J. R. *Brown Skin, White Minds: Filipino-/American Postcolonial Psychology.* Information Page Publishing, 2013.

de Jesús, Melinda Luisa. Introduction. *Pinay Power: Peminist Critical Theory. Theorizing the Filipina/American Experien*ce, edited by Melinda L. de Jesus, Routledge, 1995, pp. 1–20.

——. "Liminality and Mestiza Consciousness in Lynda Barry's *One Hundred Demons.*" *MELUS*, vol. 29, no. 1, 2004, pp. 219–52. doi:10.2307/4141803.

——. "Of Monsters and Mothers: Filipina American Identity and Maternal Legacies in Lynda Barry's *One Hundred Demons.*" *Meridians: Feminism, Race, Transnationalism*, vol. 5, no. 1, 2004, pp. 1–26. *Project Muse*, doi:10.1353/mer.2004.0051.

Desai, Karishma. "Teaching the Third World Girl: Girl Rising as a Precarious Curriculum of Empathy." *Curriculum Inquiry*, vol. 46, no. 3, 2016, pp. 248–64.

Escobar, Trinidad. *Crushed: A Graphic Memoir, Book One.* Self-published, Oakland, CA, 2018.

——. "Guest Interview: *Crushed* by Trinidad Escobar." *TAYO Literary Magazine*, 22 June 2016, www.tayoliterarymag.com/blog-2/2016/6/22/guest-interview-crushed-by-trinidad-escobar.

——. Personal interview. 14 June 2020.

——. "Silently Gathering Force," *The Brooklyn Review*, 28 February 2016, http://www.bkreview.org/plus/silently-gathering-force/.

Galang, M. Evelina. *Her Wild American Self.* Coffeehouse Press, 1996.

Gharib, Malaka. *I Was Their American Dream: A Graphic Memoir.* Clarkson Potter, 2019.

——. Personal interview. 31 May 2020.

Inness, Sherrie A. Introduction. *Delinquents and Debutantes: Twentieth-Century American Girls' Cultures*, edited by Inness, NYU Press, 1998, pp. 1–15.

Johnson, Donna Marie, and Alice Ginsberg. "Introduction: Girls' Studies: What's New?" *Difficult Dialogues about Twenty-First-Century Girls*, edited by Johnson and Ginsberg, SUNY Press, 2015, pp. 1–7.

Kelly, Erin Entrada. *Blackbird Fly.* Greenwillow, 2014.

Kingston, Maxine Hong. *The Fifth Book of Peace.* Vintage, 2004.

Mapa, Lorina. *Imelda Marcos, Duran Duran and Me: A Graphic Memoir.* Conundrum Press, 2017.

Oriel, Christina M. "Malaka Gharib's Graphic Novel 'I Was Their American Dream' Explores Identity as a Filipina-Egyptian." *Asian Journal News*, 3 July 2019, www.asianjournal.com/magazines/mdwk-magazine/malaka-gharibs-graphic-novel-i-was-their-american-dream-explores-identity-as-a-filipina-egyptian/.

Skalli, Loubna Hanna. "The Girl Factor and the (In)Security of Coloniality." *Alternatives: Global, Local, Political*, vol. 40, no. 2, 2015, pp. 174–87.

Strobel, Leny. *Coming Full Circle: The Process of Decolonization Among Post-1965 Filipino Americans*, 2nd ed., Center for Babaylan Studies, 2016.

Trenka, Jane Jeong. *The Language of Blood: A Memoir.* Graywolf Press, 2005.

Talusan, Grace. *The Body Papers: A Memoir.* Restless Books, 2019.

Whitlock, Gillian. "15. Autographics." *Comics Studies: A Guidebook*, edited by Charles Hatfield and Bart Beaty, Rutgers University Press, 2020, pp. 227–40. https://doi.org/10.36019/9780813591452-016.

PART 3

SUPERHEROES AND RACE

CHAPTER 6

Questioning the "Look" of Normalcy and the Borders of South/Asian Americans

Ms. Marvel, Kamala Khan, and the Comic Superhero

SHILPA DAVÉ

Since her character first debuted in digital and print comics in 2014, Kamala Khan's version of Ms. Marvel has been a sensation. Acclaimed by critics as a character who is representative, relatable, and embraced by global audiences, Marvel Comics doubled down on Kamala Khan's universal appeal as the first Pakistani American Muslim and woman character to headline her own comic book. The company expanded her presence onto multiple transmedia platforms. In addition to her continuing comic series, *Ms. Marvel*, and her team series, *The Champions*, Kamala Khan is the costar of the animated show *Marvel Rising* (2018) and the only "new" character in the Marvel's Avengers video game (2020). Importantly, Kamala Khan is the heart of the live-action television miniseries *Ms. Marvel* (2022) on the Disney Plus streaming platform. Bisha K. Ali directs the show as the series executive producer and newcomer Iman Vellani stars as the title character. Kamala Khan is the first Muslim and South Asian American superhero to be featured in the larger and lucrative Marvel Cinematic Universe.

Versions of this essay were presented at the 2016 Association for Asian American Studies Conference in Miami, Florida, and at the 2016 Graphic Narrative Symposium at National Hsinchu University, Taiwan.

The character of Kamala Khan stands at the intersection of two narrative genealogies that have enjoyed immense popularity in the twenty-first century—the rise of the teenage girl superhero and the emergence of a lucrative Marvel multimedia (including twenty-seven films from 2008 through 2021) and multiplatform Universe (now owned by Disney). The fact that her superpower is her ability to shapeshift solidifies the multiple roles that the character and the first collected series of books, *No Normal*, engage with in regard to racial positionality, young adult gender representations, and Asian American comics and graphic narratives.

As a comic book superhero, Kamala Khan is made for mass consumption though the public relations and marketing machine of Disney. The creation of Kamala Khan by two Muslim American women capitalizes on the popularity of the superheroine teens and a push by Marvel (and now Disney) to engage with an expanding millennial and Gen Z consumer base. Her success features a thematic change in the genre of the superhero comic rooted in twentieth-century narratives of American assimilation, nationalism, and militarism of (1) the 1930s and 1940s (known as the Golden Age of comics) and (2) representations (and critiques) of American race relations, counterculture movements, and government programs advancing experimental science and technology from the 1960s (known as the Silver Age). Adrienne Resha argues that twenty-first-century superhero comics are situated in the Blue Age of comics—a product that is digital rather than print-based. With a change in the medium of consumption, the digital comic attracts new comic book consumers (women and Black, Indigenous, and people of color) online that were previously not able to access or feel welcome in brick-and-mortar comic bookstores.

While digital comics privilege those with internet access, most of the popular characters have achieved crossover popularity in print, animation, live-action, and films. *Ms. Marvel* #1 sold out of print copies but was also the number 1 digital download in 2014. Resha identifies Kamala Khan as a prime example of the Blue Age of comics that are composed of "legacy heroes" derived from historical Marvel characters developed in the 1960s, such as Carol Danvers as Ms. Marvel ("Blue Age"). Other popular characters include Miles Morales as an Afro-Latino Spider-Man, Amadeus Cho as a Korean American Hulk, and Kate Bishop as a female Hawkeye. The characters are not new but reimagined: "This Age, thus far, [is] defined not by diversity but by diversification. New heroes (like Kamala Khan and Miles Morales) have appeared, and old heroes (like Carol Danvers and Clint Barton) have been made different" (Resha, "Blue Age" 70). Blue Age comics reconfigure the consumption, distribution, and production of print comics and appeal to a new generational demographic who have grown up in a primarily digital world.

Digital comics are read differently through guided readers that are a panel-by-panel narration that intervene in the sequencing and timing of the gutters, spaces, and big splash pages of print comics. The digital format calls for new reading practices that vary from those of print comics. There is room for the pause, but the material object is more visually dependent and per-haps geared toward apolitical consumption. And yet despite the transmedia platforms, technological innovations, and generational changes in reader-ship and superheroes, the stories reflect popular themes of isolation, differ-ence, alienation, and the hope and desire for a greater good in the world.

Kamala Khan offers an alternative narrative of an American girl, namely a Muslim Pakistani American teenager, that resonates both in the pages of the comic book and outside the book as a symbolic icon who challenges racial, gendered, and religious discrimination. The introduction of racially and religiously diverse characters in the American superhero genre of com-ics helps highlight racial and ethnic narratives in the US. These represen-tations also gesture to a generational shift of comics readers and the kind of stories twenty-first-century audiences want to consume across multiple media platforms.

Shape-Shifting the Racial Look of Normal

In US history, South Asians have been racially categorized as Caucasian, nonwhite, other, and finally, as an Asian American minority group. These multiple designations have led to a racial identity that is not easily explained or understood by mainstream culture, by racial and American groups, and even by South Asians themselves. South Asians come from diverse geog-raphies (Afghanistan, Bangladesh, Bhutan, India, the Maldives, Nepal, Pakistan, and Sri Lanka) and have a variety of religious affiliations and backgrounds that include Islam, Hinduism, Buddhism, Christianity, and others. Race, religious orientation, and nationality are often combined in the dominant culture to depict monolithic templates of Muslims, Hindus, and Buddhists. Critical race scholars such as Eduardo Bonilla Silva have shown how the conversation about and expression of racism have evolved from verbal slurs and visual cues to outright hostility. For Muslim Ameri-cans, Evelyn Alsultany argues that "though Arab and Muslim 'looks' span the racial spectrum, a conflated Arab/Muslim 'look' has been defined by the American media—one that hate crimes during the Gulf War and after

FIGURE 6.1. Carol Danvers as Captain Marvel and Kamala Khan as Ms. Marvel. © Marvel Comics.

9-11 demonstrate is often confused with Indians, Pakistanis, and Iranians" (143). This "look" is not only about skin tone but can be extended to cultural accents such as food and clothing such as the hijab and the burkini. In *Ms. Marvel*, Kamala Khan struggles with the idea of how to "look" as a hero with her ruminations over her costume design. Her costume becomes a way to show her cultural heritage. She discards the form-fitting bodysuit associated with the previous Ms. Marvel and instead heads to her own closet to fashion a costume that is a combination of a South Asian–inspired salwar kameez tunic with tights and a Muslim burkini. In her redesign, she considers the form, function, and practicality of a costume, including the lack of underwear in the original Ms. Marvel suit and the development of a uniform that will weather physical disasters. Her final outfit combines fashion and pragmatism and results in a costume that can bear the wear and tear of an active young woman who must run and save the day (see fig. 6.1).

As a South Asian American teen superhero, the character of Kamala Khan has been embraced by the South Asian diasporic community. In her discussion of the *Ms. Marvel* fan community, Winona Landis points out that Kamala Khan was "taken up" by a cross-section of South Asians, including Indian Americans, even though the character is Pakistani Muslim American.

The cosmopolitan appeal of the comic book character provides an alternative representation of Western understandings of spirituality and identity—a narrative that traverses racial, ethnic, national, and religious borders and opens dialogues among diverse audiences. Kamala Khan simultaneously embodies a Pakistani Muslim American heroine, a South Asian/American representation, an Asian American literary presence in graphic novels, and a concrete link to the superhero mythology of American culture. Scholars Sika Dagbovie-Mullins and Eric Berlatsky argue Kamala Khan's racial identity is akin to a "super"-multi-raciality or an "exceptional" mulatta narrative because she occupies so many different roles. But instead of a super-multi-raciality, I would argue Kamala Khan dis-aggregates or breaks apart the category of South/Asian/American and allows for narratives of brownness to cross racial (black/brown/white/human/inhuman) and religious and cultural categories. Kamala Khan expands the idea of what brown and/or South Asian American brownness looks like in popular culture.

The intersectionality of identities makes her appealing to a wide audience. However, as Miriam Kent asserts, emphasizing the "relatability" of her character to a mainstream audience often comes at the expense of discussing the complex and novel depiction of Kamala's everyday experience with slurs and slights about her race, religion, and nationality (524). Entitled *No Normal*, the first volume of collected issues #1–5 asserts that Kamala Khan defies the idea of a proscribed normal for her as a racial and gendered subject by popular culture and begins to reset the conventions of the Asian American and teenage coming-of-age story and the superhero genre of comics (Wilson and Alphona).

Kamala Khan's superpower is the ability to shapeshift. In her first attempts to wield her power, she tries on different body shapes and sizes as she defines her power and her role as a hero. This includes a racial transformation from a brown sixteen-year-old into the earlier manifestation of Ms. Marvel, a white, blond, and buxom Carol Danvers. Kamala believes this type of representation and embodiment will make her feel heroic until she ends up interrogating her ideal of white femininity and power when she asks herself, "So why don't I feel strong, beautiful, and confident?"[1] As Monica Chiu points out, the globality of Asian and Asian American subjects questions a US-produced "look" of race, those fantasies dictating what representations qualify as Asian American (3). Kamala Khan can literally change her look and manifest the expectations of what she thinks she is supposed to look

---

1. Unless otherwise noted, all quotes are from Wilson and Alphona.

like; what she perceives as "normal" is not what gives her strength and confidence. As she faces a popular, young, white, blond woman, Zoe, from her school she realizes that Zoe makes her feel "like I have to be someone else. Someone cool. But instead, I feel small." Despite these feelings, Zoe is the first person she rescues as Ms. Marvel. She transcends the idea of how she has defined "normal" and remembers her dad's interpretation of how the Quran can be a guide for action: "There are always people who rush in to help. And according to my dad, they are **Blessed**." In this section, Kamala draws on her faith of what her father has passed down to her. The legacy she derives is familial and spiritual knowledge that she brings to bear on her actions even as she appears as the Carol Danvers version of Ms. Marvel. Her internal thoughts and her external actions bring to the forefront her experiences and feelings as a child of immigrants in a white-majority world. The strength she gains from the same immigrant family in terms of values and religion gives her the impetus to save someone "even though she [Zoe] makes everybody feel like **crap**." Her purpose expands the idea of action and responsibility beyond the celebrity and costume and allows her to question what her family, friends, faith, and even comic book fans perceive as "normal" for the superhero genre. Chiu asserts that we can challenge the foundational norms of reading comics through caricature and symbology by "questioning if comics' typing of race presents a universal face (McCloud), provides an intellectual understanding of ethnic caricature's representation of 'an insidious cultural fiction' (Wonham), or offers an 'empathic response' (Knight)" (Chiu 9). Kamala Khan is a vehicle that allows for the questioning of norms and the expectations of how strength and heroism can be reimagined for a teenage girl.

Creator Sana Amanat is a Pakistani American woman and child of immigrants from Pakistan, and writer G. Willow Wilson is a white American female Muslim, and their perspectives shape Kamala Khan as an alternative vision of a superhero—a brown teenager from Jersey City from a loving immigrant family, and a practicing Muslim woman who can express her doubts, insecurities, and concerns to her friends, family, and elders. As a hero, she acts out of a conscious and spiritual conviction to help those in need in the community and the neighborhood around her. In figure 6.1, she is contrasted with her previous incarnation. Kamala Khan's Ms. Marvel is the local hero on the ground, who does not fly through the sky like the current Captain Marvel but is on-site on a trash heap, ready to do the dirty and unheralded work that includes addressing racial, gendered, and religious slurs and inequities. Unlike other superheroes, she is not an experiment (Captain America) or a baby male orphan of a destroyed world (Superman) or wracked by guilt (Spider-Man).[2] Her origin and journey as a super-hero are more directly related to the roots of Peter Parker, who starts as the friendly neighborhood Spider-Man and whose world expands as he grows up. Kamala Khan's role as a leader and a hero becomes more global and universal as she interacts with more characters from the Marvel Cinematic Universe. But in the opening volume, she already has a full local life that is inspired by her friends and family, her faith, and her celebrity obsession with the Avengers superhero group.

Superhero South Asian and Muslim Characters in Comics

Kamala Khan is not the first Muslim superhero to be featured in the Marvel or DC universe. Night Runner is a French Algerian Muslim black man who is part of *Batman Incorporated,* and *The 99* (a 2006 independent comic with a team that featured heroes wearing burkas) was one of the first depictions in the twenty-first century (see Hine and Higgins; Al-Mutawa). Sooraya Qadir, a mutant also known as Dust, is a Sunni Muslim woman in Afghanistan who appeared in Marvel's X-Men in 2002. Marvel has also reimagined Captain Britain in the form of Farza Hussein, a Pakistani Muslim female physician. Kamala Khan is the first Pakistani American woman to receive extended attention as an American hero.

The history of the American superhero genre is rooted in American national identity. The early superheroes such as the vigilante crime fighter Batman and Superman came out of the 1930s Depression-era politics. Super-man represents an immigrant story of assimilation under an unassuming and white American identity: Clark Kent from Smallville, Kansas, emerges as Superman—the orphan refugee from Krypton whose superpowers uphold the American way of life. Superman was created by Jewish Ameri-can writer Jerry Siegal and artist Joe Shuster, and many scholars have dis-cussed the Jewish American roots of Superman. Two other iconic heroes, Wonder Woman, a figure rooted in the world of Greek mythology and an

---

2. Spider-Man (premiered in 1962) was created as a teenage everyman—a charac-ter that had everyday problems. Kamala Khan is not becoming a hero out of tragic cir-cumstances, but her character is akin to Peter Parker. He has tragedy that forces him to use his newfound powers responsibly, but her motivation is her father's translation and application of his philosophy—her responsibility is motivated by her faith. Spider-Man is a maverick, but one who ultimately does the right thing, and so is Ms. Marvel. And yet, she acts as an individual and does not upset the system, which is a limitation of try-ing to initiate social change. For more on the legacy of Spider-Man, see Davé.

immigrant to the United States, and the supersoldier Captain America are born out of American patriotic narratives related to World War II.

The collaboration of editor Sana Amanat, who expressed her desire to create "a character that she could identify with," and writer G. Willow Wilson to create stories that express the trials and tribulations of a sixteen-year-old has been immensely popular. As an editor at Marvel Entertainment, Sana Amanat reconceived some iconic Marvel characters. In *Ultimate Comics: Spider-Man*, she was instrumental in supporting the reinterpretation of Spider-Man. Miles Morales was the first African American and Latino Spider-Man, and in the revamp of Captain Marvel, Carol Danvers took on the role of the previously male superhero. Her desire to create a positive media image of Pakistani Americans and Muslims arose from her experiences after 9/11 where she went from identifying with American images that did not look like her in the media to suddenly "seeing her culture and faith in the media identified with terrorism and violence" (Amanat). The Ms. Marvel comic works to challenge this image to the extent that when Kamala Khan first uses physical violence to stop a teenager, it is she, the hero, who ends up getting shot. Amanat and Wilson create an action hero who is reflective and self-aware of the people around her and thinks before she acts. Although Kamala Khan lives in a world where she deals with the consequences of an adverse monolithic depiction of Muslim Americans, she does not act out of rage or revenge, but she does feel alienated and isolated. Rachel Lee points out that the strength of Asian American critical studies is the ability to "personify alienated labor power or to endow technologies of living matter with personhood" (20). As a textual and graphic form, superhero comics project, reflect, and illustrate the genre crossings of science, fantasy, social and economic hierarchies, and the expression of power in multiple forms. More significantly, superhero comics have been grappling with the ideas of aliens, environmental and radioactive contamination, mutations, sexuality, power and racial exploitation, and global and counterculture movements since their inception.

One of the most recognizable and oldest superheroes, Superman, is an emblematic symbol of "truth, justice, and the American way" and an immigrant, but in the Marvel Cinematic Universe, he has been supplanted by superheroes that operate outside oversight or authority or the control of any government. In fact, many of the heroes actively resist government authority or are alienated by or persecuted by the government. Most characters are genetic mutants who don't fit into society's definitions of racial and gendered physical norms. The success of the Marvel comics franchise and the corresponding film lineup starring the *Avengers* (and its many spin-offs) feature humans, aliens, and mutants, including humans that are part of a selective breeding program of the Kree (alien) and human DNA. When individuals of this selected genetic makeup are exposed to an entity known as terragenic gas, they evolve into a new species—Inhumans, also known as Inhuminus Superior. What all these characters, enhanced humans, mutants, and Inhumans have in common is that their members are persecuted by the military, media, or society at large. In addition, they are often outsiders to the existing system who speak and fight for the defense of the basic rights of freedom and democracy. At the same time, as individuals, they wish to belong to and be accepted by a supportive community where they are seen as "normal," but they learn to embrace "no normal." Kamala Khan receives her powers though exposure to a terragenic mist that alters her DNA, making her a genetic mutant and giving her the ability to shapeshift.

Her conversion from human to Inhuman forces her to confront her existing sense of identity and community that range from her Pakistani Muslim family, her Jersey City hometown, and her role as a millennial to her new powers in the expanding universe she occupies as an Inhuman. In her case, the racialized female body transcends her role of bystander or sidekick. Her "look" is a combination of iconic American mythology with South Asian child of immigrants and Muslim spiritual and religious narratives. The sentiment of "no normal" is the negation of the status quo, and yet as a young teenager, Kamala yearns to belong to a world that will embrace her differences. The visual and structural narrative of comics allows her and the writers to open literal gateways to new ways of envisioning this conflict, but ultimately the narrative of the superhero story is to preserve the existing structures.

In the 1960s, as comics scholar Ramzi Fawaz points out, writers created new female characters such as Orono Munroe, a black woman raised in Cairo, Egypt, and Harlem, New York, who is recruited by Professor X in *The Uncanny X-Men*. As Storm, Orono controls the natural elements of the weather and is one of the most powerful X-Men, becoming one of the key leaders of the team. While Kamala Khan is a new character, the superhero identity she dons is linked to an older story, so rather than creating a new character and backstory, writers have replaced the white, blond woman with a brown, Muslim teenager. In one sense, she is constrained by old narrative, so much so that initially, Kamala Khan transforms into the older 1970s version of Ms. Marvel when she uses her powers, but as her shape-shifting settles (and she becomes more secure in her own abilities and purpose), she represents herself (not Carol Danvers and not her mother or any other avatar). The history that she steps into and the figures from whom she draws her inspiration are a biological and spiritual assembly of popular culture icons and her personal history.

Kamala Khan and Transforming the Origin Story

Kamala's encounter with the terragenic mist and her transformation into a superpowered being illustrate the different histories and genealogies that drive her. Kamala Khan is introduced as a shy and smart sixteen-year-old teenager who has a loving family and good friends. She yearns to expand her horizons and be included in the popular crowd in high school who go to parties and stay out late. Kamala is also an avid writer and consumer of Avengers fan fiction. She dreams of making a difference and having adventures with the Avengers Team, including Captain Marvel, Iron Man, Captain America, and the X-Men's Wolverine.

In comics studies, reading panels is about visually locating how time and space are mapped onto a narrative. Time is not only reflective of the past or future but combined with the narrative in Ms. Marvel; time also is about generational changes of genre and religious and racial norms. Kamala Khan is surrounded by a cast of family and community members who represent varying relationships to Islam, including her Turkish friend, Nakia, who wears a hijab; the patient Sheikh Abdullah at her local mosque; her religiously devout brother; her philosophical and loving secular father; and her strict but caring mother. Kamala engages in discussions with her community, and it is her questioning nature, which can be attributed to teenage questioning of authority and the presentation of her everyday reality as a brown girl growing up in the US, that makes her appealing to a wide audience. Her representation toes the line between accessibility, or what Miriam Kent points out as "relatability" (524), to a general audience unfamiliar with the intersectional relationships of race, gender, and religion, and a progressive representation of a young woman developing her own sense of self.

Kamala feels left out from the popular peer group because she feels her family traditions hold her back. She is not the victim of overt discrimination but bears the brunt of the slights and misinterpretations of what it means to be Muslim in the United States. In most cases, she presents herself as an apolitical Muslim who quotes her father's interpretations of Islamic scripture. She goes to the mosque and talks to her elders, but she is dissatisfied with their counsel as their answers do not fit her role as a young woman negotiating her identity. Being a Pakistani Muslim is a part of her everyday life, and it defines parts of her, but not all aspects, as she longs for a normality that disavows differences associated with culture (food, dress, family traditions) rather than nationality. The narrative focus on cultural difference draws attention to constraints of the superhero genre to challenge systemic hierarchies related to religious and racial discriminations. Kamala's definitions of difference are cultural rather than political, such as her inability to participate in health class, the different food she eats (pakoras), and the different holidays she celebrates.

The competing identities that drive Kamala Khan are revealed one night when New York (and New Jersey) is enveloped by a mysterious cloud of terragenic mist. She is visited in a hallucination (or divine visitation) by a manifestation of the former Ms. Marvel, who speaks in a hybrid form of Hindi and Urdu and is accompanied by Iron Man and Captain America, who provide English translations of the Sufi poem that describes flowering and vivid garden imagery related to change and rebirth with phrases such as "the yellow mustard is blooming in every field," and "mango buds click open." Kamala's vision is the imaginary manifestation of how her world and her worldview are going to change (see fig. 6.2).

In Kamala's moment of transformation to a being with superhuman powers, this full-page image from the comic shows how she encompasses multiple narratives or intersectional ties of identity. She is presented with these powers through a divine-like encounter. One way to think about Kamala's encounter is to draw from how Ramzi Fawaz frames the discussion of the history of mutant and racial representations of superheroes as "comic book cosmopolitics," which "describes the world-making practices of postwar superhero comic books" that privileges "cross cultural encounters" (16). Fawaz argues that the rise of group affiliations represents progressive change and challenges the economic, racial, gendered, and sexual institutional status quo. In applying Fawaz's notion of this vision as a progressive encounter, I argue that the visual illustration is less related to Islamic traditions but instead evokes a pantheon of gods reminiscent of the Hindu triumvirate or Christian trinity that includes Iron Man (a technologically enhanced human), the original Ms. Marvel (as the central goddess figure), and Captain America (a human supersoldier who was injected with an experimental drug). As a group, they are the foundational leaders of the Avengers. They are the celebrities in Kamala's world and figures that she reveres and listens to—teachers and individuals who inspire her to think beyond the borders of her everyday life. The reader is aligned with Kamala's perspective as the Avengers are situated above her, and the focus is on their act of dispensing wisdom and bestowing the roles and responsibility of being a hero to Kamala. The other figures in the image, such as the hybrid

FIGURE 6.2. Kamala's vision after exposure to terragenic mist. © Marvel Comics.

Hedge Hulk and the birds and stuffed animals, are different aspects associated with Kamala's everyday life, such as her clothing, her stuffed animals, and her imaginative sense of the world.

The progressive message that the text and images offer is an accessible form of Islam that is cultural, associated with the arts and poetry rather than a prescriptive form of worship. Although the poetry and text presented, "Sakal bul phoon rahi sarson," is derived from Islam in the thirteenth century, it is from a South Asian derivation rather than an Arab tradition. Most high literature was written/recited in Persian at this time, but this poem is spoken in "proto-Hindi/Urdu script with some words borrowed from Sanskrit" and is ascribed to the Sufi poet Amir Khusro (1253–1325) from South Asia.[3] Sufism is a mystic branch of Islam that emphasizes spirituality rather than institutionalized religion and has a different history and practice compared to Sunni and Shi'ite traditions located in the Middle East.

The poem reflects the urban or popular class of people, rather than the royal or scholarly class who pass on Islamic teachings. The book and the character, in this case, express alternative expressions of Islam (South Asian or Pakistani rather than Arab) for American audiences (see Resha, *The Embiggening* 25–26). On one hand, in an extratextual reading, it is entirely fitting that the poem (which is translated into English by Captain America and Iron Man) is a popular poem known to the masses that is presented in its contemporary counterpart of print comics. This visual also modifies the "look" of a hero's journey and combines the language of Kamala's heritage (Urdu) with the idols of her present. On the other hand, the poem evokes a coming-of-age story that is universal among teenage young women and operates to create a sense of empowerment and confidence for South Asian American women. The poem highlights the verdant images of flowers blooming and the maiden trying on new "adornments," just as Kamala is opening to new horizons and will be trying on not only her new powers but also the kind of adult she aspires to be.

The centrality of faith as the foundation of Kamala's powers and her moral compass in how she chooses to act is delivered in this scene from the comic. Kamala is stunned that Captain Marvel speaks Urdu but the figure replies, "We are **faith**. We speak all languages of beauty and hardship." Faith is rooted in the notion of confidence and trust, and while it can be applied to religion and spirituality, in this instance it is elevated beyond divine encoun-

---

3. I am indebted to Adrienne Resha for her research on the poetry in this image. Resha identifies the popular spread of Islamic works across Afghanistan, Pakistan, and India in courtly life as historical context for the representations of Muslims in graphic narratives in her master's thesis, *The Embiggening.*

ters and instead is centered solely on Kamala to instill belief in herself and purpose for her talents.

At first, she looks to others to find her confidence. When asked about her true desires, she says to Ms. Marvel, "I wish I were you," and like the person who has asked the genie or djinn, her wish is granted. She literally turns into a blond, buxom Ms. Marvel. She realizes that looking like the Carol Danvers version of Ms. Marvel does not make her feel confident, and the rest of the narrative focuses on her developing faith in herself, learning how to use her powers, and exploring how to deal with her changing size—another way of thinking of how she fits into her world after her encounter. First, she's physically small, and then her hands and then feet enlarge (like Alice in *Alice in Wonderland*). She develops her own vocabulary with words such as "Embiggen" and "Dis-embiggen" to help her focus, manage her confidence and faith in herself, and direct her energy to manipulate her powers.

Kamala Khan's questioning of authority and restrictions gently critiques Islamophobia by introducing different cultural practices and conversations around food, clothing choices such as her cousin's headscarf, and visits to the mosque. While the first five issues establish Kamala's family and her friend, Nakia, who wears a hijab (or head scarf), as the series continues, Kamala's everyday life fades as her community enlarges beyond her family, mosque, and school life to her development as a hero, by encountering first another mutant (Wolverine) and then a community of individuals who have also been transformed by terragenic mist into a community known as Inhumans.

As a teenager, the challenges and adjustments Kamala Khan faces in her everyday life and in her emerging superhero life are nonthreatening to the status quo of the social and political foreign policy of US and global histories. Kamala's first act as Ms. Marvel is to save the life of her blond teenage adversary in high school who is intoxicated after attending a party. Kamala as Ms. Marvel saves her (Zoe) from drowning when she falls off a pier. In her next attempt at heroism, she tries to stop a robbery at the convenience store where her friend Bruno is working. As Ms. Marvel, she acts as a superhero by working to save teens in her neighborhood and Jersey City from the threat of drugs, homelessness, and exploitation.

While it could be argued that Marvel has produced another wisecracking teenage superhero in the mold of Spider-Man who happens to be brown and Muslim, it can also be said that under the care of Sana Amanat and G. Willow Wilson, what works with the character and the series is an honest awareness of how her motivations are influenced by her experiences as a Muslim American woman who has faced discrimination and ethnic slurs, and who also has a loving family and community. Specifically, what is successful and heartening about the book is that the writer and artists surround Kamala Khan with a cast of family and friends and characters that showcase her successes and her frustrations in the everyday world. This world includes the trials of gym class, the temptation of eating bacon or sneaking out to a party, going to the mosque, listening to and discussing the teachings of the Quran, and rebelling against her parents' authority. She is the representative of and for a twenty-first-century generation of comic and superhero and Asian American consumers.

While the visual and narrative structure of the superhero genre has certain limitations as the representation of Kamala Khan as a progressive challenge to the status quo, it is the application of Kamala Khan's image outside of the comics universe that showcases the versatility of a comics character to go beyond the story in print and be used as a rallying cry for change in the everyday world. In San Francisco, her image was painted on buses as a call to resist Islamophobia. The popularity of her character outside the pages of comics as a rallying figure to protest the Muslim ban political rhetoric and decry Islamophobia is another shade of brown that transcends the Marvel creators and superhero narrative constraints. In effect, Kamala Khan as Ms. Marvel has shape-shifted or morphed into a South Asian American and Muslim American icon that fights racial and religious intolerance. The trajectory and emergence of Kamala Khan as a Muslim American child of immigrants and a South Asian American reframe the "look" of the superhero genre and reflect generational changes in comics readers and the nature of reading comics in a visual media–saturated world. The result of Kamala Khan's success (visual recognition and Web popularity) as Ms. Marvel is a widening platform for Asian American and South Asian/American stories, and the character inspires and creates new mediums of expression for social change.

Works Cited

Al-Mutawa, Naif. *The 99 (Ninety-Nine)*. Teshkeel Comics, 2007–14.

Alsultany, Evelyn. "Representations of Arabs and Muslims in Post 9–11 Television Dramas." *The Colorblind Screen: Television in Post-Racial America*, edited by Sarah Nilsen and Sarah E. Turner, New York University Press, 2014, pp. 140–66.

Amanat, Sana. "The Importance of Diversity in the Comic Book Universe." *TEDxTeen*, February 2014, https://www.ted.com/talks/sana_amanat_the_importance_of_diversity_in_the_comic_book_universe?utm_campaign=tedspread&utm_medium=referral&utm_source=tedcomshare.

Chiu, Monica. "Visual Realities of Race." *Drawing New Color Lines: Transnational Asian American Graphic Narratives*, edited by Chiu, Hong Kong University Press, 2014, pp. 1–23.

Dagbovie-Mullins, Sika, and Eric Berlatsky. "The Only Nerdy Pakistani-American-Slash-Inhuman in the Entire Universe: Post-Racialism and Politics in the New Ms. Marvel." *Ms. Marvel's America: No Normal*, edited by Jessica Baldanzi and Hussein Rashid, University of Mississippi Press, 2020, pp. 65–88.

Davé, Shilpa. "Spider-Man Indian and American Cultural Narratives." *Transnational Perspectives on Graphic Narratives: Comics at the Crossroads*, edited by Shane Denson et al., Bloomsbury Press, 2013, pp. 127–43.

Fawaz, Ramzi. *The New Mutants: Superheroes and the Radical Imagination of American Comics*. New York University Press, 2016.

Hine, David, and Kyle Higgins. *Detective Comics Annual #12*. DC Comics, 2011.

Kent, Miriam. "Unveiling Marvels: Ms. Marvel and the Reception of the New Muslim Superheroine." *Feminist Media Studies*, vol. 15, no. 3, 2015, pp. 522–27. *Taylor & Francis Online*, doi:10.1080/14680777.2015.1031964.

Landis, Winona Landis. "Diasporic (Dis)Identification: The Participatory Fandom of Ms. Marvel." *Journal of South Asian Popular Culture*, vol. 14, no. 1–2, 2016, pp. 33–47. *Taylor & Francis Online*, doi:10.1080/14746689.2016.1241344.

Lee, Rachel. *The Exquisite Corpse of Asian America: Biopolitics, Biosociality, and Posthuman Ecologies*. New York University Press, 2014.

Resha, Adrienne. "The Blue Age of Comic Books." *Inks: The Journal of the Comics Studies Society*, vol. 4, no. 1, 2020, pp. 66–81.

———. *The Embiggening: Marvel's Muslim Ms. Marvel and American Myth*. Master's thesis, University of Virginia, Department of Middle Eastern and South Asian Languages and Cultures, May 2016.

Wilson, G. Willow, writer, and Adrian Alphona, artist. *Ms. Marvel*, vol. 1, *No Normal*. Marvel Comics, 2014.

CHAPTER 7

(Un)Masking a Chinese American Superhero

Gene Luen Yang and Sonny Liew's *The Shadow Hero*

LAN DONG

The past few decades have seen an increased readership of comics, particularly book-length graphic narratives. Because of comics' accessibility
and intimacy, as well as its facilitation of heightened identification and the
integral role of the reader, comics has become an effective medium for promoting literacy and intellectual inquiry both in and outside of the classroom (McCloud 36, 68). In particular, comics studies scholar Derek Parker
Royal argues that comics "are well suited to dismantle . . . assumptions that
problematize ethnic representation, especially as they find form in visual
language. They achieve this by particularizing the general, thereby under-
mining any attempts at subjective erasure through universalization" (9).
Visual racial hyperbole (the "general") pervades the panels of Gene Luen
Yang and Sonny Liew's *The Shadow Hero* (2014), a graphic narrative that
challenges the vicious Chinese stereotypes in Golden Age comics while also
introducing a Chinese American superhero (the "particular"). The power
of comics as a deeply affective visual discourse, which can be both humor-

I am grateful for the feedback Monica Chiu, Stella Oh, Jeanette Roan, and Eleanor Ty
provided for an earlier draft of this essay.

ous and deadly serious,[1] is apparent in *The Shadow Hero*'s representation of the struggles of Chinese immigrants in the United States as well as in its imagination of an origin story for a Chinese American superhero. Reading Yang and Liew's graphic narrative through the lens of Asian American cultural history and racial politics in the United States, this chapter examines how *The Shadow Hero* rewrites the representation of Chinese Americans in superhero comics. It also addresses how, in reframing the images and imaginations of a Chinese American superhero, the book's fictional diegesis inextricably binds race and visual discourses in a stirring engagement with both immigration history and comics history.

Asian American scholar Monica Chiu has proposed that Yang and Liew's book "limns a history of Chinese Americans in comics" yet "falls short of challenging the racist hyperboles of racial representation"; she further questions the necessity for a Chinese American superhero (87, 102–3). This chapter argues that *The Shadow Hero* plays with Orientalist imagery but reframes the main character's Chinese American superhero identity within the family and community life of a fictional Chinatown in the 1940s, thus subverting racial typing of Chinese Americans in comics. Using historical caricatures of the Chinese in America prompts the reader to confront their discomfort with the hyperbolic imagery, an approach Yang has used in his previous works, such as *American Born Chinese* (2006). Drawing the main character's superhero persona as a process of masking, remasking, and unmasking as well as blurring the lines between his roles (as a Chinese American man and a superhero) challenges the convention of American comics superheroes living two lives separated by a particular set of costume.

Asian American artists and writers have long been practitioners in producing both mainstream comics and graphic narratives. Larry Hama and Jim Lee, for example, are well-known names in the American comics industry. Yang, author of perhaps the best-known Asian American graphic

---

1. The visual language of comics is a heavily coded medium; it relies on stereotypes to achieve narrative effectiveness (Royal 7). The power of comics to create high-stakes images is apparent in some of the twenty-first-century controversies. For example, in 2005, the Danish newspaper *Jyllands-Posten* printed cartoon depictions of Prophet Mohammad that resulted in violent protests in the Middle East as protestors objected to any visual depiction of Mohammad, especially those many deemed offensive. When a racist and sexist comic strip appeared in a 2008 issue of the *Dartmouth*, the student-run newspaper at Dartmouth College and America's oldest college newspaper, bloggers immediately expressed concerns and objections, the editor apologized for allowing it to run, and online images of the comic were removed from the Web ("Racist Comic Strip"). The terrorist attacks on French satirical magazine *Charlie Hebdo* in 2015 over its controversial portrayals of Prophet Muhammad led to further discussion of the impact of comics' visual discourses on the global scale.

narrative *American Born Chinese,* along with Adrian Tomine, Lynda Barry, Mariko Tamaki, Jillian Tamaki, GB Tran, Thi Bui, and many other writers and artists have published widely reviewed and critically acclaimed works in recent years, calling the reader's attention to nuanced portrayals of Asian and Asian American characters, themes, and settings. Asian American representation in mainstream comics, whether on the production side or within individual texts, has begun to receive more attention among artists as well as scholars. It also has been the topic of museum exhibitions and comics anthologies. For instance, "Marvels and Monsters: Unmasking Asian Images in US Comics, 1942–1986" (2011), an exhibition curated by Jeff Yang and D. Daniel Kim and produced by the Asian/Pacific/American Institute at New York University, shows the history of the representation of Asians in US mainstream comics from World War II to the mid-1980s. The display includes panels and cover images from selected comics, organized according to recurring stereotypes, alongside commentary by contemporary comics artists such as Hama and Yang. This exhibition later was featured at the Museum of Chinese in America in New York City (from September 27, 2012, to February 24, 2013) with an added accompanying exhibition, titled "Alt. comics: Asian American Artists Reinvent the Comic," curated by Jeff Yang and presenting the work of contemporary Asian American comics artists. Two anthologies, *Secret Identities: The Asian American Superhero Anthology* (2009) and *Shattered: The Asian American Comics Anthology* (2012), compiled by Jeff Yang, Parry Shen, Keith Chow, and Jerry Ma, offer an Asian American take on the superhero genre, as well as an argument that comics can be used in the expression of Asian American history and culture. These examples demonstrate what Royal has argued—comics "should be read not only as aesthetic works of narrative art, but as rich cultural documents that can truly become vehicles of American ethnoracial expression" (16–17). In this context, Yang and Liew's *The Shadow Hero* adds to the increasing creative efforts in visualizing complex characters and nuanced experiences of Asian Americans and challenging racial profiling in American comics in general and in superhero comics in particular.

Yang and Liew's graphic narrative reimagines familiar historical and cultural narratives of Asians in America by providing an origin story for the title character of Chu F. Hing's series about a superhero known as the Green Turtle.[2] Created in 1944 for Rural Home's *Blazing Comics,* Chu's short-lived wartime series grew out of the boom of the American superhero industry beginning in the late 1930s with characters such as the Flash, Hawkman,

---

2. Chu is the artist's family name, Hing his given name (Yang, "A Mistake").

Doctor Fate, the Spectre, Green Lantern, and Wonder Woman (Austin and Hamilton 20). Set in China during World War II, Chu's episodes unfold around the title character assisting Chinese guerrillas and defending China against invading Japanese troops. While the story's political underpinning is obvious and its friends-versus-foes plot echoes the shifting alliance and general wartime sentiment among Americans toward China and Japan, the Green Turtle's race is ambiguous. He wears a green cape emblazoned with a turtle insignia. His skin appears to be a pinkish color, visually differentiating him from the Chinese and Japanese characters in the narrative; his face is not only masked but also facing away or otherwise obscured from the reader. He remains costumed and masked throughout the entire series. Chu's version, which lasts merely five issues before its discontinuation, never reveals the Green Turtle's origin; neither does it explain the connection between the Green Turtle and the dark anthropomorphist turtle shadow hovering over him. It has been rumored that Chu imagined the Green Turtle as a Chinese character but was discouraged by his publisher from revealing the hero's racial identity (Yang and Liew 155). Considering that racially profiling people of color and normalizing white superiority dominated the superhero comics industry in the 1940s, the Green Turtle's "obscured racial identity reveals a continued lack of racial progress in wartime America, even as the apparent struggle over his identity leaves room for problematic attitudes to appear contested" (Austin and Hamilton 42).

A gesture toward further "racial progress," Yang and Liew's visual and textual reconstruction of the Green Turtle's identity grounds itself in a history of Chinese in America, thus a history of discrimination and typing, both humorous and serious. There is humor, for example, in the exaggerated representation of a tong's secret headquarters in *The Shadow Hero*, a gaudy bar and casino located on an island evocatively named "Coolie Hat Rock." The name of the casino, "Palace of Forbidden Fortunes," is written in Chopstix font across the front of the structure (Yang and Liew 94). The location of the casino, its name, its visual representation, and its dissembling leader render the stereotyping hyperbolic, at which point the reader laughs at the typing, an approach that works toward dismantling it.[3] The first splash image of the casino takes up nearly the entire page (Yang and Liew 94) and shows with forceful clarity the use of architectural signifiers of the exotic Orient in a building that caters to the expectations of its white patrons, who delight in

---

3. Yang has adopted a similar approach in *American Born Chinese*, in which he uses humor to poke the reader's discomfort associated with racial stereotypes through the exaggerated and deliberate name, appearance, and actions of the character cousin Chin-Kee and the sitcom-like panel borders that frame his images (Dong 238–39).

being called "foreign devils" (Yang and Liew 102). The image of the menacing Asian villain, Emperor Ten Grand, ensconced in his spectacular secret
lair, is made evident through a combination of architectural signifiers, costume, makeup, and acting. Together they fulfill popular conceptions of a
racialized identity derived from racist popular culture.

Humor in *The Shadow Hero* thus trades on readers' recognition of exag-
gerations about how to be and look Chinese.[4] When Emperor Ten Grand—
dressed in vaguely Chinese finery, with long nails and a thin, drooping
mustache—first appears, the Green Turtle mutters, "You've *got* to be kid-
ding me" (Yang and Liew 102). As Emperor Ten Grand is unmasked as a
lowly Caucasian impresario in yellowface, a white detective wonders, "The
Chinese can't find a Chinese to play Fu Manchu?"; the ersatz Emperor Ten
Grand proudly explains how he has "out-chinked the chinks" (Yang and
Liew 117). Readers familiar with Asian American texts or media representations recognize that one of the visual, racial marks of Asian Americans is
their skin color, which has othered them historically. Unmasking a yellow-
faced "Chinese" emperor who enjoys and profits from acting Chinese exemplifies Robert G. Lee's argument that "yellowface marks the Asian body as
unmistakably Oriental; it sharply defines the Oriental in a racial opposition
to whiteness" (2). In *The Shadow Hero*, in which the yellow villain is white
and the ostensibly white superhero is really yellow, masking and unmasking play a vital role in challenging and revisualizing historical images in the
contemporary moment and through popular culture. A critical engagement
with *The Shadow Hero*, in juxtaposition to its inspiration the Green Turtle
series, helps reveal how comics writers and artists subvert cultural imperialism and strive to reclaim cultural legacies. In addition, it highlights the
strategies they adopt to respond to the racial stereotypes in mainstream
American media that not only orientalize immigrants from Asia and render
them as others historically, but also shape current social perceptions of Asian
Americans in significant ways.

There are probably no better examples of the under- and misrepresenta-
tion of Asian American characters in American comics than their depictions
in superhero comics. After all, the superhero genre has a "long history of

---

4. Several reviewers have noted humor as a prominent element in *The Shadow
Hero*. For instance, Sarah Hunter remarks that in Yang and Liew's "lively, entertaining
adventure story," humor capitalizes on "the dashing bravado of golden-age comics"
(63). Elizabeth Andersen praises the artists' balanced visualization of humor, history,
and dramatic moments while tackling such themes of alienation, integrity, heritage, and
justice (65). The reviewer for *Publishers Weekly* highlights humor as one of the important
themes among racism, romance, and identity ("*The Shadow Hero*" 112).

excluding, trivializing, or 'tokening' minorities" (Singer 107). Compared to the widely known stereotypical comic images and political cartoons produced during the exclusion era and the Asian villains and sidekicks in superhero comics during the Golden Age of comics, those featuring Asian immigrants and Asian Americans as heroes seemed few and far between until they appeared in noticeable numbers in the two aforementioned anthologies spearheaded by Asian American comics artists and writers. This history is what makes Chu's Green Turtle character particularly significant. Despite its short-lived appearance, the Green Turtle was arguably the first Asian American superhero, amplified by his revisualization in Asian American comics and graphic narratives,[5] particularly *The Shadow Hero*.

The Shadow Hero connects the Green Turtle and the anthropomorphist shadow with the main character Hank's Chinese heritage literally and metaphorically through the visualization of the tortoise spirit residing in Hank's shadow. The narrative begins in 1911, when China plunged into chaos. The anthropomorphic tortoise, one of the four guardian spirits watching over the country, boards a ship bound for America in the shadow of Hank's father, a drunk and aimless young man at the time. While Hank (who was born and raised in Chinatown) aspires to be a grocer like his father, his mother is determined that he become a superhero—as if one merely decides such matters—after she is rescued by the Anchor of Justice (an epitome of American superheroes) during a robbery. After his father's murder by gangsters of a tong, the tortoise takes up residence in Hank's shadow, and Hank embarks on a journey resulting in his circuitous evolution into the Green Turtle, a costumed superhero in yellow skin who has the superpower of dodging bullets. The term "shadow hero" connects Hank's character to the spirit tortoise and to his father's shadowed past while at the same time alluding to Chu's Green Turtle, whose identity remains shadowed and ambiguous.

As comics studies scholar Hannah Miodrag reminds us, "given the staggering multi-disciplinarity of comics studies, it is vital that critics are responsive to relevant scholarly contexts if they are to engage in genuinely new thinking" (6–7). Thus, it is important for readers to examine the newly imagined origin story of the Green Turtle juxtaposed against its deliberate absence in *Blazing Comics* while also situating it within the superhero comics genre in order to reveal how *The Shadow Hero* provides an alternative visual imagination to the historical yellow peril rhetoric and images that reflect "the perception of many Americans towards their imagined exotic,

---

5. On August 4, 2014, the *Angry Asian Man* blog presented comics illustrations by twenty-seven artists to celebrate the release of *The Shadow Hero*. Each artist offers his or her own unique visualization of the Green Turtle ("27 Artists").

despotic, fascinating, and dangerous 'Orient'" (Asian/Pacific/American Institute 1). Even though images of the Chinese were turning away from those falling under the rubric of the yellow peril to those representing them as American allies and victims of Japanese military expansion during World War II, an explicit claim of a Chinese American superhero in the 1940s still grates against general perceptions of Chinese immigrants and the common practice of allowing predominantly white men to be costumed superheroes, who save the day in war and peace, in a medium that depends heavily on readership and sales.[6]

Comics studies scholar Richard Reynolds points out in his study of superheroes as a modern mythology that some key features of the superhero genre include the following: the superhero's separation from his parents, lineage from a deity to render him a man-god, devotion to justice, superpower(s) and invulnerability, actions in tandem with the politics of the day (fighting Nazis in the 1940s, for example), his secret identity, and his combination of science and magic (12–16). In particular, the costume plays a significant role in shaping the superhero; it not only visually distinguishes a superhero from other characters and the ordinary world but also functions as a narrative device and suggests the superhero's mode of operation (Reynolds 26). *The Shadow Hero* follows such a tradition in portraying a Chinese American superhero in costume; yet, in masking, remasking, and unmasking the Green Turtle, Yang and Liew's graphic narrative challenges the system of *langue* (the structure of costume conventions and the rules that dictate what the character wears) and *parole* (individual costumes as "specific utterance" within the structure) (Reynolds 26). The construction and reconstruction of Hank's costume parallels the formation of the shadow hero. Similar to most superheroes in American comics, the Green Turtle is inseparable from his costume, which functions as more than a disguise to hide his identity (Reynolds 29). Rather, the evolution of his wardrobe reflects the process of his superhero identity formation: from Hank (a Chinese American young man growing up in Chinatown and feeling a strong sense of belonging in his family's store and community), to Golden Man of Bravery (a repeated and failed attempt by his mother to make a superhero out of him), to Jade Tortoise (who seeks revenge for his father's murder), and finally to the Green

---

6. The publication of *Action Comics* 1 in June 1938 not only indicated the birth of Superman but also launched the long-lasting existence of the costumed superhero in American comics. While a sizeable number of characters were created during the Golden Age of comics from the 1930s to the 1940s, the bulk of the superhero comics folded rather quickly due to falling readerships, with a few exceptions such as Batman, Spider-Man, and Wonder Woman, among others (Reynolds 8).

Turtle (who joins forces with other superheroes to uphold justice and the law as well as to serve his country in the looming war).

Taking advantage of what Marianne Hirsch describes as the visuality and materiality of words and the discursivity and narrativity of images, *The Shadow Hero* uses Hank's costume to visually and metaphorically represent his superhero persona (or lack thereof) early in the story. In her 2004 editor's column for *PMLA*, Hirsch writes: "Asking us to read back and forth between images and words, comics reveal the visuality and thus the materiality of words and the discursivity and narrativity of images. . . . Comics highlight both the individual frames and the space between them, calling attention to the compulsion to transcend the frame in the act of seeing" (1213). Hank's mother Hua designs his original costume: a light-green full-body suit with a dark green cape, conforming to the American superhero tradition and thus implying her effort at making him "one of them." On his debut as his mother's so-named "Golden Man of Bravery," the reader cannot help but notice the disjunction between Hank and his superhero persona, symbolized by a separation between the superhero and his mask. Unlike most superheroes in American comics, it is his mother Hua who wears the green mask that is an essential part of Hank's costume.[7] In the panel, a masked Hua dominates the foreground while an unmasked Hank trails behind, blending into the background (Yang and Liew 38). The interior door, shelves, and counters of their family grocery store frame Hank within the space, which is where he believes he belongs. In this scene, the frame-within-frame structure of the panel achieves "a successful cross-breeding of illustration and prose" (Eisner 2). The only word bubble, uttered by Hua, covers the doorplate positioned above Hank. The reader has already been informed on previous pages that the doorplate features the Chinese characters for "turtle." In spite of the mask, Hua's enthusiasm, as expressed through her facial features and her words—"Hurry! I've got the car right outside!"—presents a sharp contrast to Hank's uncertainty and lack of excitement visible through his body language. This moment reminds the reader that it is Hua who conceived Hank's superhero persona and imposed it on him. It also foreshadows the upcoming failure of his first attempt to fight for justice. A costumed Hank without a mask appears repeatedly in the book, blending the charac-

---

7. Some readers will note that Hua as the masked driver provides another intertextual reference to superheroes and Asians in American popular culture. For example, Bruce Lee's character Kato, as a sidekick, drives the title character around in *The Green Hornet*. Yang and Liew have published another comic retelling the story of an Asian American sidekick and subverting the norm of the white hero and his Asian aid in the aforementioned collection *Secret Identities*: "The Blue Scorpion and Chung."

ter's dual personas and setting him apart from the superhero convention in American comics.

Chinatown, visually represented in the interior space of Hank's family store (Yang and Liew 38) as well as the exterior streets and buildings (Yang and Liew 87), highlights the connection between comics and racial registers. After his father's murder, the tortoise spirit switches residence to Hank's shadow, an inheritance from his father literally and metaphorically. Initially driven by revenge, Hank decides to become a superhero on his own terms and reconstructs his costume, substituting the Chinese character for gold featured on his original costume for a green turtle insignia and fashioning a mask. The altered costume marks his rebirth "as a superhero" (Yang and Liew 87). The full-page panel shown below situates Hank against the backdrop of Chinatown on a rainy night, facing away from the reader (see fig. 7.1). Such a posture highlights the cape's green turtle insignia, which occupies the focal point in the panel. The character is positioned between the signs, stores, and buildings in Chinatown. Even though Hank's figure is no longer within the confines of the family store selling Chinese goods, Chinatown buildings frame his character on this page. The visual entity of the page is interrupted by an insert (a panel contained within a larger panel), in which a thought bubble announces: "Just my luck" (Yang and Liew 87), referencing the result of his mother's many scientific experiments in her effort to mold him into a superhero. His skin turns pink when it gets wet. The mother's accidental "pinkification" of Hank is of particular significance when read alongside the yellow-faced Emperor Ten Grand and the predominantly white superheroes in American comics. This "scientific" modification of Hank's appearance visually highlights his skin color. Hank's masking and changing skin tone visually erase one physical feature of his Asianness. Thus, the pink skin becomes part of his costume—a fabrication—that allows him to disguise his race, albeit temporarily. Two pages later, he identifies himself as the Jade Tortoise, the name of their family grocery store, connecting his newly formed persona with his previous aspiration—to become a grocer in Chinatown just like his father, who "would wake up every morning knowing exactly where [he] belonged" (Yang and Liew 10). The disjunction between the visual erasure of Hank's Asianness and the self-identification with his Asianness foreshadows the concluding page of the book, where he appears as a yellow-skinned superhero.

If Hank's rebirth as the Jade Tortoise—masked, pink-skinned, and with his back facing the reader—pays tribute to historical images from *Blazing Comics*, his metamorphosis into the Green Turtle is marked by his face, at first masked and then unmasked, in full display at the Palace of Forbidden

FIGURE 7.1. Hank/the Green Turtle in Gene Luen Yang and Sonny Liew's *The Shadow Hero* (87). © MacMillan.

Fortunes, the underground tong's headquarters. The Green Turtle first appears not only masked, but also wet and therefore pink-skinned, suggesting a separation between Hank and his self-made superhero persona. Peter Coogan considers mission, powers, and identity to be the core of the superhero comic genre (39). He further contends:

> A heroic character with a selfless, pro-social mission; with superpowers—extraordinary abilities, advanced technology, or highly developed physical, mental, or mystical skills; who has a superhero identity embodied in a codename and iconic costume, which typically express his biography, character, powers, or origin (transformation from ordinary person to superhero); and who is genetically distinct, i.e., can be distinguished from characters of related genres (fantasy, science fiction, detective, etc.) by a preponderance of generic conventions. Often superheroes have dual identities, the ordinary one of which is usually a closely guarded secret. (Coogan 30)

If typical American superheroes are distinguished by their (white) skin and flamboyant costumes, Hank fits this cultural trope only so far. Different from Golden Age superheroes whose characters tend to romanticize "human collaboration with technological advancement in the promotion of American liberal and democratic belief" (Fawaz 6–7), the Green Turtle ultimately resorts to his ethnic and cultural heritage for his extraordinary power. As the story unfolds, the unmasking of the superhero in confrontation with the gangsters symbolically brings together Hank's split identities and consolidates his Chinese heritage with his American superhero persona by visually portraying Hank with yellow skin and robed in his Green Turtle costume, his face in display. The appearance of the Green Turtle's "unmistakably Asian face, masked in the original comic, bears witness to the American comic industry's progress from a time when Asianness could only be rendered pejoratively or surreptitiously hinted at to a moment in which visibly Asian American superheroes are no longer novelties" (Cheang 82). The hero's unmasking is particularly meaningful when read together with the conclusion's revelation of the being behind the archetypical American superhero in the book, the Anchor of Justice.

The last sequence in *The Shadow Hero* reveals the Anchor of Justice's identity through a "productive interaction," in which text and image "contextualize each other, to the extent that each actually alters the way we interpret the other" (Miodrag 85). While the Anchor of Justice's words—"my parents aren't from around here, either" (Yang and Liew 152)—are suggestive yet vague, a visual presentation of his unmasking reveals his likely alien origin beneath his human mask (fig. 7.2). The revelation is portrayed against the backdrop of the sky, punctuating his superpower to fly. Such a setting evokes the common recognition among readers of the connection between aliens and other planets. It also alludes to Asians as "undesirable aliens" in American immigration history. Some masks, just like some racial registers, are more visible than others. It is their differences as much as their common identities that connect the Green Turtle to the Anchor of Justice. It is through such "productive interaction" that *The Shadow Hero* destabilizes the historical racialization of Asian Americans as well as the convention of white superheroes in American comics. As Miodrag insists, what is unique to the visual narrative is that "spatial arrangement informs the way text reads, assisting in creating literary effects" (66). The arrangement of the top-right panels on the last page breaks away from the convention of the left-to-right reading sequence, prompting the reader to read the panels vertically. The inter-frame space, or gutter, is crucial for the process of "closure" (McCloud 66–67), accomplished through the Anchor of Justice's unmasking as well as the Green Turtle's witnessing. Such an ending not only reminds the reader that renowned American comics superheroes are commonly different in one way or another, but it also reasserts the important role immigration has played in American history and the founding of the nation.

Juxtaposing early comics like Chu's *The Green Turtle* with contemporary graphic narratives such as Yang and Liew's *The Shadow Hero* allows readers to scrutinize how visual representations of Asians and Asian Americans evolve in different historical, cultural, and political contexts and helps them make connections between history and reality. *The Shadow Hero* ends with a splash panel in which illustration runs to the edge of the page. Here, a masked, yellow-skinned Hank is launching a new adventure to serve his country, the tortoise spirit hovering behind him, both a visual reference to Chu's comics and a symbolic connection to Hank's father and their ancestral roots in China. As the making of the shadow hero demonstrates, discourses of racial visibility—how we read and interpret race—are reawakened and examined in contemporary Asian American graphic narratives. As a popular cultural form, comics still has a "problematic relationship to ethnic difference" (Royal 8), despite all the leaps and bounds we have seen in recent years. Yang and Liew's reimagination of a Golden Age comic book hero as Asian American begins in China and concludes in America, as the Green Turtle and the Anchor of Justice prepare to bolster morale among American troops and to defend allies in Europe and Asia, illuminating racial (and perhaps species) acceptance and transnational (and perhaps transuniversal) connections between the characters.

FIGURE 7.2. The Anchor of Justice showing his face in Gene Luen Yang and Sonny Liew's *The Shadow Hero* (152). © MacMillan.

Works Cited

"27 Artists Celebrate the First Asian American Superhero: Epic Fan Art Gallery Dedicated to Gene Luen Yang and Sonny Liew's 'The Shadow Hero.'" *Angry Asian Man*, 4 August 2014, http://blog.angryasianman.com/2014/08/27-artists-celebrate-first-asian.html. Accessed 27 March 2022.

Andersen, Elizabeth. "*The Shadow Hero*." *Library Media Connection*, November/December 2014, p. 65.

Asian/Pacific/American Institute. *Yellow Peril: Collecting Xenophobia*. Asian/Pacific/American Institute, New York University, 2007.

Austin, Allan W., and Patrick L. Hamilton. *All New, All Different?: A History of Race and the American Superhero*. University of Texas Press, 2019.

Cheang, Kai Hang. "Restaging the Superhero Spectacle: Green Turtle's Shame, *The Shadow Hero*'s Reparative Aesthetics, and the Chinese Diaspora's Speculative Historiography of Golden Age Comics." *MELUS: Multi-Ethnic Literature of the US*, vol. 43, no. 4, 2018, pp. 80–103.

Chiu, Monica. "Who Needs a Chinese American Superhero?: Gene Luen Yang and Sonny Liew's *The Shadow Hero* as Asian American Historiography." *Redrawing the Historical Past: History, Memory, and Multiethnic Graphic Novels*, edited by Martha J. Cutter and Cathy J. Schlund-Vials, University of Georgia Press, 2017, pp. 87–105.

Coogan, Peter. *Superhero: The Secret Origin of a Genre*. Monkey Brain Books, 2006.

Dong, Lan. "Reimagining the Monkey King in Comics: Gene Luen Yang's *American Born Chinese*." *Oxford Handbook of Children's Literature*, edited by Lynne Vallone and Julia Mickenberg, Oxford University Press, 2011, pp. 231–51.

Eisner, Will. *Comics & Sequential Art*. Poorhouse Press, 2001.

Fawaz, Ramzi. *The New Mutants: Superheroes and the Radical Imagination of American Comics*. New York University Press, 2016.

Hirsch, Marianne. "Editor's Column: Collateral Damage." *PMLA*, vol. 119, no. 5, 2004, pp. 1209–15.

Hunter, Sarah. "*The Shadow Hero*." *Booklist*, 1 and 15 June 2014, pp. 62–63.

Lee, Robert G. *Orientals: Asian Americans in Popular Culture*. Temple University Press, 1999.

McCloud, Scott. *Understanding Comics: The Invisible Art*. Kitchen Sink Press, 1993.

Miodrag, Hannah. *Comics and Language: Reimagining Critical Discourse on the Form*. University Press of Mississippi, 2013.

"Racist Comic Strip in the Dartmouth." *Angry Asian Man*, 28 April 2008, http://blog.angryasianman.com/2008/04/racist-comic-strip-in-dartmouth.html. Accessed 27 March 2022.

Reynolds, Richard. *Superheroes: A Modern Mythology*. University Press of Mississippi, 1992.

Royal, Derek Parker. "Introduction: Coloring America: Multi-Ethnic Engagements with Graphic Narrative." *MELUS*, vol. 32, no. 3, 2007, pp. 7–22.

"*The Shadow Hero*." *Publishers Weekly*, 2014, p. 112.

Singer, Marc. "Black Skins and White Masks: Comic Books and the Secret of Race." *African American Review*, vol. 36, no. 1, 2002, pp. 107–19.

Yang, Gene Luen. "A Mistake in The Shadow Hero." *Diversity in YA*, https://diversity-inya.tumblr.com/post/104604090974/a-mistake-in-the-shadow-hero. Accessed 27 March 2022.

Yang, Gene Luen, and Sonny Liew. *The Shadow Hero*. First Second, 2014.

PART 4

ECOLOGY, OTHERNESS, AND INCLUSIVITY

CHAPTER 8

Posthumanist Critique in Jillian Tamaki's *Boundless*

ELEANOR TY

Best known as the co-creator of *Skim* with her cousin Mariko Tamaki, Jillian Tamaki is a mixed-race Asian Canadian and American cartoonist and illustrator who has lived and worked in New York and Toronto. In an interview with Shelagh Rogers on CBC (Canadian Broadcasting Corporation) Radio's *The Next Chapter*, Tamaki talked about how her racialized identity is important to her art: "I grew up in a very white part of Calgary. In the 1980s, there were not a lot of mixed-race kids so I was constantly looking around for images of myself. Now that I'm in the position of being an image maker, it's something that I take seriously" ("Why"). While *Skim* features a mixed-race Japanese Canadian teenager, most of the short stories in Jillian Tamaki's *Boundless* (2017) do not feature racialized characters. They are predominantly white, living in the privileged position Ruth Frankenberg observes as "unmarked and unnamed" (1) in contemporary society. The one exception is the story "Darla!," whose protagonist, a starlet named Darla Nakamura, is "a young Midwestern single just arrived in New York City" (139). She is presumably part-Japanese because of her surname. Race, however, is not a key element in the short story, which is about the nostalgia for a failed sitcom produced in the 1990s. Nevertheless, Tamaki's *Boundless* is very much an Asian American work because of its consideration of categories of otherness.

159

Since the 1970s, beginning with *Aiiieeeee! An Anthology of Asian-American Writers*, edited by Frank Chin, Jeffery Paul Chan, Lawson Fusao Inada, Shawn Wong, and others, Asian American literature has been defined as works by people of Asian descent, and typically, about Asian Americans and their experiences. How we classify works by Asian American authors who write literature with "unmarked" characters remains problematic for readers because we expect our Asian American writers to write about racialized experiences and ethnic stories. But as Stephen Sohn notes, "this authenticity paradigm circumscribes Asian American writers by assuming unification among the author, narrative perspective, and narrative content. . . . Narrative perspective is therefore under incredible pressure to exhibit ethnoracial authenticity" (5). Jillian Tamaki's *Boundless*, like Adrian Tomine's *Killing and Dying*, is a collection of short comics that do not always feature Asian American protagonists or issues. Both works go beyond the iconic and the expected by not reacting to specific racial stereotypes, sometimes by erasing racial markers altogether. In Tamaki's case, she goes beyond the icon by looking at various "others," by questioning the boundaries between human, animal, plants, machines. Jean-François Staszak has defined otherness as "the result of a discursive process by which a dominant in-group ('Us,' the Self) constructs one or many dominated out-groups ('Them,' Other) by stigmatizing a difference—real or imagined—presented as a negation of identity and thus a motive for potential discrimination" (43). Through vignettes and short narratives, Tamaki makes insightful and ironic observations about our contemporary society, how we have constructed others, and important issues like ecology, capitalism, and the durability of relationships, but also about minor irritations, or what Sianne Ngai calls "ugly feelings," such as "envy, irritation, paranoia, or anxiety" (5). Using images as well as text, she engages with urgent political and popular debates about representation, the distribution of power and resources, and the sexualization of women's bodies, using a variety of protagonists to express her views. It is a prime example of how Asian North Americans participate in larger conversations about the current state of our world.

Boundless, named by NPR and *Publishers Weekly* as "one of the best graphic novels of the year" in 2017 ("Best Books"), tells a range of stories, including those about the "interior lives of unexpected subjects: the writer of a pornographic sitcom, a shrinking woman, a plant-nursery employee with an internet doppelganger, even a fly" (Buchanan). As the title suggests, it is "boundless" in its attempts to break conventional categories in important ways: of gender, of genre, and of the species of the protagonists. Stylistically, Jillian Tamaki does not follow common graphic narrative layouts, which consist usually of the waffle grid, "six to twelve panels spread across three or four tiers" (Postema 29). Instead, some of the illustrations take up a full-page or even two full-page splashes. Most are pencil sketches and carefully detailed. The drawings vary in shape and size, and the color palettes change from story to story. In some stories, the illustrations seem disconnected from the textual narrative, so that the diegetic narrative is different from that of the mimetic. Rowan Buchanan notes that the graphic narrative borrows from different genres, "from speculative fiction to domestic drama to magical realism"; it is visually breathtaking, with images spilling over pages, images that are "vague, almost symbolic," and sometimes, seemingly unrelated to the words. Thematically, the stories are "quirky and ephemeral" but are "indelible in the mind," as another reviewer, Rachel Cooke, notes. They highlight the point of view of those we have been othered in society—women, animals, Indigenous people, the inanimate. Tamaki breaks conventions of the genre to comment on our modern world: our reliance on technology and social media; our attitudes to romance, marriage, and sexuality; our relationship with the other beings that live in our world. In keeping with posthumanist theories, which reject the belief that human beings occupy a central place in the universe, the work breaks down binaries and categories that we are used to—animal/human, male/female, real/virtual, us/them, science fiction/social reality—engaging in a revolutionary kind of "worldmaking" (Goodman 1) and reenvisioning of our earth. Often, Tamaki's slightly surreal images provide a strong counterpoint to the narrative voice.

This chapter reads four of Tamaki's graphic short narratives that demonstrate posthumanist and ecological concerns. Posthumanism is used to apply to a range of theoretical positions, but one general definition that I find useful is that "it seeks to undermine the traditional boundaries between the human, the animal, and the technological" (Bolter 1). According to Cary Wolfe, posthumanism engages directly with the problem of "anthropocentrism and speciesism and how practices of thinking and reading must change in light of their critique" (xviii). Wolfe encourages us to rethink the human/animal divide, and to question our assumptions that we are superior to animals because of our possession of language. Instead, Wolfe notes that different autopoietic life-forms, systems that reproduce and maintain themselves, all share what Maturana and Varela call a "consensual domain" (xxiii), a complex and heterogenous environment. Mel Y. Chen argues in *Animacies* that the "fragile division between animate and inanimate—that is, beyond human and animal—is relentlessly produced and policed" by language, by culture, by binary systems of difference (2). In *Boundless*, sto-

ries such as "World-Class City," "Bedbugs," and "Boundless" all force us
to rethink our relationship with nonhuman animals, our responsibilities to
our environment, and the implications of our actions on the world around
us, while "1.Jenny" humorously and ironically reviews our obsession with
social media and the way technologies are embedded in our everyday lives.[1]
These four stories are linked by their critique of anthropocentrism through
the juxtaposition of the grand and the everyday, the fantastic and the real,
and the interactions between human, animal, and technology.

In response to climate and environmental deterioration, as well as global
capitalist practices that have made living unsustainable in the twenty-first
century, feminist scholars have advocated the necessity of discontinuing the
practice of privileging the human species to the detriment of all other entities. Feminist posthumanist scholars have encouraged us to critique "the
rule of Anthropos," where "an exceptional species can claim the central
position in contemporary, technologically mediated knowledge production systems" (Braidotti 26). Following Donna Haraway, who offered the
cyborg as a figure that rejects rigid boundaries between human and animal
and human and machine in her oft-cited "A Cyborg Manifesto" (Haraway),
feminist posthumanist scholars also encourage going beyond dualisms—of
nature and culture, self and other. Nick Fox and Pam Alldred argue that
environmental sustainability "needs to overcome anthropocentric privileging of the human over the non-human—to develop a perspective on the
environment that—rather than differentiating the realms of human and nonhuman—draws culture and nature into one affective assemblage" (121). In
her "Four Theses on Posthuman Feminism," Rosi Braidotti proposes "species egalitarianism, which opens up productive possibilities of relations, alli-
ances, and mutual specification" (32).

One technique Jillian Tamaki uses is the decentering of the human and
the highlighting of the nonhuman. In *Boundless*, "Bedbugs" is the only story
where the animal or insect is featured in the title but not shown in the visuals. "Bedbugs" is a story about the slow disintegration of a couple's relationship, about irritation, infidelity, and change. The degeneration of the
relationship is aggravated by and metaphorically revealed through the
almost invisible bedbugs. The title page of the story has the word "bedbug"
imprinted almost imperceptibly at the bottom left-hand corner of the page to
show how small they are. At the outset of the story, Tamaki reveals the fray-

---

1. A YA graphic novel that also deals with the use of social media by Gen Z is *Snotgirl* by Brian Lee O'Malley and Leslie Hung. The writer, O'Malley, calls it "a comedic
soap opera set among people who spend a lot of time online" (Alverson).

ing bond between Jeremy and Angela by introducing the main characters in separate panels rather than together in the same room. Jeremy and Angela are featured in circular panels with jagged or torn edges, to suggest their tattered relationship. When they are talking to each other, Tamaki uses a shot/reverse shot emphasizing their disconnectedness. "Bedbugs" represents the literal and metaphorical upheaval of the lives of this couple, precipitated by the discovery of the "small, oval, brownish insects that live on the blood of animals or humans" (Dunkin) in their home. These bugs are so tiny that they are difficult to see, but they are a nuisance because they are difficult to evict. Also, bedbugs are pesky because they procreate quickly and can spread rapidly in one's home. They are active at night, and their bites cause itching and welts. After discovering the infestation, Jeremy and Angela have to examine every item of clothing, piece of furniture, and article of bedding in their home to decide whether to "toss" or keep (153). The question of whether to "toss" personal and household items is suggestive of the larger question of whether or not the couple's relationship is worth salvaging. The distress and chaos caused by the bedbugs serve to reveal the existing fractures and rough edges in Jeremy and Angela's marriage.

Though minuscule, the bedbugs unsettle the couple's relationship, and consequently, unsettle our notion of the superiority and domination of the human. In modern cities, we tend to ignore, for the most part, animals: how they manage to live, and what other forms of autopoietic life exist. Or else, they are domesticated and fully under our control. We decide when to feed them, when to clean them, and when to exercise them. They do not run our lives. I am not arguing here for the rights of bedbugs, rather that the story reminds us that even tiny creatures have powers and ways of being that may be in conflict with our own.

The invisible bedbugs overturn Angela and Jeremy's domestic life in unexpected ways. When they find bites in "tell-tale rows" on their lower legs, they are shocked but also ashamed. Angela muses, "We couldn't tell our coworkers. People treat you like you have Ebola, not that I blame them. But I swear, we were being responsible" (152). The bedbugs render them abject figures, unclean others in society. They wonder how and where they could have gotten them: "Neither of us had travelled recently. We hadn't had a houseguest in over a year" (154). Angela's thoughts, revealed through her internal monologue, reveal that bedbugs, like infectious diseases, are assumed to be "foreign," originating from some exotic place that one has traveled to, or brought by some guest. Instead, the infestation creates paranoia about their home, forces them to rethink boundaries between us and them, inside and outside, clean and unclean. Through this story, Tamaki show how easily our sense of order and chaos, self and other can be undone by a tiny, unseen creature.

In *Strangers to Ourselves,* Julia Kristeva discusses the difficulties of living as a foreigner who experiences exclusion and feelings of nonbelonging. However, Kristeva also notes that the foreigner is not always a stranger, but that "the foreigner lives within us: he is the hidden face of our identity, the space that wrecks our abode" (1). She argues, "By recognizing him within ourselves, we are spared detesting him in himself" (1). She explains how we can feel an "uncanny strangeness" in certain situations: "Confronting the foreigner whom I reject and with whom at the same time I identify, I lose my boundaries, I no longer have a container, the memory of experiences when I had been abandoned overwhelm me. I lose my composure. I feel 'lost,' 'indistinct,' 'hazy'" (187). In Tamaki's story "Bedbugs," Angela and Jeremy are forced to look inside and outside, to feel the plight of the other, albeit temporarily, as they feel estranged from their usual ways of living, the comfort of their domestic space. During the infestation, they have to wear different clothing because of the bedbug bites: "Despite the warming weather, we continued to wear pants and long-sleeved shirts whenever we weren't home" (163). This experience of "uncanny strangeness" ought to make the couple closer to each other, but instead, it makes Angela reassess her marriage.

The title, "Bedbugs," thus can also be read as a pun on the bugs or difficulties in Angela's marital bed. In the course of cleaning up their bedroom and telling the story about the bedbug infestation, Angela, a lecturer, reveals that she has had an affair with a TA in her English first-year class. This surprising fact seems to emerge out of nowhere, yet by implication, it is prompted by the couple's examination of their home and possessions. Greg, the TA, is mentioned after Angela remarks that bedbugs are "everywhere now . . . Fancy hotels, park benches, train seats" (155). Tamaki represents the passing of time in the two-page splash where the bed is in the middle, but where Angela is featured twice, once picking up clothing from the floor and once putting on earrings in front of a mirror (154–55). The scene then moves away from the disheveled bed to scenes in a classroom, where Greg may or may not be among the students sitting in class. Though Angela is continuing her recollection of the affair, talking about how they "usually fucked at his shitty apartment near campus, but sometimes other places too" (156), the images are not about the affair. They do not depict sexual scenes or passion. Instead, they are situated in the classroom, focusing on Angela as a lecturer. The images show her animated and successful in her job, as she seems to be able to entertain her students and make them laugh (156–57). These are followed by two pages of close-ups of Angela sitting at a desk and marking papers (158–59). In these pages, Angela is reflecting about the reasons why she embarked on the affair, but the images are hardly romantic. Instead, the close-ups show Angela's fingers itching her body, first on one spot behind her ear, and then another on her shoulder blade. The textual and the visual narrative do not seem to be in sync, yet they are suggestive, linking the floundering marriage with an itch and an anxiety.

In an essay on "Comics as Literature," Hillary Chute has remarked that "comics contain 'double vision' in their structural hybridity, their double (but nonsynthesized) narratives of words and images. In one frame of comics, the images and the words may mean differently, and thus the work sends out double-coded narratives or semantics" (459). In the scenes where Angela is musing about why she had an affair, the images of her itching herself while marking papers are presented in small panels, while the text reads, "I should probably say that I was unfulfilled. That I was not engaging my 'whole' self. That my husband and I stopped having 'new experiences'" (158). The small panels suggest the increasing smallness of her marriage and daily life. Tamaki playfully alludes to "the seven-year itch," a common reference to the way happiness in a relationship declines after around seven years of marriage, or the scenes could also refer to scabies, a contagious skin infestation by a mite that can last for months or years. In any case, as Chute says, the scene is a "double-coded narrative" where the images show the tedium and limitations of Angela's domestic life compared to her memories of the affair. Tamaki shows the difference between Angela's feelings about her dull marriage and the liberating affair through the use of small panels in the first set of memories, and the removal of borders in the latter.

Later, the illustrations that accompany Angela's recollection of the affair, two months after it ended, are the only ones in the short story where Angela is represented as unfettered and relaxed. There are no borders or frames around the images of Angela, naked and in sensual poses, with a look of pleasure on her face (164–65). The borderless images reflect Angela's feeling of expansiveness during the affair, as she says that during it, "the rules didn't apply to me anymore" (172). In all the other images where she is at home or out with Jeremy, Angela's face is worried, bored, or nonexpressive. Though Jeremy never finds out about the affair, and they eventually rid themselves of the bedbugs, along with some of their belongings and their bed, we are left with a sense that for Angela, everything will not be back to normal. Tamaki is able to encapsulate the many ways their relationship is bugged or broken through her illustrations of their day-to-day interactions. For example, when they stop for pizza in a place that was "shitty, as was the pizza" (170), the couple is represented again in two separate panels even though they are sitting at the same table. A close-up of Jeremy shows him staring moodily at his phone, eating his pizza with no relish or pleasure. The two are not talking, and Angela, depicted as an observer, stares at him morosely. There is no dialogue, but we see the emotional paucity of the relationship.

In the concluding panel, Jeremy embraces Angela and says, "We beat those little fuckers" (177). But Angela's furrowed brows show doubt and worry, not about the bedbugs, but about their lives, or her infidelity. Angela's expression, shown only to readers, contradicts Jeremy's assumptions, revealing the incongruities of their life together. The tiny insects did not, by themselves, cause marital discord, but they were a catalyst for Angela's realization about the bugs or irritations in her marriage and in her life. The story shows how small, insignificant things can trigger or reveal more crucial fissures in life. The ending is noncathartic, revealing instead what Ngai calls a "flatness or ongoingness" of unsatisfactory domestic relationships (7).

The first story of the collection, "World-Class City," uses defamiliarization and also the disjunction between texts and images to comment about animals, the environment, and the place of Indigenous people in our contemporary society. The term "world-class city" usually evokes images of skyscrapers, a cosmopolitan city of glass, and concrete structures. However, Tamaki's images are the opposite of what readers expect. In an interview with Chris Randle, Tamaki said that "world-class city" was definitely about New York because she wrote it before moving to Toronto (Randle). First, in this as well as the final story, Tamaki draws her images vertically, rather than horizontally, so we are forced to turn the book sideways to read it. Our usual reading practices are disturbed and so are graphic narrative conventions. The entire story consists of drawings without borders, and the images often run from one page to the top or bottom of the next.

Second, it is unclear who is the speaker or narrator. It could be the figure on the first page, an androgynous-looking male with a long braid, who is peering in and looking at some strange-looking creatures that seem to be evolving from amphibians to land animals. This figure is not dressed as a modern-day city dweller but is unclothed from the waist up. The diegetic narrative does not match the mimetic narrative, leading us to question our assumptions about cosmopolitanism, power, and control. He could be an Indigenous person, or someone from the past, except that he wears a watch. But the voice could also come from the two figures in the middle of the story who are humanlike, except for the wings that come out of one figure's

FIGURE 8.1. World-Class City in *Boundless*. © Jillian Tamaki. Used with permission from Drawn & Quarterly.

breasts (12–13, see fig. 8.1). Tamaki plays with our notions of the real and the fantastic, a technique that formalist critic Viktor Shklovsky has described as defamiliarization. Shklovsky notes, "The technique of art is to make objects 'unfamiliar' to make forms difficult, to increase the difficulty and length of perception because the process of perception is an aesthetic end in itself and must be prolonged" (18). By making these figures strange, Tamaki asks us to see "things out of their normal context" (Shklovsky 20) so we question our conventional assumptions and beliefs. Who is entitled to live in the "world-class city"? Who have we displaced when we build our "world-class city"?

In this short story, the drawings of the inhabitants of the world-class city resemble animals and humans, but the drawings contain elements of the fantastic and the strange. Reading the story through the lens of posthumanism, one could read its depiction of different life-forms to show (1) the possible existence of different "autopoietic life forms" (Wolfe xxiii) of which we are unaware, or (2) the disappearance of Indigenous peoples and animals that may have existed in history. Tamaki's drawing of the frog-like creatures (8–9) that seem to be evolving support the first reading, while the two-page illustration of a male figure with a machete cutting down a spiky plant is suggestive of an Indigenous way of life. What is jarring on these pages is the diegetic narrative that accompanies the picture, which sounds very contemporary: "And I'm going to be respected and so important, the type of person who eats yogurt and nuts" (16–17). Using François Jost's terminology, the "ocularization," "what the camera shows and what the characters are presumed to be seeing" (74), contains elements of the fantastic, while the narrative voice employs a discourse of a contemporary chic urban dweller. David Sandner notes of fantastic literature: "The fundamental characteristic of the fantastic is displacement; the fantastic signifier does not point, even superficially, to any clear signified and so causes the reader to experience a lack, a disruption inviting (if not provoking) an interpretation" (9). Tamaki forces us to rethink the consequences of our world-class cities, our tendency to flatten the earth and all the inhabitants in it in order to suit human needs in the modern world.

To emphasize the destructiveness of our "world-class" cities, Tamaki inserts a two-page drawing of a skeleton holding a candle and inviting us: "Come visit me in my World-Class City / The crime's not so bad in my World-Class City" (18–19). The friendly invitation becomes ironic because it comes from a skeleton, creating confusion and doubt in readers who associate skeletons with death. In this story, what Jost calls the "focalization . . . the cognitive point of view adopted by the narrative" (74), switches several times: from an Indigenous-looking person to creatures that look like frogs, to humanlike forms with wings, to a skeleton. We are not certain whether it is one character who is narrating the story or if there are several voices. The story asks us to contemplate questions such as, Who can we believe about the state of our world when it comes to contemporary urban development and building cities over our earth? What dies and what forms of life have we lost when we build world-class cities? The images—of Indigeneity, of death, of extinct animals—ask us to think about the ghostly "others" that we have repressed and forgotten in our compulsion to build the cosmopolitan city.

Similarly, in the third story, called "Boundless," Tamaki tells the story from the perspective of several nonhuman animals, including some birds, a squirrel, and a fly. The theme of boundlessness unites the narratives told by different animals, though freedom in each case is curtailed by one or more dangers. For example, birds are creatures often associated with freedom and transcendence in literature, but the birds have their obstacles. The bird says, "Humans think flying must feel very free. And they're right! It does" (212–13). But the bird warns of the dangers of spider webs, because "the smallest bit of web can cause our feathers to stick together and can fatally inhibit flight" (217). Similarly, the squirrel talks about being able to "move about the land when and where I want. I bound across roofs and yards—fences are irrelevant. It's all the same to me" (222–23). However, he cannot cross into fellow squirrel Gerry's territory, because Gerry is larger than him. In these stories, both the verbal and pictorial elements feature animal focalization; humans have no dialogue or narration in these stories and are seemingly displaced. The animals, like humans, express feelings of liberation, but also those of anxiety and envy. They, rather than humans, are the focus of the story.

Furthermore, the drawing techniques of these stories reflect the theme of boundlessness, as the story lacks panels, frames, or any type of drawn border. As in "World-Class City," the images are drawn vertically, rather than horizontally, forcing the reader to hold the book in an unfamiliar way. Tamaki includes a couple of close-ups of animals drawn in double-page splashes—the Canada goose with its outstretched wings (212–13); spiders looking rather ominous in their web (216); Gerry, the extra-large squirrel, who guards his territory fiercely (228–29); and the fly with his large, bulging eyes (236–37). Through the animals' focalization, Tamaki calls our attention to details about our world that we normally ignore, the beauty and splendor of animals, as well as some of the challenges they face. Through the focalization on animals, she challenges our tendency to see humans as the only species that has a right to master the earth, to make use of the air, and to occupy the land. Rosi Braidotti argues that the posthuman offers "an expanded relational vision of the self, as a nomadic transversal assemblage engendered by the cumulative effect of multiple relational bonds. The relational capacity of the posthuman subject is not confined within our species, but it includes all nonanthropomorphic elements, starting from the air we breathe" (33). She notes, "This vitalist approach to living matter displaces the boundary between the portion of life—both organic and discursive—that has traditionally been reserved for Anthropos, that is to say, *bios,* and the wider scope of animal and nonhuman life, also known as *zoe.* The dynamic, self-organizing structure of life as *zoe* stands for generative vitality" (32). In her stories, Tamaki questions our anthropomorphism, our feelings of superiority, by suggesting how the lives of animals, human and nonhuman, are similar. Like the squirrel, we too have our strengths, our skills, but also limitations in our lives, our petty squabbles with other people. We get a glimpse of animals and their worlds, their concerns about entrapment and competition, their special abilities. They exist as autopoietic life-forms, in spite of the boundaries we and other animals construct. We feel awe as these animals are able to transcend boundaries, such as fences and walls, constructed by humans, and are able to defy our earth-bound bodies.

At the same time, there is a bit of irony in the story, as Tamaki shifts perspectives. By taking the perspective of animals and insects, Tamaki makes them larger than life, suggesting that they have anxieties, like humans. She makes their size matter less than their worries that link them to humans. Toward the end of the story, it is a female reader who kills the fly with her book as she sits in a library. What kills animals and insects is not just thoughtlessness, but also centuries of learning and cultural conditioning. We have been taught not to value other autopoietic life-forms, and our instinct is to destroy what gets in our way. The last two pages are drawn with dark backgrounds. The book is ghostly white, and the woman's arm is extended in an eerie fashion. The motion lines indicate the strength and ferocity with which the fly is killed when the woman closes her book on it. Ironically, the fly has read Hobbes. We are selfish and are "driven by fear of death and the hope of personal gain," says Hobbes. By having the fly able to quote a well-known Western philosopher, Tamaki sets up a parallel between the insect and the human, putting them both at the same level. The story reminds us to pay attention to animals around us, but also of the precarity of their existence. Because they are shown to be thinking like human beings, there is a suggestion that we are like them. We believe in our grandeur and beauty, but we can also be envious, petty, and small. We each have our special talents and powers, but we, like the Canada geese, spiders, and squirrels, are not impervious to dangers, to the insensitive action of others. In our competitive, neoliberal world, we are not so far away from leading the "solitary, poor, nasty, brutish, and short" life that Hobbes described (Yale Books).

Another strand of posthumanism is the belief that humans have increasingly become reliant on technology, to the point that our identities are, in many ways, constituted by algorithms and machines. N. Katherine Hayles contends that "there are no essential differences or absolute demarcations between bodily existence and computer simulation, cybernetic mechanism and biological organism, robot teleology and human goals" (3). One of the most interesting stories in *Boundless* is a kind of "Black Mirror"–like piece (*Black Mirror*) about how technology and social media have taken over our lives. In "1.Jenny," the protagonist Jenny discovers one day that a mirror

Facebook page has been created for her and a few of her friends. The mirror Facebook "looked like an exact duplicate of the main Facebook" except that "small changes started to appear in everyone's profiles" (74). Their identities on the mirror Facebook are slightly inconsistent with their original online profiles. Jonah, who is sixteen and openly gay, finds that 1.Jonah is married to 1.Caroline (76). Jenny finds herself fascinated with her mirror self, of which she has no control. Even though 1.Jenny's life "seemed as relentlessly ordinary as her own" (83), Jenny finds herself surreptitiously checking her phone as much as possible to find out what her mirror self is up to. For example, in the mirror Facebook, a certain man, 1.Robert, begins to appear in photos with 1.Jenny, which annoys Jenny because it reminds her of her former boyfriend, and the fact that she is not seeing anyone at present. Then, it shows 1.Jenny about to go on vacation with the man Jenny just met. The mirror Facebook makes her "acutely aware of some sort of lost momentum" (93), reminds her of what she does not have and/or what she lost. She feels envy, one of the paradigmatic "ugly feelings" Ngai discusses. Eu Jin Chua notes that "ugly feelings, according to Ngai, operate at the border between internal feeling and objective reality, between affective consciousness and material political conditions." Jenny cannot direct her anger at an other because 1.Jenny is intimately connected to her; 1.Jenny is her. Through this story, Tamaki represents common affects that many of us feel as social media users: curiosity, envy, competitiveness, and disappointment. The feelings of restlessness are within, rather than directed at others. Our subjectivities contains those others that we attempt to ignore, to exclude.

The story is fascinating for a number of other reasons. Tamaki comments on our society's obsession with social media, and how our lives online are sometimes more exciting than our actual lives. The mirror Facebook makes Jenny envious of 1.Jenny's life and also arouses desires in her that she has hidden, even to herself. While some studies have shown that using many social media platforms is linked to depression and anxiety (see Zagorski), Tamaki's story reveals a more nuanced understanding of the way social media works. At the beginning, the mirror Facebook does make Jenny depressed and aware of what she lacks, but her interaction with her mirror Facebook identity shows how using social networking sites can become an act of self-formation, where the self is "constituted and reconstituted constantly" (Sauter 826). In her article, Theresa Sauter links writing on Facebook to earlier forms of writing, such as the Christian confessional, Romantic autobiography, and transgressive self-writing (827–29). She writes, "Facebook users are incited to record and reflect on their personal experiences, successes, failures and faults and to make these reflections publicly accessible" (830). In the story, Jenny is initially irritated by and jealous of her mirror counterpart. But Jenny decides to see a therapist, who recommends that she take up an activity where she can't use her phone, so she starts swimming. The regular exercise makes her feel better and calms her down. When she is no longer so anxious about what the other Jenny is doing, she peeks at mirror Facebook again and discovers that 1.Jenny has become single again, and has posted, "any SINGLE ppl want to grab some fuckin pizza" (111). Seeing this, "Jenny felt victorious. Also terrible—she was well aware that her delight equated to 1.Jenny's misery. That made her bad. Still, she achieved a personal best in the pool that morning" (112). In Jenny's world, it seems like her increased stability and well-being, which she achieves from refraining to go on Facebook, has a direct inverse effect on her mirror self. Her happiness equates with the diminished happiness of the mirror self. Tamaki suggests that we ought to dwell less in social media and lead more active lives, but interestingly, there is a dark undertone to the story: that our secret pleasure can also come from seeing others' unhappiness. Guessing that her mirror counterpart has experienced a breakup with Robert, Jenny concludes by reflecting coolly about their relationship: "Cruelty isn't that unusual."

Sauter has an expansive notion of the benefits of self-writing on Facebook. She argues that self-writing on social networking sites "can be employed as a way for people to understand and work on themselves and their relations to others" (836). People "make meaning of their existence in the world and navigate its complexities. . . . They form relations to self and others by exposing themselves to others and obtaining their feedback" (836). In Tamaki's story, Jenny reacts to the posts made by her mirror self, as well as her friends' comments about what she sees. Through 1.Jenny's posts, she realizes that she is using her past failed relationship as an "excuse to avoid dating" and decides to do something positive for herself, which leads to a healthier lifestyle and developing a stronger body. By comparing herself to 1.Jenny, she begins to understand what she herself has to do and feels better when she sees that the other Jenny also experiences disappointments and heartbreaks.

Another reason the story is fascinating is its unusual graphiation. According to Jan Baetens and Hugo Frey, graphiation is the "drawing style of the graphic novel," or "the visual enunciation or graphic expression" (137). They point out that "the hand and the body—as well as the whole personality of an artist—is visible in the way he or she gives a visual representation of a certain object, character, setting, or event" (137). In Tamaki's *Boundless*, however, the book encompasses many styles. The stories each have very different graphiation, which makes it difficult to talk about one specific drawing style of the artist. In the story "1.Jenny," Tamaki uses a brown pencil sketch to draw the story of Jenny and 1.Jenny. The images do not fit into traditional graphic panels but are sprawling, sometimes with smaller insets within the page to illustrate what is shown on her Facebook pages. In a story about the use and misuse of technology, one would expect a style that mimics computerization, focused on a screen or phone, but instead, the drawings feature organic, rather than technological items, surrealist-looking exotic plants and a garden. They represent growing, biological things in the greenhouse where Jenny works. Instead of a distrust of technology, Tamaki's story reveals social media and the internet as a fascinating and natural growth of our contemporary culture that is so saturated with images and mediated representations.

Initially, there seems to be little connection between the text and the visual imagery. Once the reader figures out that the setting is a garden center, the presences of the plants are logical, but their sizes are deliberately unrealistic, so some things make sense, while others do not. Exotic plants tower over the protagonist, so she is hidden in the "flowering bush department" (78). In a two-page spread where Jenny talks about how the two Facebook profiles of one user diverge, there is no human figure in the drawing, only giant cacti and 1.Jenny's statements enclosed in rectangular boxes (82–83). The plants and their treatment are sometimes used to suggest her state of mind. When Jenny is disgusted with 1.Jenny attempting to feminize herself by growing out her hair, Tamaki draws a pair of pruning shears cutting off the end of a tropical bloom (104–5). In another two-page spread depicting Jenny swimming, the curve of her arms echoes the spread of shrubs (108–9). The graphiation in the story creates links between the human and the nonhuman environment, suggesting that we grow and thrive similarly to plants, and that we need the same kind of care and sunlit conditions to bloom (see fig. 8.2).

However, the garden center/hothouse nursery setting also adds to the complicated division between real versus artificial, nature versus technology. Tamaki blurs the boundaries between them, suggesting that they are entangled, rather than opposites. The mirror counterparts exist only virtually but are derived from actual names and people. At the same time, since so much of social media is performative, in that users are able to shape their identities by controlling what they post, both the original profiles and the mirror profiles can be said to be fantasies. One is not more "real" than the other.

Similarly, it is significant that the elements of "nature" (plants, flowers, trees) shown in the story do not grow in meadows, farm fields, or mountains,

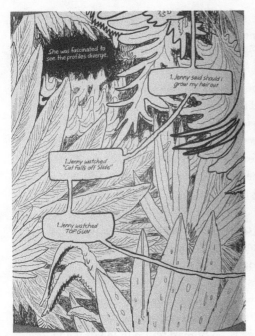

FIGURES 8.2A AND B. Tropical plants in *Boundless*. © Jillian Tamaki. Used with permission from Drawn & Quarterly.

but in a greenhouse. Because Jenny is an extension of the greenery through the similarities in drawing styles that depict her arms and the plants in the greenhouse, Tamaki suggests that human beings, like plants in a greenhouse, are artificially cultivated and dependent on structures, buildings, shelter, the care of other beings, science, technology. Our identities have been shaped by careful pruning to be marketable and presentable, contradicting beliefs in humanist notions of individual freedom and autonomy.

Another issue raised by the visual imagery is the representation of the female body and femininity. Significantly, Jenny is not depicted as a traditionally feminine woman in "1.Jenny." Tamaki is very aware of the way women are represented and sexualized in the media. In an interview with Suzette Smith about her book *SuperMutant Magic Academy*, Jillian Tamaki said, "I'm trying to be conscious and to present women's issues and be conscious of the bigger feminist picture in all areas of my life: my personal life, my professional life, my political life" (Smith). Jenny is not depicted in a way that contemporary advertising and media represent beautiful women— thin, sexualized, and glamorous. Rather, she is strong and sturdy and is able to lift large planters and bags of mulch. Jenny wears her hair short and wears work boots. Tamaki's depiction of women challenges us to see our world differently, less in traditional binary terms of masculine and feminine. The fact that Jenny's arms are drawn to suggest the tendrils of plants makes humans more connected with vegetation, animals, and our environment.

Taken together, these stories stress a theme of connectedness among humans, animals, plants, and the environment. They show Tamaki's resistance to binary modes of thinking and her attempt to re-view our existing "ways of seeing" (Berger)—that offer a more all-encompassing vision of our world, and our consideration and engagement with the other. They offer important commentary on the ways we have been using and misusing our natural resources, environment, technology, and social media. Through Tamaki's surreal illustrations, the stories question the traditional divide between human and nonhuman animals, nature and technology, the way we tend to practice speciesism in our culture. Mel Y. Chen points out, "Animacy hierarchies have broad ramifications for issues of ecology and environment, since objects, animals, substances, and spaces are assigned constrained zones of possibility and agency by extant grammars of animacy" (13). We assume that only human beings have a right to live in a "world-class city," and that the world is made for our use and comfort. We forget that our world-class cities still need flora and fauna, and that we, too, are animals. Evolutionary biologist Richard Dawkins argued against speciesism, observing that we tend to have a "discontinuous mind" because we refuse to see the links between humans and apes. In Tamaki's drawings, lines are blurred between the human, the animal, and the vegetation, encouraging us to see similarities rather than difference between species. *Boundless* challenges us to read and see differently, to reflect on the unexpected, and to radically reassess our ways of seeing the world around us and inside us.

Works Cited

Alverson, Brigid. "There Is a Graphic Novel Called 'Snotgirl.' Here's Why." *Publishers Weekly*, 23 February 2017, https://www.publishersweekly.com/pw/by-topic/industry-news/tip-sheet/article/72853-o-malley-and-hung-take-on-fashion-social-media-in-snotgirl.html.

Baetens, Jan, and Hugo Frey. *The Graphic Novel: An Introduction*. Cambridge University Press, 2015.

Berger, John. *Ways of Seeing*. 1972. Penguin Kindle Edition, 2008.

"Best Books of 2017 Publishers Weekly." *Publishers Weekly*, https://best-books.publishersweekly.com/pw/best-books/2017/comics.

Black Mirror. TV mini-series. Created by Charlie Brooker, Channel 4/ Netflix, 2011–19.

Bolter, Jay David. "Posthumanism." *The International Encyclopedia of Communication Theory and Philosophy*, edited by Klaus Bruhn Jensen and Robert T. Craig, John Wiley and Sons, 2016, *Wiley Online Library*, doi:10.1002/9781118766804.wbiect220.

Braidotti, Rosi. "Four Theses on Posthuman Feminism." *Anthropocene Feminism*, edited by Richard Grusin, University of Minnesota Press, 2017, pp. 21–48.

Buchanan, Rowan Hisayo. "The Cartoonist Who Makes You Look Twice." *The Atlantic*, 18 June 2017, https://www.theatlantic.com/entertainment/archive/2017/06/the-cartoonist-who-makes-you-look-twice/529842/.

Chen, Mel Y. *Animacies: Biopolitics, Racial Mattering, and Queer Affect*. Duke University Press, 2012.

Chin, Frank, et al., editors. *Aiiieeeee! An Anthology of Asian American Writers*. 1974. 3rd ed., University of Washington Press, 2019.

Chua, Eu Jin. Review of *Ugly Feelings* by Sianne Ngai. *Bryn Mawr Review of Comparative Literature*, vol. 6, no. 2, Fall 2007, http://www.brynmawr.edu/bmrcl/Ugly%20Feelings.htm.

Chute, Hillary. "Comics as Literature? Reading Graphic Narrative." *PMLA*, vol. 123, no. 2, 2008, pp. 452–65.

Cooke, Rachel. "*Boundless* by Jillian Tamaki Review—Picture-Perfect Short Stories." *The Guardian*, 17 July 2017, https://www.theguardian.com/books/2017/jul/17/boundless-jillian-tamaki-review-picture-perfect-short-stories-graphic-novel-jenny-bedbug.

Dawkins, Richard. "Gaps in the Mind." *The Great Ape Project*, edited by Paola Cavalieri and Peter Singer, St. Martin's Griffin, 1993, pp. 81–87.

Dunkin, Mary Anne. "Bedbugs." *WebMD*, 2020, https://www.webmd.com/skin-problems-and-treatments/guide/bedbugs-infestation#1.

Fox, Nick J., and Pam Alldred. "Sustainability, Feminist Posthumanism and the Unusual Capacities of (Post)Humans." *Environmental Sociology*, vol. 6, no. 2, 2020, pp. 121–31.

Frankenberg, Ruth. *The Social Construction of Whiteness: White Women, Race Matters*. University of Minnesota Press, 1993.

Goodman, Nelson. *Ways of Worldmaking*. Hackett Publishing, 1978.

Haraway, Donna. "A Cyborg Manifesto: Science, Technology, and Socialist-Feminism in the Late Twentieth Century." *Simians, Cyborgs, and Women: The Reinvention of Nature*, Routledge, 1991, pp. 149–81. https://theanarchistlibrary.org/library/donna-harroway-a-cyborg-manifesto-1.

Hayles, N. Katherine. *How We Became Posthuman: Virtual Bodies in Cybernetics, Literature, and Informatics*. University of Chicago Press, 1999.

Jost, François. "The Look: From Film to Novel. An Essay in Comparative Narratology." *A Companion to Literature and Film*, edited by Robert Stam and Alessandra Raenge, Blackwell Wiley, 2004, pp. 71–80.

Kristeva, Julia. *Strangers to Ourselves*. Translated by Leon S. Roudiez, Columbia University Press, 1991.

Ngai, Sianne. *Ugly Feelings*. Harvard University Press, 2007.

O'Malley, Bryan Lee, and Leslie Hung. *Snotgirl*. Vol. 1, Image Comics, 2017.

Postema, Barbara. *Narrative Structure in Comics: Making Sense of Fragments*. RIT Press, 2013.

Randle, Chris. "A Conversation with Jillian Tamaki, a Cartoonist Who Explores the Distance between Desire and Reality." *Drawn and Quarterly*, 1 July 2017, https://drawnandquarterly.com/press/2017/07/jezebel-interviews-jillian-tamaki.

Sandner, David. *Fantastic Literature: A Critical Reader*. Greenwood, 2004.

Sauter, Theresa. "'What's on Your Mind?' Writing on Facebook as a Tool for Self-Formation." *New Media and Society*, vol. 15, no. 5, 2014, pp. 823–39.

Shklovsky, Viktor. "Art as Technique." *Literary Theory: An Anthology*, edited by Julie Rivkin and Michael Ryan, Blackwell, 1998, pp. 17–23.

Smith, Suzette. "Jillian Tamaki Talks Comics, Mutants, and Why Canada Is Awesome." Bitch Media, 23 April 2015, https://www.bitchmedia.org/post/jillian-tamaki-talks-comics-mutants-and-why-canada-is-awesome.

Sohn, Stephen Hong. *Racial Asymmetries: Asian American Fictional Worlds*. New York University Press, 2014.

Staszak, Jean-François. "Other/Otherness." *International Encyclopedia of Human Geography*, edited by Rob Kitchin and Nigel Thrift, Vol. 8, Elsevier Science, 2009, pp. 43–47.

Tamaki, Jillian. *Boundless*. Drawn and Quarterly, 2017.

Tomine, Adrian. *Killing and Dying*. Drawn and Quarterly, 2015.

"Why Jillian Tamaki Believes in the Power of Comics." Interview of Jillian Tamaki by Shelagh Rogers, *CBC Radio*, 1 September 2017, https://www.cbc.ca/radio/thenextchapter/full-episode-june-25-2018-1.4271806/why-jillian-tamaki-believes-in-the-power-of-comics-1.4271824.

Wolfe, Cary. *What Is Posthumanism?* 2009. University of Minnesota Press, 2010.

Yale Books. "Thomas Hobbes: 'Solitary, Poor, Nasty, Brutish, and Short.'" *Yale University Press Official London Blog*, 5 April 2013, https://yalebooksblog.co.uk/2013/04/05/thomas-hobbes-solitary-poor-nasty-brutish-and-short/.

Zagorski, Nick. "Using Social Media Platforms Linked with Depression, Anxiety Risk." *Psychiatric News: American Psychiatric Association*, 17 January 2017.

CHAPTER 9

Drawing Disease and Disability

Ethical Optics and Space in Adrian Tomine's
Killing and Dying

STELLA OH

Comics depends on the interplay between verbal and visual modalities combining text and image in sequence and utilizing a vocabulary of icons, frames, gutters, panels, and word balloons. By employing such various forms, comics engages in expressive storytelling. Comics studies is inherently interdisciplinary, overlapping with cultural studies, ethnic studies, gender studies, literary studies, and most recently with the field of disability studies. Comics creates opportunities and prompts new ways of imagining current discourses about differences and our connections and encounters with one another. A growing number of scholars have interrogated the portrayal of disability in comics and alternative mediums to narrate stories and experiences of illness and disability.[1] However, while the field of disability studies has grown, conversations on the intersections of disability studies with race and comic studies have remained largely absent. In this essay, I explore the ways in which comics can overturn assumptions and expectations to write identity in particular, acceptable ways. Forging new modes of thinking about seeing and being seen, comics offers alternative modes of theorizing ethical engagements with what it means to be disabled and

---

1. See Holmes; Jacobs and Dolmage; Smith and Alaniz

dismissible in society. Adrian Tomine's graphic narrative *Killing and Dying*, illustrates our dis-ease as well as our desire to connect with marginalized bodies that are racialized and disabled.[2] In the narrative, disability aligns with other marginalized identities in a nexus of power relations. Tomine's work illustrates the complexities of addressing and challenging dominant racial and medical narratives while situated under the pressures of its normative gaze.

Ethical Optics and Space

Marginalized bodies are visually represented and situated as objects of spectacle; yet, they are located at safe distances. Uneasiness with bodily difference also triggers emotions such as anxiety or disgust that contribute to implicit negative biases toward minority groups.[3] Visually signaling out different bodies through medical scrutiny or racial staring further distances those who are marginalized. Such distancing not only raises questions regarding critical articulations and constructions of the Other, but also interrogates our ethical viewing practices. Ethical optics gestures to our relational capacities and challenges as we desire communication and connection with others, yet struggle with the distance inherent in encountering others.

Emmanuel Levinas is useful for thinking about the ethical dimensions of the visual. In *Totality and Infinity*, Levinas writes that "ethics is an optics" creating a significant connection between the ethical and optical (23). Levinas argues that the face of the Other presents "a rupture of being" that is located outside the self and offers an alternative structure that demands an ethical response (*Ethics* 87). Learning to see the Other involves disrupting our habits of looking and being keenly aware of alternative structures of perception. Levinas inquires, "How does one 'see' the Other if the Other is precisely other by being 'otherwise than being'?" (qtd. in Simmons 23). Engaging with an ethical optics entails movements of both proximity and distance from the Other. The ethical response to move toward an understanding of the Other is necessary, while simultaneously such understanding is always already out of our grasp. Nevertheless, in this movement between the inevitable distance of the Other and our desire to know the Other lies our ethical response.

---

2. Adrian Tomine has authored over nine book-length projects and the comic series *Optic Nerve* and is an illustrator for *The New Yorker* magazine.

3. See Nussbaum, who suggests that notions of disgust have shaped public opinion and legislation and argues for the need for imaginative engagement with others.

While we cannot deny the importance of visual capacities in constructing our perceptions and informing our ethical sense of responsibility, visual metaphors for ethical optics are inadequate. In *Otherwise and Being*, Levinas suggests that ethical responsibility is articulated not merely through vision but also through aurality and bodily contact that provide possibilities of moving closer while also being estranged. The following discussion focuses on absent presences of being, what Levinas calls a "complicated hiddenness in the heart of visibility" (qtd. in Simmons 23). Here, I look at ethical optics that signal to not only what is visible and pictorially embodied but also the absent and missing that challenge us toward ethical responsibility as we strive to engage meaningfully with difference. Playing with the dialectic of absence and presence, fragment and whole, the visible and nonvisible, artistic reimaginings break down stereotypes and binary categories and help us critically review the ways we see and engage with one another.

Graphic narratives have the potential to move us beyond distanced spectacles to genuine encounters with the experience of disability and marginalization. Several scholars have argued for the suitability of graphic narratives as a medium for representing disabled experience.[4] Susan Honeyman, for example, notes that graphic narratives and comics "have the potential to disrupt the medical and normative gaze by making individual experience more sympathetically visible and comprehensible as alternatively abled" (20). Such "pictorial embodiments" of bodily discomforts in graphic narratives also make it an ideal form in which to visually and affectively depict marginalized bodies (El Refaie 51). Graphic narratives engage in an ethical optics of representing uneasiness associated with bodily difference and other forms of marginalization. Through the use of panels and the gutters (space between panels), Tomine's *Killing and Dying* opens up different ways of talking about disabled and diseased bodies and the spaces they occupy.

Through its thematic focus on disability and disease, Tomine's graphic narrative *Killing and Dying* expands critical conversations between comics theory and disability studies into what scholars have called "graphic medicine."[5] There are three main characters in the story—the mother, father, and their fourteen-year-old daughter Jessie. Jessie's age is made explicit in the story, emphasizing the emotional teen years as she transitions into adult-

---

4. See Orbán; Squier, "So Long."

5. Recently, there has been scholarship that explores how comics can be utilized to impart critical approaches to medicine and medicalization. For further reading on comics and medicalization, see Green; Vaccarella. The publication of the graphic narrative series *Crazy Hospital* in 2013 by medical practitioners in Taiwan gained popularity and publicity.

hood. This period in which Jessie develops an independent identity separate from her parents is marked by two forms of disease—Jessie's speech impediment and the illness and sudden death of her mother. *Killing and Dying* underscores an urgent desire to understand Jessie's disability as well as cope with the mother's disease and death. However, the narrative refuses to offer easy resolutions and explores the "complicated hiddenness in the heart of visibility" in our attempt to meaningfully engage with disease and disability and feelings of depression that surround them (Simmons 23).

"Dying" in the Space of the Home

Killing and Dying offers new spaces and ways of representing disease and disability. The illness of the mother does not occur at a hospital setting, but rather at home. Jessie's difficulty with speech also does not occur at a medical office or hospital but within the space of her home and the comedy club. Such spatial positioning offers alternative spaces where we can hold conversations about illness. These spaces signal to the complexities of illness and differing abilities that affect not only one's medical and physical conditions but also one's personal, emotional, and intimate situations. There are no images of doctor's offices or hospitals in Tomine's narrative, thus taking authority away from institutionalized powers and instilling them on the characters who experience the illness. Such a move challenges us to rethink the ways we speak about illness and who has authority to speak about illness and disability. As Ann Cvetkovich notes, "comics give voice to those who are often not heard" (2). Instead of a sterilized medical office or the white walls of the hospital, *Killing and Dying* takes place at the family home and at a comedy club. While traditionally the medical establishment has had authority over how illness was visualized, "graphic medicine seeks to disrupt this power imbalance" (Czerwiec et al. 3).

Technologies of medicine have also traditionally been masculine and dominated by male doctors, while discourses of care and caregiving have been largely feminized and performed by women. Challenging us to critically think about the gendered dimensions of medicine, graphic narratives offers what Susan Squier argues is a "more inclusive perspective of medicine, illness, disability, caregiving, and being cared for" ("Introduction" 2). Associated with disrupting linear and traditional modes of storytelling, graphic medicine provides apt spaces for challenging traditional ways of thinking about medicine and caregiving and is "ideal for exploring taboo or forbidden areas of illness and healthcare" (Squier, "Introduction" 3). In *Kill-*

ing and Dying, Tomine not only illustrates the disability of the daughter and the illness and eventual death of the mother, but also challenges traditional gender roles of care and caregiving.

It is the father who acts as the caregiver in the family and is most closely associated with the family home. When we are first introduced to the father on the first page of the comic, he is wearing yellow kitchen gloves and washing the dishes. It is not the financial provisions for the family that are central here, but the gendered performance of care. We never see the mother figure or Jessie engage in any traditional domestic activities such as washing the dishes, preparing food, or cleaning the house. Images depicting the father as the caregiver are repeated often in the narrative and are almost always adjacent to images of the family home. The family home plays a key role in the narrative. There are multiple images of the home lit up, indicating an occupied home that is lived in rather than just a house. In fact, the story is framed with images of the family home lit up at night. The beginning and ending panels of the graphic narrative illustrate the importance of home and its material and subjective meanings, what political philosopher Iris Marion Young calls a "material anchor" (7). Having a home serves as a foundation for a politics of identity where subjectivities can be constructed with some detachment from the pressures of dominant social structures. Here, the family home becomes a space of respite from the constraints of society, the spectacle of medical staring, and the medical discourse of illness.

A typical page in a graphic narrative is composed of an average of eight panels. In *Killing and Dying,* the pages are arranged so that each page consists of twenty identical panels, producing a crammed effect. Such a claustrophobic architectural structure echoes the stifling emotional tension that permeates the text. This pattern of twenty panels on a page is abruptly interrupted midway through the narrative with the sudden death of the mother. If one is not careful, it is easy to miss her death since the characters do not spend time verbally mourning the loss of the mother figure. Stylistically the mother's death leaves a hole in the hearts as well as in the physical space of the narrative. An empty space produces a gaping hole in the middle of the page, visually indicating her departure and absence from the story. Panels that are completely black or white typically signal an ineffable loss and are referred to as "blind panels" by comic scholars (Groensteen, "The Monstrator" 11). Such panels gesture toward an event or emotion that is extremely painful and refuses to be sufficiently represented by image or text. Here, the panel that indicates the death and loss of the mother is represented by a white blank space rather than a darkened black area, as found in other graphic narratives, such as Joe Sacco's *Footnotes in Gaza* or Marjane Satrapi's *The Complete Persepolis*. In leaving the paneling and its frames blank, Tomine encourages the reader to fill in the gaps and engage in a process of closure at the mother's sudden absence. Scott McCloud and critics citing his work promote the idea that comics rests on this process of closure that "fills in" the gaps between sequential panels and "demand[s] active interpretation" and participation from the audience (136). The degree of the reader's engagement with the text influences our willingness to empathize with the characters.[6] Kate Polak discusses the nexus between empathy and ethics in graphic narratives and suggests that the reader's perspective and their level of engagement greatly impacts their ability to affectively identify with the character's grief. According to Polak, graphic narratives represent at a metacognitive level, and how we read images has a profound effect on the reader's ability to empathize with the characters. The comic architecture urges the reader to imagine and engage, providing a uniquely productive framework in which "to theorize and practice new ethical and affective relationships and responses" (Gardner 1).

The missing panel visualizes the emotional loss and depression that affect the father and Jessie throughout the remainder of the story. Similar to the characters of the father and daughter, the audience is left with the difficult and messy task of interpreting and working through loss in the narrative. The ability to examine each separate panel and read the entire page at once offers a mode of reading that simultaneously makes visible the absence of the mother as well as the emotive memories of her that are sequentially experienced. In one particular sequence of panels, there are five related frames depicting the mother and Jessie in a highly emotional interchange of anger and sadness that culminates in a loving embrace. Although there is no dialogue that accompanies these panels, the visual elements of composition and layout underscore the scene's emotional significance. The visual ellipses that precede the embrace between the mother and daughter are used to visualize emotions that make up our registers of memory (see fig. 9.1).

Memory consists not only of previous actions and words but also of feeling and emotions.[7] In dealing with loss, the archive of memory is an emotive one in which "one is undone, in the face of the other, by the touch, by the scent, by the feel, by the prospect of the touch, by the memory of the feel" (Butler 23). Pain of loss is world-breaking in that as socially constituted individuals who are attached to and have relationships with others, we are all subject to such feelings of loss. Such a loss is indicative of "a rupture

---

6. See Polak.

7. For more on the relationship between emotions and memory, see H. T. Schupp et al.; S. B. Hamann et al.; W. R. Walker et al.

FIGURE 9.1. Loss of the mother in *Killing and Dying*. © Adrian Tomine. Used with permission from Drawn & Quarterly and Faber and Faber UK.

of being" that is located outside the self and demands an ethical response (Levinas, *Ethics* 87). And hence, our relations with others is ethical insomuch as it dispossesses us rather than constitutes us. The pain and overwhelming depression that ensues is world-breaking but also word-breaking for the father and daughter who remain behind. As Elaine Scarry has powerfully argued, "pain does not simply resist language but actively destroys it, bringing about an immediate reversion to a state anterior to language, to the cries a human being makes before language is learned" (4). This sentiment is echoed by Squier, who suggests that "comics make that narrative most fully possible because they include its pre-verbal components: the gestural, embodied physicality of disabled alterity in its precise and valuable specificity" ("So Long" 85–86). The sequence of scenes in which mother and daughter share a final embrace is followed by the father looking despondently at a hospital door that the mother had entered through. It is an eerily silent yet powerful sequence of images that affectively captures a landscape of pain and distress.

In *Killing and Dying*, there are two pages that contain a missing panel. The first occurrence takes place to mark the mother's abrupt absence and death. The only other time this spatial abnormality occurs in the page layout is to gesture to the escalation of the father's depression and distress after his wife's death. The father bashes his head against the wall as he holds a framed photograph of his wife. Sobbing, he cries, "All your goddamn fault! God! Damn! God! Damn! God!" before he collapses to the ground, only to be found by his daughter (109). Grieving with loss and frustrated by the weight of parenting his daughter without his wife, the father figure lays bare the emotional and physical trauma associated with death, disease, and disability. Through the interplay between image and text, comics convey a "far richer sense of the different magnitudes at which we experience any performance of illness, disability, medical treatment, or healing" (Squier, "Literature" 131). In this scene, we witness how death, disease, and disability intrude into the space of the family home, affecting the physical, mental, and emotional state of its family members.

"Killing It" in the Space of the Comedy Club

The difficulty of expressing the emotional loss of her mother is echoed in Jessie's difficulty with speech. The mother's illness and Jessie's speech disability signal to contemporary calls, particularly from medical humanities, to critically think of new discourses on illness and ability. Recent scholarship on critical health studies are attuned to the intersectional factors that influence the relationships between patient, doctor, and caregiver, as well as the power imbalances of gender, race, age, and class. In *The System of Comics*, Thierry Groensteen uses a medical term "arthrology," the study of joints and their functions, to indicate the compositional relationships of comic paneling, underscoring "the link between graphic narrative as a semantic structure based on (abled) embodiment" (Whalen et al. 7). Conventional cultural norms and images of normativity are encoded through visual idioms. Such motifs and archetypal narratives of abled bodies direct our point of view and provide a lens through which to see the world. Such approaches also attend to the possibilities of nontraditional media, including comics, to contribute to medical humanities scholarship.

Here, I look at the visual rhythms that punctuate the structure of *Killing and Dying* and syncopate the cadences of our ordinary ways of thinking about illness and disability. While the space of the home serves as a framing anchor for *Killing and Dying*, the space of the comedy club is where Jessie ventures courageously to seek her own identity as an aspiring stand-up comedian. When Jessie is onstage doing her stand-up comic routine, the panels with images are interlaced with panels with just text written in parentheses. The visual rhythm of the organization of the panels with text mimics the stuttering rhythm in Jessie's speech pattern. The visual sounds of "(silence)" and "(tension-breaking laughter)" provide haptic representations evoked through rhythmic visual cadences (105). Here, time is represented visually and spatially through the stops and starts of silence and laughter. Signaling to what Groensteen refers to as the "spatio-temporal apparatus" of comics, the punctuated spaces and temporality of the page layout mimic the time it takes for Jessie to speak (*System* 25). Temporal and spatial representations are interlaced as the audience gets to hear, witness, and take time processing through the difficulty of Jessie's speech with its stutters, pauses, and misunderstandings. Hence, the panels are both visually and aurally effective, communicating in unique ways how theories of embodiment and identity derived from disability studies speak to the rhetoric of comics (see fig. 9.2).

Jessie's insistence on pursuing a career as a stand-up comedian despite her disability puts her onstage in front of an audience that gazes upon her as a spectacle of difference, emphasizing the "unfamiliar, unseen, the freak show, and reinforcing the position of the disabled and racialized other" (Mitchell and Snyder 10). However, Jessie's performance on stage challenges oppressive cultural constraints that marginalize women and people of color and see them not as the creators of jokes but as the butt of jokes. Jessie's presence onstage as an Asian American female comedian challenges our scopophilic ways of seeing and the politics of staring at people of color and those who are disabled. Her embodiment as a woman of color who has a speech impediment not only raises questions regarding the critical articulation of disability but also critiques representations of other fundamental categories of difference and identity, such as race and gender. Notions of stuttering and speaking disability not only apply to Jessie's speech impediment but also signal to stereotypical perceptions of Asian Americans as a silent minority who are not able to speak English well.

Although Jessie courageously takes the stage, she is not successful as a stand-up comedian. Her act does not generate laughter and is painfully wrought. When she tries to make a joke regarding someone who is overweight in the audience, another audience member strikes back at her, remarking, "Wait . . . You're going to take a shot at somebody because of their looks?" (105). The interaction between the audience and a disabled female comedian of color does not generate the desired affective response. Jessie's intended joke is redirected at her as her looks become the butt of the joke. Audiences are used to viewing certain types of bodies—usually young, male, and able-bodied—on the comedy stage. When a woman of color with a disability performs, the audience perceives the performer through a lens of pity and dis-ease. Hence, getting the audience to laugh at Jessie's jokes is situationally challenging. Rather than laughing with the comedian at her joke, the audience reacts with pitiful chuckles of "tension breaking laughter" and intermittent moments of deafening "silence" (105). The complex process of effectively communicating and executing the joke is clouded by gender bias, racism, and ableism.

Jessie's courage to take the stage despite her speech impediment alters her relationship with a world that perceives disability as a negative trait. Tomine's work calls attention not only to meanings associated with disability but to meanings generated by disability. Hence, the narrative of *Killing and Dying* recognizes various notions of disability and its potential as a source of creativity and invention. Jessie's determination to pursue a career in stand-up comedy despite her disability speaks to what disability studies scholars have called disability gain. While disability is often seen as representing loss, the concept of disability gain embraces "what a person can gain when they 'lose'; the creativity of working around obstacles, fueled by necessity, instead of becoming creative *in spite* of your disability; you become creative *because* of it" (Barker 195). A creative form of communicative meaning is developed in *Killing and Dying* through the disabilities of Jessie and her mother.

In Tomine's graphic narrative, diseased and disabled bodies move in a disabling world through the creative architecture of comics. Racialized, female, and disabled bodies relay specific histories and contexts and are constituted with signification and value that reflect larger discursive structures of power.[8] As such, the mobility of marginalized bodies is largely contingent on social structures and circumstances. The experimental and creative structure of comics allows for a revisioning of the spatial properties of embodiment and illness and who has authority over narratives and representations of disease and disability. As Tobin Siebers observes, "The emerging field of disability studies defines disability not as an individual defect but as the project of social injustice, one that requires not the cure or elimination of the defective person but significant changes in the social and build environ-

---

8. Sara Ahmed argues that emotions generate meaning in the world and as material rhetoric have affective power. This link between emotions and power allows us to discuss the politics of emotions. Following Franz Fanon, Ahmed argues that due to the legacy of colonialism, the body that stems from a certain familiar position is white, and nonwhite bodies are constantly stopped and their bodies stick with various signs of disgust, terror, and fear within the nation-state.

FIGURE 9.2. Comedy club scene in *Killing and Dying*. © Adrian Tomine. Used with permission from Drawn & Quarterly and Faber and Faber UK.

ment" (3). The composition of comics offers a creative venue through which we can imagine changes in structures and environments that bodies inhabit.

The narrative of *Killing and Dying* does not end with recovery from ailments that the characters experience. The mother does not recover from her illness, the father continues to struggle with depression, and Jessie still has her speech impediment. Rather, the narrative develops forms of nonconventional communication, urging us to move beyond illness, disability, and our dis-ease with difference. The story represents a powerful performance that addresses disease and disability through the visual architecture of comics. Framed by images of family and home, Tomine's graphic narrative integrates both physical and emotional angst associated with disease and disability and fills in where linguistic capacity cannot. The reader experiences the tension and unease of gazing at bodies that are considered deviant— the female, Asian, sick, dying, depressed, and disabled. Yet, it is a productive tension that engages in an ethical dimension of vision that is a "vision without image," in which sensuous metaphors of sight, hearing, and touch are intertwined, allowing us to see more than what is merely visible to the eye (Levinas, *Totality* 23). Disrupting our habits of looking and engaging in alternative structures, Tomine's work urges us to disable stereotypes and problematize the hegemonic gaze that has silenced, muted, and stuttered the voices of marginalized communities. Similar to the form of the improv comedy that is dependent on the active "c-c-colla . . . collabor . . . ARGH! Collaboration w-w-with the audience," Tomine's graphic narrative provides spaces for pause and revision in which we are able to negotiate our distance, desire, and dis-ease with difference (Tomine 101). This endeavor is a collaborative one in which the reader is encouraged not only to engage in the act of closure connecting and constructing meaning but also to be aware of gaps, silences, and contradictions that emerge. *Killing and Dying* provide spaces for us to critically consider how we negotiate our desire to understand, as well as our dis-ease and distance from difference.

Works Cited

Ahmed, Sara. "Happy Objects." *The Affect Theory Reader*, edited by Melissa Gregg and Gregory J. Seigworth, Duke University Press, 2010, pp. 29–51.

Barker, Nicole C. S. "What Will You Gain When You Lose?: Deafness, Disability Gain, Creativity, and Human Difference." *Beginning with Disability: A Primer*, edited by Lennard J. Davis, Routledge, 2018, pp. 195–200.

Butler, Judith. *Precarious Life: The Powers of Mourning and Violence*. Verso, 2004.

Cvetkovich, Ann. *An Archive of Feelings: Trauma, Sexuality, and Lesbian Public Cultures.* Duke University Press, 2003.

Czerwiec, MK, et al. *Graphic Medicine Manifesto.* Penn State University, 2015.

El Refaie, Elisabeth. *Autobiographical Comics: Life Writing in Pictures.* University Press of Mississippi, 2012.

Fanon, Franz. *The Wretched of the Earth.* Grove Press, 1963.

Gardner, Jared. "Autobiography's Biography, 1972–2007." *Biography: An Interdisciplinary Quarterly,* vol. 31, no. 1, Winter 2008, pp. 1–26.

Green, Michael J. "Teaching with Comics: A Course for Fourth-Year Medical Students." *Journal of Medical Humanities,* vol. 34, no. 4, 2013, pp. 471–76.

Groensteen, Thierry. "The Monstrator, the Recitant, and the Shadow of the Narrator." *European Comic Art,* vol. 3, 2010, pp. 1–21.

———. *The System of Comics.* Translated by Bart Beaty and Nick Nguyen, University of Mississippi, 2007.

Hamann, S. B., et al. "Amygdala Activated Related to Enhanced Memory for Pleasant and Aversive Stimuli." *Nature Neuroscience,* vol. 2, 1999, pp. 289–93.

Holmes, Martha Stoddard. "Narrating Cancer through Sequential Art." *Tulsa Studies in Women's Literature,* vol. 32, no. 2, 2014, pp. 147–62.

Honeyman, Susan. "Pain Proxies, Migraine, and Invisible Disability in Renée French *H Day.*" *Disability Arts and Culture: Methods and Approaches,* edited by Petra Kuppers, University of Chicago Press, 2019, pp. 15–36.

Jacobs, Dale, and Jay Dolmage. "Accessible Articulations: Comics and Disability Rhetorics in *Hawkeye #19.*" *Inks: The Journal of the Comics Studies Society,* vol. 2, no. 3, 2018, pp. 353–68.

Levinas, Emmanuel. *Ethics and Infinity: Conversations with Philipe Nemo.* Translated by Richard A. Cohen, Duquesne University Press, 1985.

———. *Otherwise and Being: Or Beyond Essence.* Translated by Alphonso Lingis, Duquesne University Press, 1998.

———. *Totality and Infinity.* Duquesne University Press, 1969.

McCloud, Scott. *Understanding Comics: The Invisible Art.* Harper Perennial, 1994.

Mitchell, David T., and Sharon L. Snyder. "Introduction: Disability Studies and the Double Bind of Representation." *The Body and Physical Difference, Discourses of Disability,* edited by Mitchell and Snyder, University of Michigan Press, 1997, pp. 1–31.

Nussbaum, Martha. *From Disgust to Humanity: Sexual Orientation and the Law.* Oxford University Press, 2010.

Orbán, Katalin. "Trauma and Visuality: Art Spiegelman's Maus and In the Shadow of No Towers." *Representations,* vol. 97, no. 1, 2007, pp. 57–89.

Polak, Kate. *Ethics in the Gutter: Empathy and Historical Fiction in Comics.* Ohio State University Press, 2017.

Sacco, Joe. *Footnotes in Gaza: A Graphic Novel.* Metropolitan Books, 2010.

Satrapi, Marjane. *The Complete Persepolis.* Pantheon, 2004.

Scarry, Elaine. *The Body in Pain: The Making and Unmaking of the World.* Oxford University Press, 1985.

Schupp, H. T., et al. "Selective Visual Attention to Emotion." *The Journal of Neuroscience,* vol. 27, no. 5, 2007, pp. 1082–89.

Siebers, Tobin. *Disability Theory.* University of Michigan Press, 2008.

Simmons, J. Aaron. "'Vision without Image': A Levinasian Topology." *Southwest Philosophy Review,* vol. 25, no. 1, 2009, pp. 23–31.

Smith, Scott T., and José Alaniz. *Uncanny Bodies: Superhero Comics and Disability.* Penn State University Press, 2019.

Squier, Susan Merrill. "Introduction." *Graphic Medicine Manifesto,* edited by MK Czerwiec et al., Penn State University, 2015, pp. 1–20.

———. "Literature and Medicine, Future Tense: Making it Graphic." *Literature and Medicine,* vol. 27, no. 2, 2008, pp. 124–52.

———. "So Long as They Grow Out of It: Comics, the Discourse of Developmental Normalcy, and Disability." *Journal of Medical Humanities,* vol. 29, no. 2, 2008, pp. 71–88.

Tomine, Adrian. *Killing and Dying.* Drawn & Quarterly, 2015.

Vaccarella, Maria. "Exploring Graphic Pathographies in the Medical Humanities." *Medical Humanities,* vol. 39, no. 1, 2013, pp. 70–71.

Walker, W. R., et al. "Why People Rehearse Their Memories: Frequency of Use and Relations to the Intensity of Emotions Associated with Autobiographical Memories." *Memory,* vol. 17, no. 7, 2009, pp. 760–73.

Whalen, Zach, et al. "Introduction: From Feats of Clay to Narrative Prose/thesis." *Disability in Comic Books and Graphic Narratives,* edited by Zach Whalen et al., Palgrave McMillan, 2016, pp. 1–13.

Young, Iris Marion. *Intersecting Voices: Dilemmas of Gender, Political Philosophy and Policy.* Princeton University Press, 1997.

CONTRIBUTORS

MONICA CHIU is a professor of English at the University of New Hampshire, where she teaches courses in Asian American studies, American studies, and comics and graphic narrative. A recent 2019 Fulbright Specialist Award took her to Minan Normal University in Fujian, China, where she offered a series of lectures, for four weeks, in her areas of expertise. She currently is working on a book in the arena of graphic medicine: graphic narratives about subjects who are ill.

SHILPA DAVÉ is an assistant dean in the College of Arts and Sciences and an assistant professor in the Department of Media Studies and American Studies at the University of Virginia. She is the author of *Indian Accents: Brown Voice and Racial Performance in American Television and Film* (University of Illinois Press, 2013) and a coeditor of *Global Asian American Popular Cultures* (NYU Press, 2016) and *East Main Street: Asian American Popular Culture* (NYU Press, 2005). She researches and teaches about representations of race and gender in media and popular culture from superhero stories to animated narratives, as well as American cultural narratives of immigration and border crossings, and comparative American studies specializing in Asian American and South Asian American studies.

MELINDA LUISA DE JESÚS is an associate professor and former chair of diversity studies at California College of the Arts. She writes and teaches about

Filipinx/American cultural production, girl culture, monsters, and race/ethnicity in the United States. She edited *Pinay Power: Peminist Critical Theory,* the first collection of Filipina/American feminisms (Routledge, 2005); her first collection of poetry, *peminology,* was published by Paloma Press in 2018. De Jesús is also a classically trained mezzo-soprano, an Aquarian, and a mom who loves hard liquor and admits an obsession with Hello Kitty. More about her at peminist.com.

LAN DONG is the Louise Hartman and Karl Schewe Endowed Professor and interim dean of the College of Liberal Arts and Sciences at the University of Illinois Springfield. She teaches Asian American literature, world literature, comics and graphic narratives, and children's and young adult literature and has published numerous articles and essays in these areas. She is the author or editor of several books, including *Reading Amy Tan, Mulan's Legend and Legacy in China and the United States, Transnationalism and the Asian American Heroine, Teaching Comics and Graphic Narratives, Asian American Culture: From Anime to Tiger Moms,* and *25 Events That Shaped Asian American History.*

JIN LEE is an assistant professor of American and British Literature at Myongji University. She specializes in American and Asian American literature, with an emphasis on trauma studies, postcolonial literary studies, and visual culture (graphic narratives). Her research has appeared or is forthcoming in *The Comics Grid: Journal of Comics Scholarship;* the journal *American, British and Canadian Studies;* the *Journal of Literature and Trauma Studies; CLCWeb: Comparative Literature and Culture;* and *Graphic Novels and Comics as World Literature.*

ERIN KHUÊ NINH is an associate professor of Asian American studies at the University of California, Santa Barbara. She is the author of *Ingratitude: The Debt-Bound Daughter in Asian American Literature* (NYU Press, 2011; recognized for Best Literary Criticism by the Association for Asian American Studies in 2013), and more recently, *Passing for Perfect: College Impostors and Other Model Minorities* (Temple University Press, 2021). With Shireen Roshanravan, she edited the special issue of the *Journal of Asian American Studies* on sexual violence, entitled #WeToo: A Reader (2021).

STELLA OH is a professor of women's and gender studies at Loyola Marymount University. Her areas of expertise are Asian American literature, graphic novels, trauma studies, and gender studies. She has published her research in over thirty academic journals and anthologies. Her most recent publications appear in *Gendering the Transpacific World* (Brill Press, 2017), *Ethnicity and Kinship in North American Literature* (Routledge, 2021), and *Asian American Literature in Transition, 1996–2020* (Cambridge University Press, 2021).

JEANETTE ROAN is an associate professor in the History of Art and Visual Culture Program and the graduate program in Visual and Critical Studies at California College of the Arts. She is the author of *Envisioning Asia: On Loca-*

tion, Travel, and the Cinematic Geography of U.S. Orientalism (University of Michigan Press, 2010). Her comics studies scholarship addresses issues of Asian American representation, aesthetics, and visual studies methodologies. She was recently appointed an associate editor of *Inks,* the journal of the Comics Studies Society.

ELEANOR TY, fellow of the Royal Society of Canada, is a professor of English at Wilfrid Laurier University. She was a Fulbright Canada Visiting Research Chair at the University of California, Santa Barbara, in 2019 and has published on Asian North American literature, graphic novel, life writing, and eighteenth-century British women writers. Her most recent book, *Asianfail: Narratives of Disenchantment and the Model Minority* (University of Illinois Press, 2017), won the Asian/Pacific American Librarians Association Award for Literature in Adult Non-Fiction Category for 2017. She coedited a special issue of *a/b: Auto/Biography Studies: Migration, Exile and Diaspora in Graphic Life Narratives* in spring 2020.

INDEX

9/11 (September 11 terrorist attack), 99–100, 128

Abbott, Lawrence L., 85n3

abjection, 8, 14, 163, 179, 189; Filipina, 19

ableism, 179–87, 188 fig. 9.2, 189

abuse, 14, 114–16, 118

adolescence, 17

adoption, 20, 115–16; and adoptee gratitude, 56; and adoptee trauma, 115; and birth families, 114–18; interracial, 56; Korean adoptees, 115; in the Philippines, 115; transnational, 57, 114–15, 118

African American women, 20, 68–72; bodies of, 72–73

Ahmed, Sara, 17, 31n3, 44, 44n19, 187n8

Ali, Bisha K., 125

Alldred, Pam, 162

Alsultany, Evelyn, 127

Amanat, Sana, 130, 132, 138

American Born Chinese (Yang), 15–16, 83, 85–96, 100–101, 142–44, 144n3

American Dream, 109–13; and masculinity, 50. *See also* assimilation; exceptionalism, American

Andersen, Elizabeth, 145n4

anthropocentrism, 21, 161–62, 169

anthropomorphism, 21

anti-Asian racism: during COVID-19 pandemic, 2, 120; murder, 97; and racial slurs, 97–98. *See also* Orientalism

anti-Black racism, 99, 120; police brutality, 120

Asian North Americans: activism, 5; as aliens, 5, 99, 152; and "bamboo ceiling," 98, 98n21; as children, 15; families of, 9; hierarchy of, 111; history, 85, 92, 142–43; identity, 6, 9, 15; and indebtedness, 61; intergenerational issues, 14–15, 46, 50, 115; and masculinity, 7–8, 16; mixed-race, 12, 20, 85, 96, 159 (*see also* Filipina Americans: mestiza); othering of, 9; resistance, 7; self-representation, 13, 55–57, 111, 114, 118, 143; subjectivity, 15–16; as

Creef, Elena, 32, 33n6, 40n16
Cruz, Denise, 108
Cutter, Martha, 4, 18
Cvetkovich, Ann, 181

Dagbovie-Mullins, Sika, 129
Danvers, Carol, 21, 67, 126–27, 128 fig.
    6.1, 129–30, 132–33, 138. *See also*
    superheroes: Ms. Marvel
Davé, Shilpa, 21
David, E. J. R., 108
Dawkins, Richard, 175
DC Comics, 21
death, 181–85
decolonization, 104, 107–8, 111, 118–19,
    121
DeConnick, Kelly Sue, 67, 69; *Bitch
    Planet*, 19–20, 67–81
de Jésus, Melinda Luisa, 13, 20
De Landro, Valentine, 79; *Bitch Planet*,
    19–20, 67–81
De Leon, Adrien, 2
diasporic subjectivity, 50
disability, 22, 178–82, 184–87, 189; speech
    impediment, 181, 185–87, 188 fig.
    9.2, 189
Disney, 125–26
Dong, Lan, 15, 21
Douglas, Mary, 46

ecology, 160–62, 166, 168–70, 173, 175
education, colonial, 8
Egyptian culture, 110
Eisinger, Justin, 18
Eisner, Will, 6
Escobar, Trinidad, 20, 103, 107–8, 113,
    119; *Crushed: Book One*, 113–15,
    118–19; "Silently Gathering Force,"
    113, 116–19
ethical optics, 179–80, 189
exceptionalism, American, 50
exoticization. *See* race: and fetishization
extinction, 168

family: daughter, 9, 13n3, 183–84;
    extended, 111; father, 130, 149, 182–

85, 189; grandmother, 13; mother, 12,
    13n3, 14, 148–49, 180–85, 187, 189
Fanon, Franz, 187n8
Fawaz, Ramzi, 133, 135, 151
femininity, 7, 16, 70–74, 80, 129, 174–75
feminism: and Asian North American
    novels, 7, 13, 174; and graphic nar-
    ratives, 19, 58, 67–68; intersectional,
    105; posthumanism and (*see* posthu-
    manism). *See also* girls' studies
Filipina Americans, 13; aesthetics of, 20,
    114; girlhood of, 114, 119; mestiza,
    109–12 (*see also* Asian North Ameri-
    cans: mixed-race); as graphic artists,
    20, 104; and peminisms (Filipina/
    American feminisms), 104, 107–8,
    118–21; and representation, 107; and
    trauma, 108, 115. *See also* Philippines
Filipinx (Filipino) Americans, 6, 103, 108;
    as characters, 70–71; culture of, 110;
    and Filipinx American studies, 103–
    4, 107–8, 110, 112, 120; graphic nar-
    ratives by, 10, 104, 121; mixed-race
    (*See* Asian North Americans: mixed-
    race); and precolonial belief systems,
    118. *See also* Philippines
film, 10; women-in-prison films, 69–71,
    77, 79
Fleetwood, Nicole, 73
Floyd, George, 120
folklore. *See* supernatural beings
food, 46, 110, 135, 138, 166
Fox, Nick, 162
Frankenberg, Ruth, 159
Frey, Hugo, 172
Fu Manchu, 5, 5n1, 90, 93, 145
futurity, 9

Galang, M. Evelina, 107
Gharib, Malaka, 20, 103, 107–13, 119; *I
    Was Their American Dream*, 109–13,
    119
ghosts. *See* supernatural beings
Gibbon, Dave: *Watchmen*, 6
Gilmore, Leigh, 12
Ginsberg, Alice, 105
girls' studies, 103–8, 119–20; Global
    South girlhoods, 105–6; Western
    girlhoods, 106; white hegemony in,
    104–6

O'Malley, Brian Lee: *Snotgirl*, 162
One! Hundred! Demons! (Barry), 10–15, 52, 104, 107n5, 109, 114–15, 115n8, 118–19
Orange Is the New Black, 71n4
Orientalism, 4, 71, 74–76, 92, 97, 142, 144, 147; yellowface, 4–5, 89n12, 145; yellow peril, 5, 146–47
Otsuka, Julie: *When the Emperor Was Divine*, 39–40

Park, Jane Chi Hyun, 16
patriarchy, 7, 20, 68, 72–75; male gaze, 71–72, 77, 79
Pearl Harbor, 18, 29, 34–35, 36 fig.1.1a, 37 fig. 1.1b, 38, 87, 98, 100
Petersen, Robert, 3, 6
Philippines: relations with US, 20. *See also* Filipina Americans; Filipinx Americans
photography: Japanese internment camps and, 32nn4–5, 33, 40n16. *See also* Japanese internment camps
Pinay/Pinoy. *See* Filipina Americans; Filipinx Americans
plants, 173–74, 174 fig. 8.2a–b, 175
Polak, Kate, 183
pornography, 70
Postema, Barbara, 13, 70n3, 161
posthumanism, 21–22, 160–62, 168–70, 175
postmemory, 50–51, 60. *See also* Hirsch, Marianne
postracism, 85
poverty, 10, 13, 86n8, 115–16
Pratt, Henry John, 10
prostitution, 2

Qadir, Sooraya. *See* superheroes: Dust
queerness: and Asian North American subjectivity, 17; and diaspora, 8; and identity, 17, 113

race: in American history, 84, 91–92; and Black-white relations, 71; and coalition building, 71; and colorism, 112; and fetishization, 2, 20, 74–77; hierarchy of (*see* Asian North Americans: hierarchy of); and segregation, 20,

42, 86, 92; and solidarity, 94; and stereotypes (*see* stereotypes: racial)
refugees, 53, 55; children as, 19, 55; and family separation, 53, 55; and global crisis, 53, 55; "good," 61–62; and gratitude, 19, 56, 60–62. *See also* Vietnamese Americans: as refugees
Resha, Adrienne, 126, 137n3
Reynolds, Richard, 147, 147n6
Roan, Jeanette, 1, 19–20
Rohmer, Sax, 5
Royal, Derek Parker, 3, 15, 141, 142n1, 143, 152

Sacco, Joe, 33n6, 182
Salkowitz, Rob, 1
Sandner, David, 168
Satrapi, Marjane, 12, 182; *Persepolis*, 6, 183
Sauter, Theresa, 171–72
Scarry, Elaine, 184
Schaub, Grace, 32n4
Schleitwiler, Vince, 96n19
Schlund-Vials, Cathy, 4, 18
Scott, Steven, 18
September 11. *See* 9/11
The Shadow Hero (Yang and Liew), 21, 141–53
Shimizu, Celine Pareñas, 16
Shklovsky, Viktor, 167
Shuster, Joe, 131
Siebers, Tobin, 187
Siegal, Jerry, 131
Silva, Eduardo Bonilla, 127
Skalli, Loubna Hanna, 106, 106n3
Skim (Tamaki and Tamaki), 17, 21, 159
Smith, Sidonie, 7
Smyth, Heather, 96n19
social media, 21, 103, 161–62, 162n1, 170–73, 174 fig. 8.2a–b, 175; and identity, 171; and self-writing, 171–72
speciesism. *See* posthumanism
Spiegelman, Art, 90; *Maus*, 6, 52, 85, 92–93
Sohn, Stephen, 160
Soma, Taki, 73n5
Song, Min Hyoung, 3, 15–16, 90–91, 93–94

STUDIES IN COMICS AND CARTOONS

Jared Gardner, Charles Hatfield, and Rebecca Wanzo, Series Editors
Lucy Shelton Caswell, Founding Editor Emerita

Books published in Studies in Comics and Cartoons focus exclusively on comics and graphic literature, highlighting their relation to literary studies. The series includes monographs and edited collections that cover the history of comics and cartoons from the editorial cartoon and early sequential comics of the nineteenth century through webcomics of the twenty-first. Studies that focus on international comics are also considered.